WORLD HUNGER AND MORALITY

Second Edition

Edited by

William Aiken
Chatham College

and

Hugh LaFollette
East Tennessee State University

Prentice Hall
Upper Saddle River, New Jersey 07458

Library of Congress Cataloging-in-Publication Data

World hunger and morality/edited by William Aiken and Hugh
 LaFollette—2nd ed.
   p. cm.
 Rev. ed. of: World Hunger and moral obligation. c 1977.
 Includes bibliographical references.
 ISBN 0-13-448284-0
   1. Food supply. 2. Food relief—Moral and ethical aspects.
 I. Aiken, William. II. LaFollette, Hugh III. World hunger and moral obligation.
 HD9000.6.W63 1996
 363.8'83—dc20

95-23514
CIP

Acquisitions editor: *Ted Bolen/Charlyce Jones Owen*
Editorial assistant: *Meg McGuane*
Production editor: *Jean Lapidus*
Copy editor: *Maria Caruso*
Buyer: *Lynn Pearlman*
Cover design: *Wendy Alling Judy*

©1996 by Prentice-Hall, Inc.
Simon & Schuster/A Viacom Company
Upper Saddle River, New Jersey 07458

Printed in the United States of America

10   9   8   7   6   5   4   3   2   1

ISBN 0-13-448284-0

Prentice-Hall International (UK) Limited, *London*
Prentice-Hall of Australia Pty. Limited, *Sydney*
Prentice-Hall Canada Inc., *Toronto*
Prentice-Hall Hispanoamericana, S.A., *Mexico*
Prentice-Hall of India Private Limited, *New Delhi*
Prentice-Hall of Japan, Inc., *Tokyo*
Simon & Schuster Asia Pte. Ltd., *Singapore*
Editora Prentice-Hall do Brasil, Ltda., *Rio de Janeiro*

CONTENTS

PART IV. Justice and Development

PART V. Hunger and the Environment

Introduction

Why a Second Edition?

When we assembled the first edition of this anthology (*World Hunger and Moral Obligation*) in 1976, the debate over famine relief was raging in the popular press. We believed reasoned moral argument could play a significant role in this debate—that such reasoning could lead people (especially students) living in the affluent "northern" societies, to substantially alter their beliefs, choices, and life-styles. We were optimistic that world hunger could be, and would be, eliminated, if only the rich peoples of the world would listen to "right reason," share their abundance, and muster the political will to create the necessary political, social, economic, and technological changes.

It is now 20 years later and the world is a very different place: more geopolitically complex, environmentally fragile, and economically interconnected. The "cold war" mentality, which for so many decades divided the world into the good guys and the bad guys, obsessively drove foreign policy decisions, and distorted budget priorities, has finally (we hope) slipped away. There are signs of a new, earnest commitment to international dialogue and cooperation between the peoples of developed and developing nations. In the past 4 years there have been four significant United Nations conferences: the earth summit at Rio in 1992, the conference on population and development in Cairo in 1994, and the 1995 conferences on social development in Copenhagen and on women in Beijing. Getting government representatives and leaders of nongovernmental organizations to come together to explore, thrash out, and sign agreements of mutual intent on these issues is an important first step toward the actual implementation of much needed changes. Indeed there are signs that the twenty-first century will see the well-being of the globe's peoples enhanced in an environmentally sustainable and nature-respecting way.

Why, then, do we feel it necessary to create a second edition of an anthology specifically on world hunger and moral responsibility? Because, unfortunately, chronic hunger is still with us. Other things have changed, but it remains. As much as a fifth of the world's 5.5 billion people live in the type of extreme poverty that makes them vulnerable to undernourishment and thereby prey to debilitating or life-destroying diseases. Most of these one billion people are innocent young children. This life-robbing poverty may be abating, but not at a rapid rate.

This problem will not go away by ignoring it. It does no good for individuals, communities, or leaders of nations to simply divert attention from human misery, and to direct energies and resources to more "manageable" problems. The extreme poverty which creates world hunger is a persistent and deeply rooted global problem. To tolerate it as an economic, environmental, or political reality which should be "accepted" is to take a moral stance. So, too, is judging it "unacceptable" and in need of remedial action. The issues of global poverty and world hunger have clear moral dimensions.

That is why, after these 20 years, we still believe that moral argument has an important role to play in the discussions about world hunger. It is important to carefully scrutinize, from the moral point of view, not only what, if anything, is to be done, but also how and why it is to be done, and by whom. Rational moral argumentation remains an important intellectual tool for critiquing normative beliefs and assessing consequent actions. However, it will be vividly apparent to anyone familiar with the original volume, that the moral questions are currently framed and discussed in rather different ways than they were two decades ago.

The Essays in this Volume

Six of the essays in this volume have been published previously: Hardin, Aiken, Singer, Arthur, O'Neill, and Sen; three of these appeared in the first edition. The remaining nine are original essays, written specifically for this volume. The essays are divided into five units.

The first unit, **Lifeboat Ethics**, considers the popular metaphor of nations as lifeboats, presented in Garrett Hardin's 1974 essay "Lifeboat Ethics: The Case Against Helping the Poor." He describes the "tragedy of the commons" and likens nations to lifeboats with limited carrying capacities which must be protected from over-crowding. Aiken's 1980 "The 'Carrying Capacity' Equivocation" challenges Hardin's application of the biological concept of carrying capacity to human populations within nation states.

The second unit, **A Responsibility to Aid**, focuses on whether affluent people have a moral responsibility to provide assistance to people in need in other lands. Peter Singer, in his famous 1972 essay, "Famine, Affluence, and Morality," argues that we should assist the starving since, if is in our power to prevent something bad from happening without thereby sacrificing anything of comparable moral importance, we ought, morally, to do it. In response to Singer, John Arthur's 1977 essay, "Rights and the Duty to Bring Aid" argues that utilitarian theories like Singer's fail to give sufficient weight to the rights of the affluent. Any duty to bring aid, Arthur claims, is rightly seen as a duty of benevolence. In "'The Life-Saving Analogy," Garrett Cullity defends the widely used analogy that compares the failure to contribute money to aid agencies with the failure to save the life of a person right in front of you. Cullity claims this analogy is apt; the criticisms, unconvincing. He responds to those critics who say that giving aid is either useless or unduly demanding. Hugh LaFollette and Larry May in "Suffer the Little Children" build on the prephilosophical feeling of responsibility evoked by the suffering of seriously undernourished children. The moral debate, they argue, should focus on the plight of children, who are paradigms of vulnerability and innocence. Onora O'Neill's 1993 essay "Ending World Hunger" presents the Kantian approach in which she demonstrates what Kantian thinking requires of us with regard to the vulnerable, on both grounds of beneficence and of justice. She emphasizes the importance of respecting, fostering, and securing others' capacity for autonomous action. Since people's autonomy can be eroded by poverty and malnutrition, the Kantian approach requires that we create economic and social security sufficient to protect it.

The third unit, **Rights and Justice**, shifts the attention from potential benefactors to the actual sufferers of hunger. Henry Shue argues, in "Solidarity among Strangers and The Right to Food,"that people have a basic right to food because their vitally important interest in food justifies holding others to have a duty. These rights have an underlying social character. Because they depend on solidarity across the community for their protection, their implementation involves consideration of the interests of potential duty-bearers, reciprocity among right-bearers, and creation of the necessary social institutions. In "Global Justice," James Sterba sets out to show that adherents to a libertarian theory of justice, to be consistent with their principles, should endorse a right to welfare, including a right to a minimum satisfaction of basic needs, including food. These rights extend to distant peoples and future generations. In "Making Sense of the Right to Food," Xiaorong Li argues that the need-based right to food is a right to access to the means to procure food. This right must be supported by social practices conducive to a stable social and economic order. Society, through government, is predominately responsibility for insuring the conditions necessary for the exercise of this right. James Nickel in "A Human Rights Approach to World Hunger" appeals to the norms and institutions of the international rights movement which emphasizes self-help, agency, and responsibility by the malnourished themselves. He combines the right to adequate food with a variety of other civil and political rights which facilitate political participation and economic action. The virtue of this approach is its flexibility to deal with changing circumstances, and with both individuals' and institutional failures.

The fourth unit, **Justice and Development**, emphasizes the point so effectively established in the work of economist Amartya Sen, that it is poverty, not a shortage of food, which causes starvation. In his 1983 essay "Goods and People," he argues that hunger and starvation depend on the nature of the entitlement system operating in the economy in question and the ability of individuals within that system to command entitlements to food and to complementary goods and services such as health services and education. Abolishing hunger is linked to insuring these entitlements and thereby expanding peoples' capabilities. Adopting Sen's capabilities approach to development, David Crocker argues in "Hunger, Capability, and Development" that the predominant "ethics of aid" evoked by most moral philosophers should be replaced with an "ethics of development". This latter approach widens and reframes the questions of world hunger and moral responsibility to focus on the prevention of persistent malnutrition and the integration of food entitlements into a capabilities-based model of development. Radhika Balakrishnan and Uma Narayan similarly criticize the popular western moral discourse on world hunger. In "Combining Justice with Development: Rethinking Rights and Responsibilities in the Context of World Hunger and Poverty," they stress the role of past and current economic policies in creating poverty and resilient hunger. They dispute the attempt to explain chronic poverty by blaming poor women for overpopulation; they also chronicle the costs of current market-driven development policies to women. Elimination of hunger and poverty is a matter of social and international justice, not charity.

The sole essay in the final unit, **Hunger and the Environment**, Holmes Rolston's "Feeding People versus Saving Nature?" explores the question: can we ever say that we should save nature rather than feed people? He argues that given the complexity created by many factors such as unsustainable consumption, maldistribution of wealth, and exploding human populations, sometimes we ought to preserve natural values—like endangered species and tropical rain forest biodiversity—even if it might cost human lives because of hunger through the omission of development.

I. LIFEBOAT ETHICS

Lifeboat Ethics
The Case Against Helping
the Poor*

GARRETT HARDIN

Garrett Hardin received the 1989 Humanist Distinguished Service award from the American Humanist Association for his lifelong dedication to population growth control. Hardin taught biology and human ecology at the University of California at Santa Barbara. His books include *Mandatory Motherhood, Exploring New Ethics for Survival*, and *Population, Evolution, and Birth Control*.

Environmentalists use the metaphor of the earth as a "spaceship" in trying to persuade countries, industries, and people to stop wasting and polluting our natural resources. Since we all share life on this planet, they argue, no single person or institution has the right to destroy, waste, or use more than a fair share of its resources.

But does everyone on earth have an equal fight to an equal share of its resources? The spaceship metaphor can be dangerous when used by misguided idealists to justify suicidal policies for sharing our resources through uncontrolled immigration and foreign aid. In their enthusiastic but unrealistic generosity, they confuse the ethics of a spaceship with those of a lifeboat.

A true spaceship would have to be under the control of a captain, since no ship could possibly survive if its course were determined by committee. Spaceship Earth certainly has no captain; the United Nations is merely a toothless tiger, with little power to enforce any policy on its bickering members.

If we divide the world crudely into rich nations and poor nations, two thirds of them are desperately poor, and only one third comparatively rich, with the United States the wealthiest of all. Metaphorically each rich nation can be seen as a lifeboat full of comparatively rich people. In the ocean outside each lifeboat swim the poor of the world, who would like to get in, or at least to share some of the wealth. What should the lifeboat passengers do?

First, we must recognize the limited capacity of any lifeboat. For example, a nation's land has a limited capacity to support a population and as the current energy crisis has shown us, in some ways we have already exceeded the carrying capacity of our land.

Adrift in a Moral Sea

So here we sit, say fifty people in our lifeboat. To be generous, let us assume it has room for ten more, making a total capacity of sixty. Suppose the fifty of us in the lifeboat see 100 others swimming in the water outside, begging for admission to our boat or for handouts. We have several options: we may be tempted to try to live by the Christian ideal of being "our brother's keeper," or by the Marxist ideal of "to each according to his needs." Since the needs of all in the water are the same, and since they can all be seen as "our brothers," we could take them all into our boat, making a total of 150 in a boat designed for sixty. The boat swamps, everyone drowns. Complete justice, complete catastrophe.

Since the boat has an unused excess capacity of ten more passengers, we could admit just ten more to it. But which ten do we let in? How do we choose? Do we pick the best ten, the neediest ten, "first come, first served"? And what do we say to the ninety we exclude? If we do let an extra ten into our lifeboat, we will have lost our "safety factor," an engineering principle of critical importance. For example, if we don't leave room for excess capacity as a safety factor in our country's agriculture, a new plant disease or a bad change in the weather could have disastrous consequences.

Suppose we decide to preserve our small safety factor and admit no more to the lifeboat. Our survival is then possible, although we shall have to be constantly on guard against boarding parties.

While this last solution clearly offers the only means of our survival, it is morally abhorrent to many people. Some say they feel guilty about their good luck. My reply is simple: "Get out and yield your place to others." This may solve the problem of the guilt-ridden person's conscience, but it does not change the ethics of the lifeboat. The needy person to whom the guilt-ridden person yields his place will not himself feel guilty about his good luck. If he did, he would not climb aboard. The net result of conscience-stricken people giving up their unjustly held seats is the elimination of that sort of conscience from the lifeboat.

This is the basic metaphor within which we must work out our solutions. Let us now enrich the image, step-by-step, with substantive additions from the real world, a world that must solve real and pressing problems of overpopulation and hunger.

The harsh ethics of the lifeboat become even harsher when we consider the reproductive differences between the rich nations and the poor nations. The people inside the lifeboats are doubling in numbers every 87 years; those swimming around outside are doubling, on the average, every 35 years, more than twice as fast as the rich. And since the world's resources are dwindling, the difference in prosperity between the rich and the poor can only increase.

As of 1973, the United States had a population of 210 million people, who were increasing by 0.8 percent per year. Outside our lifeboat; let us imagine another 210 million people, (say the combined populations of Colombia, Ecuador, Venezuela, Morocco, Pakistan, Thailand, and the Philippines) who are increasing at a rate of 3.3 percent per year. Put differently, the doubling time for this aggregate population is 21 years, compared to 87 years for the United States.

Multiplying the Rich and the Poor

Now suppose the United States agreed to pool its resources with those seven countries, with everyone receiving an equal share. Initially, the ratio of Americans to non-Americans in this model would be one-to-one. But consider what the ratio would be after 87 years, by which time the Americans would have doubled to a population of 420 million. By then, doubling every twenty-one years, the other group would have swollen to 354 billion. Each American would have to share the available resources with more than eight people.

But, one could argue, this discussion assumes that current population trends will continue, and they may not. Quite so. Most likely the rate of population increase will decline much faster in the United States than it will in the other countries, and there does not seem to be much we can do about it. In sharing with "each according to his needs," we must recognize that needs are determined by population size, which is determined by the rate of reproduction, which at present is regarded as a sovereign right of every nation, poor or not. This being so, the philanthropic load created by the sharing ethic of the spaceship can only increase.

The Tragedy of the Commons

The fundamental error of spaceship ethics, and the sharing it requires, is that it leads to what I call "the tragedy of the commons." Under a system of private property, the men who own property recognize their responsibility to care for it, for if they don't they will eventually suffer. A farmer, for instance, will allow no more cattle in a pasture than its carrying capacity justifies. If he overloads it, erosion sets in, weeds take over, and he loses the use of the pasture.

If a pasture becomes a commons open to all, the right of each to use it may not be matched by a corresponding responsibility to protect it. Asking everyone to use it with discretion will hardly do, for the considerate herdsman who refrains from overloading the commons suffers more than a selfish one who says his needs are greater. If everyone would restrain himself, all would be well; but it takes only one less than everyone to ruin a system of voluntary restraint. In a crowded world of less than perfect human beings, mutual ruin is inevitable if there are no controls. This is the tragedy of the commons.

One of the major tasks of education today should be the creation of such an acute awareness of the dangers of the commons that people will recognize its many varieties. For example, the air and water have become polluted because they are treated as commons. Further growth in the population or per capita conversion of natural resources into pollutants will only make the problem worse. The same holds true for the fish of the oceans. Fishing fleets have nearly disappeared in many parts of the world, technological improvements in the art of fishing are hastening the day of complete ruin. Only the replacement of the system of the commons with a responsible system of control will save the land, air, water, and oceanic fisheries.

The World Food Bank

In recent years there has been a push to create a new commons called a World Food Bank, an international depository of food reserves to which nations would contribute according to their abilities and from which they would draw according to their needs. This humanitarian proposal has received support from many liberal international groups, and from such prominent citizens as Margaret Mead, U.N. Secretary General Kurt Waldheim, and Senators Edward Kennedy and George McGovern.

A world food bank appeals powerfully to our humanitarian impulses. But before we rush ahead with such a plan, let us recognize where the greatest political push comes from, lest we be disillusioned later. Our experience with the "Food for Peace program," or Public Law 480, gives us the answer. This program moved billions of dollars worth of U.S. surplus grain to food-short, population-long countries during the past two decades. But when P.L. 480 first became law, a headline in the business magazine Forbes revealed the real power behind it: "Feeding the World's Hungry Millions: How It Will Mean Billions for U.S. Business."

And indeed it did. In the years 1960 to 1970, U.S. taxpayers spent a total of $7.9 billion on the Food for Peace program. Between 1948 and 1970, they also paid an additional $50 billion for other economic-aid programs, some of which went for food and food-producing machinery and technology. Though all U.S. taxpayers were forced to contribute to the cost of P.L. 480, certain special interest groups gained handsomely under the program. Farmers did not have to contribute the grain; the Government, or rather the taxpayers, bought it from them at full market prices. The increased demand raised prices of farm products generally. The manufacturers of farm machinery, fertilizers, and pesticides benefited by the farmers' extra efforts to grow more food. Grain elevators profited from storing the surplus until it could be shipped. Railroads made money hauling it to ports, and shipping lines profited from carrying it overseas. The implementation of P.L. 480 required the creation of a vast Government bureaucracy, which then acquired its own vested interest in continuing the program regardless of its merits.

Extracting Dollars

Those who proposed and defended the Food for Peace program in public rarely mentioned its importance to any of these special interests. The public emphasis was always on its humanitarian effects. The combination of silent selfish interests and highly vocal humanitarian apologists made a powerful and successful lobby for extracting money from taxpayers. We can expect the same lobby to push now for the creation of a World Food Bank.

However great the potential benefit to selfish interests, it should not be a decisive argument against a truly humanitarian program. We must ask if such a program would actually do more good than harm, not only momentarily but also in the long run. Those who propose the food bank usually refer to a current "emergency" or "crisis" in terms of world food supply. But what is an emergency? Although they may be infrequent and sudden, everyone knows that emergencies will occur from time to time. A well-run family, company, organization, or country prepares for the likelihood of accidents and emergencies. It expects them, it budgets for them, it saves for them.

Learning the Hard Way

What happens if some organizations or countries budget for accidents and others do not? If each country is solely responsible for its own well-being, poorly managed ones will suffer. But they can learn from experience. They may mend their ways, and learn to budget for infrequent but certain emergencies. For example, the weather varies from year-to-year, and periodic crop failures are certain. A wise and competent government saves out of the production of the good years in anticipation of bad years to come. Joseph taught this policy to Pharaoh in Egypt more than 2,000 years ago. Yet the great majority of the governments in the world today do not follow such a policy. They lack either the wisdom or the competence, or both. Should those nations that do manage to put something aside be forced to come to the rescue each time an emergency occurs among the poor nations?

"But it isn't their fault!" some kindhearted liberals argue. "How can we blame the poor people who are caught in an emergency? Why must they suffer for the sins of their governments?" The concept of blame is simply not relevant here. The real question is, what are the operational consequences of establishing a world food bank? If it is open to every country every time a need develops, slovenly rulers will not be motivated to take Joseph's advice. Someone will always come to their aid. Some countries will deposit food in the world food bank, and others will withdraw it. There will be almost no overlap. As a result of such solutions to food shortage emergencies, the poor countries will not learn to mend their ways, and will suffer progressively greater emergencies as their populations grow.

Population Control the Crude Way

On the average, poor countries undergo a 2.5 percent increase in population each year; rich countries, about 0.8 percent. Only rich countries have anything in the way of food reserves set aside, and even they do not have as much as they should. Poor countries have none. If poor countries received no food from the outside, the rate of their population growth would be periodically checked by crop failures and famines. But if they can always draw on a world food bank in time of need, their population can continue to grow unchecked, and so will their "need" for aid. In the short run, a world food bank may diminish that need, but in the long run it actually increases the need without limit.

Without some system of worldwide food sharing, the proportion of people in the rich and poor nations might eventually stabilize. The overpopulated poor countries would decrease in numbers, while the rich countries that had room for more people would increase. But with a well-meaning system of sharing, such as a world food bank, the growth differential between the rich and the poor countries will not only persist, it will increase. Because of the higher rate of population growth in the poor countries of the world, 88 percent of today's children are born poor, and only 12 percent rich. Year-by-year the ratio becomes worse, as the fast-reproducing poor outnumber the slow-reproducing rich.

A world food bank is thus a commons in disguise. People will have more motivation to draw from it than to add to any common store. The less provident and less able will multiply at the expense of the abler and more provident, bringing eventual ruin upon all who share in the commons. Besides, any system of "sharing" that amounts to foreign aid from the rich nations to the poor nations will carry the taint of charity, which will contribute little to the world peace so devoutly desired by those who support the idea of a world food bank.

As past U.S. foreign-aid programs have amply and depressingly demonstrated, international charity frequently inspires mistrust and antagonism rather than gratitude on the part of the recipient nation.

Chinese Fish and Miracle Rice

The modern approach to foreign aid stresses the export of technology and advice, rather than money and food. As an ancient Chinese proverb goes: "Give a man a fish and he will eat for a day; teach him how to fish and he will eat for the rest of his days." Acting on this advice, the Rockefeller and Ford Foundations have financed a number of programs for improving agriculture in the hungry nations. Known as the "Green Revolution," these programs have led to the development of "miracle rice" and "miracle wheat," new strains that offer bigger harvests and greater resistance to crop damage. Norman Borlaug, the Nobel Prize winning agronomist who, supported by the Rockefeller Foundation, developed "miracle wheat," is one of the most prominent advocates of a world food bank.

Whether or not the Green Revolution can increase food production as much as its champions claim is a debatable but possibly irrelevant point. Those who support this well-intended humanitarian effort should first consider some of the fundamentals of human ecology. Ironically, one man who did was the late Alan Gregg, a vice president of the Rockefeller Foundation. Two decades ago he expressed strong doubts about the wisdom of such attempts to increase food production. He likened the growth and spread of humanity over the surface of the earth to the spread of cancer in the human body, remarking that "cancerous growths demand food; but, as far as I know, they have never been cured by getting it."

Overloading the Environment

Every human born constitutes a draft on all aspects of the environment: food, air, water, forests, beaches, wildlife, scenery, and solitude. Food can, perhaps, be significantly increased to meet a growing demand. But what about clean beaches, unspoiled forests, and solitude? If we satisfy a growing population's need for food, we necessarily decrease its per capita supply of the other resources needed by men.

India, for example, now has a population of 600 million, which increases by 15 million each year. This population already puts a huge load on a relatively impoverished environment. The country's forests are now only a small fraction of what they were three centuries ago, and floods and erosion continually destroy the insufficient farmland that remains. Every one of the 15 million new lives added to India's population puts an additional burden on the environment, and increases the economic and social costs of crowding. However humanitarian our intent, every Indian life saved through medical or nutritional assistance from abroad diminishes the quality of life for those who remain, and for subsequent generations. If rich countries make it possible, through foreign aid, for 600 million Indians to swell to 1.2 billion in a mere 28 years, as their current growth rate threatens, will future generations of Indians thank us for hastening the destruction of their environment? Will our good intentions be sufficient excuse for the consequences of our actions?

My final example of a commons in action is one for which the public has the least desire for rational discussion—immigration. Anyone who publicly questions the wisdom of current U.S. immigration policy is promptly charged with bigotry, prejudice, ethnocentrism, chauvinism, isolationism, or selfishness. Rather than encounter such accusations, one would rather talk about other matters, leaving immigration policy to wallow in the crosscurrents of special interests that take no account of the good of the whole, or the interests of posterity.

Perhaps we still feel guilty about things we said in the past. Two generations ago the popular press frequently referred to Dagos, Wops, Polacks, Chinks, and Krauts, in articles about how America was being "overrun" by foreigners of supposedly inferior genetic stock. But because the implied inferiority of foreigners was used then as justification for keeping them out, people now assume that restrictive policies could only be based on such misguided notions. There are other grounds.

A Nation of Immigrants

Just consider the numbers involved. Our government acknowledges a net inflow of 400,000 immigrants a year. While we have no hard data on the extent of illegal entries, educated guesses put the figure at about 600,000 a year. Since the natural increase (excess of births over deaths) of the resident population now runs about 1.7 million per year, the yearly gain from immigration amounts to at least 19 percent of the total annual increase, and may be as much as 37 percent if we include the estimate for illegal immigrants. Considering the growing use of birth-control devices, the potential effect of educational campaigns by such organizations as Planned Parenthood Federation of America and Zero Population Growth, and the influence of inflation and the housing shortage, the fertility rate of American women may decline so much that immigration could account for all the yearly increase in population. Should we not at least ask if that is what we want?

For the sake of those who worry about whether the "quality" of the average immigrant compares favorably with the quality of the average resident, let us assume that immigrants and nativeborn citizens are of exactly equal quality, however one defines that term. We will focus here only on quantity; and since our conclusions will depend on nothing else, all charges of bigotry and chauvinism become irrelevant.

Immigration versus Food Supply

World food banks move food to the people, hastening the exhaustion of the environment of the poor countries. Unrestricted immigration, on the other hand, moves people to the food, thus speeding up the destruction of the environment of the rich countries. We can easily understand why poor people should want to make this latter transfer, but why should rich hosts encourage it?

As in the case of foreign-aid programs, immigration receives support from selfish interests and humanitarian impulses. The primary selfish interest in unimpeded immigration is the desire of employers for cheap labor, particularly in industries and trades that offer degrading work. In the past, one wave of foreigners after another was brought into the United States to work at wretched jobs for wretched wages. In recent years the Cubans, Puerto Ricans, and Mexicans have had this dubious honor. The interests of the employers of cheap labor mesh well with the guilty silence of the country's liberal intelligentsia. White Anglo-Saxon Protestants are particularly reluctant to call for a closing of the doors to immigration for fear of being called bigots.

But not all countries have such reluctant leadership. Most educated Hawaiians, for example, are keenly aware of the limits of their environment, particularly in terms of population growth. There is only so much room on the islands, and the islanders know it. To Hawaiians, immigrants from the other forty-nine states present as great a threat as those from other nations. At a recent meeting of Hawaiian government officials in Honolulu, I had the ironic delight of hearing a speaker, who like most of his audience was of Japanese ancestry, ask how the country might practically and constitutionally close its doors to further immigration. One member of the audience countered: "How can we shut the doors now? We have many friends and relatives in Japan that we'd like to bring here some day so that they can enjoy Hawaii too." The Japanese-American speaker smiled sympathetically and answered: "Yes, but we have children now, and someday we'll have grandchildren too. We can bring more people here from Japan only by giving away some of the land that we hope to pass on to our grandchildren some day. What right do we have to do that?"

At this point, I can hear U.S. liberals asking: "How can you justify slamming the door once you're inside? You say that immigrants should be kept out. But aren't we all immigrants, or the descendents of immigrants? If we insist on staying, must we not admit all others?" Our craving for intellectual order leads us to seek and prefer symmetrical rules and morals: a single rule for me and everybody else; the same rule yesterday, today, and tomorrow. Justice, we feel, should not change with time and place.

We Americans of non-Native American ancestry can look upon ourselves as the descendants of thieves who are guilty morally, if not legally, of stealing this land from its Indian owners. Should we then give back the land to the now living American descendants of those Native Americans? However morally or logically sound this proposal may be, I, for one, am unwilling to live by it and I know no one else who is. Besides, the logical consequence would be absurd. Suppose that, intoxicated with a sense of pure justice, we should decide to turn our land over to the Native Americans. Since all our wealth has also been derived from the land, wouldn't we be morally obliged to give that back to the Native Americans too?

Pure Justice versus Reality

Clearly, the concept of pure justice produces an infinite regression to absurdity. Centuries ago, wise men invented statutes of limitations to justify the rejection of such pure justice, in the interest of preventing continual disorder. The law zealously defends property rights, but only relatively recent property rights. Drawing a line after an arbitrary time has elapsed may be unjust, but the alternatives are worse.

We are all the descendants of thieves, and the world's resources are inequitably distributed. But we must begin the journey to tomorrow from the point where we are today. We cannot remake the past. We cannot safely divide the wealth equitably among all peoples so long as people reproduce at different rates. To do so would guarantee that our grandchildren, and everyone else's grandchildren, would have only a ruined world to inhabit.

To be generous with one's own possessions is quite different from being generous with those of posterity. We should call this point to the attention of those who, from a commendable love of justice and equality, would institute a system of the commons, either in the form of a world food bank, or of unrestricted immigration. We must convince them if we wish to save at least some parts of the world from environmental ruin.

Without a true world government to control reproduction and the use of available resources, the sharing ethic of the spaceship is impossible. For the foreseeable future, our survival demands that we govern our actions by the ethics of a lifeboat, harsh though they may be. Posterity will be satisfied with nothing less.

The "Carrying Capacity" Equivocation*

WILLIAM AIKEN

William Aiken is Professor of Philosophy at Chatham College. He has published essays in applied ethics on a variety of topics, such as world hunger, agricultural research, human rights, and the environment.

Offering assistance to innocent persons in need of either a good or a service and assisting them, if they choose to accept the offer, is presumed to be morally permissible.[1] Such action can only be questioned, from a moral point of view, when there is evidence demonstrating that the assistance will result, not in benefit, but in harm. The burden of proof is placed on those who claim that what is apparently beneficent (assisting the needy) will, in a particular case, turn out to be harmful. In order to show this, a morally relevant difference between the particular case and cases of genuine assistance must be found.

The challenge of demonstration has been accepted by certain Neo-Malthusians and "ecologically oriented ethicists" with respect to offering and rendering food aid to members of certain nation states. They argue that membership in certain nation states disqualifies one from receiving assistance; that although assisting members of these nation states "appears" to be both beneficent and morally permissible, it is, in fact, neither. The morally relevant difference cited involves the notion of "carrying capacity."

The argument used to support this position, which I will call Argument T (since it is sometimes associated with the policy known as "triage") is derived from a maxim in biologist Garrett Hardin's "New Decalogue," that, "Thou shalt not exceed the carrying capacity of any environment."[2] The argument is as follows:

*© *Social Theory and Practice*, Vol. 6, No. 1 (Spring 1980). pp. 1–11. Reprinted by permission of the author and publisher.

Argument T

1. Every nation has a carrying capacity (that is, the maximum human population which its territory can support without irreparable damage; that is, damage which would result in its diminishing capability to support a population).

2. Some nations threaten to exceed, or have already exceeded, their carrying capacity by increasing their population (either through increased birth rate or decreased death rate).

3. Giving food to starving persons in such a nation will both decrease the death rate (by interfering with the outcome of starvation) and eventually increase the birth rate (those presently saved from death will later procreate) and thus it will either contribute to that nation's exceeding its carrying capacity or it will assist it to further exceed its carrying capacity.

4. Contributing to a nation's exceeding its carrying capacity, or assisting it to exceed this limit further, is morally wrong according to the maxim. "Thou shalt not exceed the carrying capacity of any environment."

5. *Therefore*, giving food to starving persons in nations which threaten to exceed or have already exceeded their carrying capacity is morally wrong (we ought not to do it even if we could do it with little or no cost to ourselves). and so we ought not to assist such persons.[3]

Although generally it may be morally permissible to offer and render assistance, it is not, by Argument T, morally permissible to assist members of some nation states because there is a morally relevant difference between those persons who live in a nation which has exceeded its carrying capacity and those who live in a nation which has not.

The entire framework of Argument T as established in the first premise can be challenged. The selection of nation states as the units of classification appears to be somewhat arbitrary from both a biological perspective and a moral perspective. From the former perspective, populations are examined in relation to their natural ecosystems, but since the natural environments with which populations interact can be smaller or larger than those circumscribed by ecologically irrelevant political boundaries, the adoption of political entities as environmental units requires justification. From the moral perspective, it is not clear that the fulfillment of basic human needs should be discussed in terms of groups at all—particularly such apparently morally irrelevant *groups* as those defined by political boundaries. It is not obvious, from a moral point of view, that membership in any geographically defined group could morally disqualify a needy innocent person from receiving assistance. In spite of these difficulties with the entire framework of Argument T, I will not pursue them here, but will rather demonstrate that even granting the questionable framework, Argument T fails to make a convincing case against food assistance because it is a defective argument. It is defective, as I will show, because it rests on an equivocation on the central concept, "carrying capacity."[4]

There is no question that Argument T is very persuasive. It appears to be realistic, sensible, and "hard-headed." Its appeal is due primarily to the apparent empirical basis of the concept *carrying capacity*. In general, this notion has a nice scientific ring to it. The carrying capacity of a vehicle (for example, an elevator, boat, or truck) can be accurately determined by dividing the average size or weight per individual unit into the maximum total space or weight for which the vehicle was designed to safely operate. This limit may be accurately predicted through a calculation of mechanical and physical forces. It is a natural physical limit of the vehicle's capability. Although this "objective physical limit" connotation of "carrying capacity" carries over into the use of the concept in ecological contexts (for example, deer, rabbit, or lemming populations within a specific territorial environment), it is obvious that a natural environment is neither intentionally designed nor inalterably constrained by physical forces to carry only a specific number of units.[5] In an ecological context, the carrying capacity of the environment is approximated by dividing the calculated "living space" required per individual organism (which is primarily determined by assessment of the extent and suitability of the renewable food and water supply available) into the total range of environment under examination. If a given area can support only x number of deer (its carrying capacity), then $x + n$ number of deer will "overgraze" and damage the environment, thereby increasing the living space per individual organism required and thus reducing the environment's carrying capacity. The determination and prediction of an environment's carrying capacity for animal populations can be made with relative precision (even though it is not as precise as is that of a vehicle's carrying capacity). It, too, is a natural limiting factor of sorts, a "biological fact" about the environment and the species involved. When animal populations reach this limit, the pending crisis of overpopulation can be forestalled by migration or by territorial expansion. Normally, however, this crisis is not forestalled, and starvation and concomitant disease reduce the population to a level which the damaged environment will tolerate—that is, to the new carrying capacity of the damaged environment.

Argument T applies this "biological limit" meaning of carrying capacity to human populations. The specifiable environment whose toleration limits are determined is the territory ruled by a sovereign nation state. By comparing the human population to the nation's available foodstuffs, a carrying capacity for that nation is determined. As in the case of deer, it is implied that if the limit is threatened, then migration, territorial expansion, or death by starvation and disease will restore the population to within the tolerable limits of the nation's environmental carrying capacity. It is the application of the notion of carrying capacity to human populations which generates Argument T with its conclusion that we must not interfere with the effects of starvation.[6]

Like the carrying capacity of a vehicle or a territorial ecosystem, the application of carrying capacity in Argument T has a nice "scientific" ring to it—it is apparently based on hard data, is easily predicted, and is unambiguously determined. But Argument T only gives the appearance of being based on hard facts. When the concept of carrying capacity is applied to human populations within a nation state's territory, it is not a natural fixed ratio of organism to environment. Unlike nonhuman animals, humans have the ability to artificially extend the carrying capacity of their environment.

One method humans use to extend their environment's carrying capacity is to increase agricultural productivity (through technological advances and increased efficiency) and to increase efficiency in storage and transportation. If a given region can produce and preserve more food, it will be able to support more people. Much of the debate surrounding the notion of carrying capacity has focused on the ability of technological advances to keep up with population growth. Supporters of the Green Revolution, algae-based protein advocates, and the "technological optimists" square off against the Neo-Malthusians, the "limits of growth" prophets, and the defenders of "quality" versus mere quantity of life. Although perhaps relevant to an examination of the entire globe's carrying capacity, this debate is irrelevant to the type of application of carrying capacity which Argument T makes, that is, the carrying capacity of a particular nation. No matter how advanced agricultural technology becomes, if a nation cannot afford to buy this technology it is useless to them as a means of providing food for their expanding population. Buying technology, however, is neither an environmental nor a technological matter. It is an economic matter.

This points to the second and most important method which humans use to extend the carrying capacity of their nation's environment: trade and negotiation with other nations who either have advanced agricultural technology to sell or who, because their agricultural productivity exceeds their population's demand, have food to sell. Once trade is introduced into the social environment of humans, a number of additional factors must be examined: national wealth, general productivity and distribution of goods, purchasing power, natural resource development potential, strategic military location, international bargaining power, and so on. Inclusion of these factors alters the notion of carrying capacity. It is no longer merely a biological concept. Now it is determined by a nation's ability not only to produce, but also to trade for the necessary agricultural products and technology required to feed its population. Any country which can afford to purchase these necessary goods has *not* exceeded its carrying capacity. The carrying capacity of a densely populated nation like the Netherlands is much higher than that of the sparsely populated sub-Sahara nations, not because of the amount of indigenous produce per capita, but because of the wealth per capita.

To demonstrate just how far from a "biological fact" the notion of carrying capacity is when applied to nation states, consider the following. If Argument T views human populations in nation states in the same way that nonhuman populations in territorial regions are viewed, then would it not follow that it would be immoral to *sell* food to any nation which needed it for human consumption? Presumably a nation would not buy food unless its own agricultural productivity was incapable of supporting its population. By selling food for human consumption, we would be assisting that nation (be it Japan or Saudi Arabia) to exceed its carrying capacity which, according to Hardin's maxim, is immoral. But for the advocates of Argument T this is absurd, for they assume that any nation which can buy food or essential agricultural technology has not yet exceeded its carrying capacity. International purchasing power extends a nation's carrying capacity because this is not a biological limit—it is a complex social, economic and political limit. It is not fixed by "nature" but by trade practices (for example, protective tariffs, currency exchange rates, concessionary prices, multinational corporation interests, militarily motivated "loans") by the international market in terms of who has what to sell (goods, resources, alliances), who wants to buy it, what price you can get for what you have to sell, and by the influence of international interests on indigenous production and distribution (for example, neo-colonialism with its emphasis upon the mass production of nonfood export crops).

It is important to stress the fact that the carrying capacity of a nation is not just a "biological fact" about a population and its environment. If a nation's carrying capacity were a "biological fact," the implicit assumption of Argument T (that a nation's carrying capacity can be determined) would not need justification. However, when the carrying capacity is seen as a socioeconomic limit, this assumption must be examined. Can we determine the carrying capacity of a nation, and, if so, are the assumptions which must be made to arrive at this calculation reasonable ones to make? I will divide my discussion into the two cases suggested by Argument T: those nations which have not yet, but threaten to, exceed their carrying capacity, and those nations which have already exceeded their carrying capacity.

In the former case, the determination of carrying capacity of a nation must be predicted, that is, at time t_1 a judgment must be made that at some future time t_2, the maximum population a nation can withstand will have been reached, and that any further increase in population will exceed the carrying capacity. Such predictions are calculated by assuming the maintenance of all present conditions, projecting the continuation of current trends, and by either reducing all potential variables to constants or eliminating consideration of them by the "other things being equal" assumption. Such predictions are hypothetical in form; that is, if conditions remain unaltered, then the carrying capacity will be reached at time t_2. In dealing with nonhuman populations, which are incapable of intentional action to alter conditions, effect changes in trends, or actualize options, the truth of the antecedent may be safely assumed. Animals cannot alter their conditions. But such predictions are at least questionable when dealing with human populations, for it is not obvious that the antecedent can be reasonably expected to be true over an extended time period. The multitude of factors which must be taken into account and held to be constant over time is enormous, but the accuracy of the calculation of socioeconomic carrying capacity is entirely contingent upon the constancy of these factors. This is not to say that it is impossible to determine a nation's carrying capacity before it is exceeded; only that it is not nearly so simple a matter as is the determination of biological carrying capacity. The longer the range of prediction (the longer time period over which the maintenance of the status quo is assumed), the less likely the antecedent is to be true. Consequently, the accuracy of the determination of carrying capacity on which Argument T relies is in inverse relation to the length of time covered in the prediction.

It is morally wrong, according to Argument T, to contribute to a nation's exceeding its carrying capacity by giving food aid. The present act of keeping people alive does not in itself increase the population; it merely prevents an anticipated decrease. It would appear then that the immediate effect of food aid does not contribute to a nation's exceeding its carrying capacity; thus, in the "short run," assistance would be permissible. It could be argued, however, that for some nations, the threat of exceeding the carrying capacity is (other things being equal) so severe that preventing any deaths would contribute to a decline in the death rate and, thus, would contribute to that nation's exceeding its carrying capacity. (But then not only would food aid be prohibited by Argument T, but so, too, would any act which resulted in fewer deaths—for example, trade with that nation in life-preserving commodities such as medical supplies and services, sanitation technology.) It may be that the fewer deaths resulting from assistance do decrease the overall annual death rate, but this must be clearly shown to be the case (for such assistance may only prevent an increase in death rate), and it must be shown that the decreasing death rate will not be offset by other factors (for example, rise in per capita income) which would increase the nation's carrying capacity. In these cases of severe threat, where the prediction of exceeding carrying capacity is a short-range prediction, the relationship of food aid to exceeding carrying capacity is not a direct causal one. Giving assistance "contributes" to that event only in the sense that it is one of many antecedent conditions which, given the entire set of relevant factors, is contingently necessary for the event. So even if a short-range prediction of exceeding carrying capacity were to be made, it could not be immediately inferred that acts of assistance which prevent deaths would "contribute" in a significant way to this event.

But the force of Argument T lies not in short-range predictions. It lies in long-range predictions of the geometric increase in population which results from keeping people alive. As Malthus demonstrated so well, populations multiply geometrically over generations so that, in 20 years, the effect of keeping people alive now will be a sharp increase in total population. So by Argument T, we should refuse to assist now in order to prevent a population increase in 20 years, and thus to avoid contributing to that nation's exceeding its carrying capacity in the next generation. Yet here we must rely upon a long-range prediction of socioeconomic carrying capacity which assumes that all current socioeconomic factors will remain unaltered for 20 years. It is these predictions which, given the multitude of factors which can change, are questionable. Even if a determination of socioeconomic carrying capacity is made and the event of exceeding it is predicted, the status of that prediction will be far below the level of "scientific accuracy" enjoyed by predictions of biological carrying capacity (due to the difference in credibility of the "other things being equal" assumption between human and nonhuman animals). Given these difficulties in predicting the socioeconomic carrying capacity of nations which have not yet exceeded that limit, Argument T is not convincing in its proscription against assisting these nations.

But what about those nations which have *already* exceeded their carrying capacity? Argument T clearly prohibits assisting them. The problems of prediction and determination need not be considered here, for even if a nation's carrying capacity may not be accurately determined in advance of its being exceeded, at least we can know when it has been exceeded by simply observing the fact that large numbers of people in that nation are dying of starvation. Should we not refuse assistance to at least these nations? The strange thing about this criterion (that people are starving in a nation) is that it disregards other potential causes for the starvation such as the economic factors within that nation (for example, production and distribution of wealth, land, and capital ownership, effective social services), the political factors within that nation (for example, expenditure on arms development is given priority over food or population control programs), and the social factors within that nation (for example, the maintenance of an affluent elite at the cost of the impoverished masses). It looks only at the *result* of economic, political, and social arrangements in its judgment of carrying capacity. To ignore these other relevant causes of starvation within a nation merely reduces the statement, "Nation x has exceeded its carrying capacity," to the statement. "There is starvation in nation x." But then what is the use of this quasi-scientific circumlocution? Why not just assert that we ought not to assist any nation in which starvation is occurring? Why make it sound so objective and so reasonable?

Still there may be some nations in which massive starvation is indeed unavoidable—in which no amount of internal change could avert famine. Surely these should not be given assistance. They are doomed to their fate. Yet even these nations, of what Joseph Fletcher calls the *Fifth World*, are doomed only by present international market practices.[7] They do not have anything to sell which someone else wants, so their population capacity is very low, dependent entirely upon what their indigenous agricultural productivity can support. They are forced into the same situation which animal populations are; that is, they are unable to extend their carrying capacity through trade and exchange. It is this group of nations which Argument T zeroes in on and of whom it boldly asserts that. "Thou shalt not assist any nation in which there are starving people who cannot afford to buy food at current market prices," and that, "It is immoral to give people what they cannot afford to buy." Yet it must be repeated again, the carrying capacity of such a nation is not in any way a biological limit, rather it is an economic limit. Its purchasing power determines whether or not its environment's carrying capacity can be extended. If oil is discovered within its territory, the supposed limit on population suddenly bolts upward to whatever extent the oil reserves last. A *nation's* carrying capacity is a by-product of the market—nothing more. It is never merely a biological limit.

In spite of this, Argument T gives the impression that the same notion of carrying capacity which applies to deer and lemmings also applies to humans within a nation state. The maxim, "Thou shalt not exceed the carrying capacity of any environment," suggests the primary biological meaning of the concept. Argument T applies this notion to humans within nation states. In this application there is an ambiguity in the concept since, as I have shown, human populations produce artificial carrying capacities according to socio-economic laws, not biological ones. Two different meanings of the term are simultaneously implied: one means population versus available renewable foodstuffs, the other means population versus international bargaining power. Argument T must either stick to the primary biological meaning of the term and conclude that it is immoral to trade, exchange, sell, or lend food or agricultural assistance to any nation which needs it (at which point it becomes an absurd argument), or it must surrender the quasi-scientific connotation of biological carrying capacity and address the economic factors which determine the extent to which a nation can increase its population. By trying to do both, it equivocates on the term and thus renders the argument fallacious. If it were to stick purely to the economic connotation, Argument T would boil down to the claim that it is morally wrong to interfere with the free market and the "natural" consequences which result from lack of interference with that market (*à la* Adam Smith). In other words, it is immoral to assist a nation which is unsuccessful in trade—a claim which I find to be morally unjustifiable. But because Argument T equivocates between the biological and the socioeconomic meanings, it implies that not only can a nation's socioeconomic carrying capacity be accurately determined, but that, if that nation exceeds its socioeconomic carrying capacity, the same inevitable disaster will occur which occurs when animal populations exceed the biological carrying capacity of their territorial environment; that is, the increased population will deplete the resources and so increase the "living space" per unit required, and consequently increase the concomitant suffering and starvation. Without the equivocation, Argument T would never be seriously considered a *moral* argument. It would be seen for what it is, an attempted moral justification for present world trade practices and allocation of economic goods. Those nations which do not fare well in this arrangement are said to be doomed to suffering and starvation while those who prosper can ease their conscience by the assurance that it would be, after all, immoral to interfere.

By showing that Argument T is defective, I have answered the popular challenge of the Neo-Malthusians and have undercut their claim of exception to the general moral permissibility of benevolence. There may, of course, be other arguments which proscribe assisting the needy in other nations (for example, Lappé and Collins' claim that food-aid assistance reinforces unjust social structures and prevents the indigenous power alterations necessary to obtain self-reliance[8]). But, by exposing the confusion in the supposedly "scientific" basis of the Neo-Malthusian arguments, I have at least cleared the way for the debate over the moral permissibility of giving food aid to be waged in its appropriate context–the world of social, political, and economic structures.

NOTES

1. In order to respect the autonomy of potential assistees, the possibility of refusing the assistance must be kept open.

2. Garrett Hardin, "Carrying Capacity as an Ethical Concept," in *Lifeboat Ethics: The Moral Dilemmas of World Hunger*, edited by George Lucas and Thomas Ogletree (New York: Harper and Row, 1976), p. 134.

3. Argument T is not Hardin's formulation, but it puts his comments on "situation ethics" into argument form.

4. There are several other ways to attack this argument from within its framework which I will not develop here, for instance: (a) it relies on the procedure of calculating utility over future generations, thus granting the interests of potential persons the same weight as living persons, and (b) it ignores alternative methods of reducing birth rates to avoid exceeding the carrying capacity of a nation (for example, birth control, demographic transition, alleviating the economic and social need for large families).

5. This is important to remember because no matter how often the "lifeboat" metaphor is used by Hardin and company, an environment simply is not a boat which will "sink" when x number of extra people are added to it.

6. Hardin has anticipated the other two standard population reactions by advocating that the "lifeboat" of the United States close its doors to all immigration and build up its defenses against invasion (to prevent territorial expansion). See Garrett Hardin, "Lifeboat Ethics: The Case Against Helping the Poor," in *World Hunger and Moral Obligation*, edited by William Aiken and Hugh LaFollette, Englewood Cliffs, NJ: Prentice-Hall, 1977, pp. 11-21.

7. Joseph Fletcher, "Give If It Helps But Not If It Hurts," in *World Hunger and Moral Obligation*, p. 108.

8. Frances Moore Lappé and Joseph Collins, *Food First: Beyond the Myth of Scarcity.* Boston: Houghton Mifflin Company, 1977.

II. A RESPONSIBILITY TO AID

Famine, Affluence, and Morality*

PETER SINGER

Peter Singer is Professor of Philosophy and Director of the center for Human Bioethics at the University of Monash, Melbourne. He is author of *Democracy and Disobedience, Marx, Hegel, Animal Liberation, The Expanding Circle,* and *Practical Ethics.* He is also co-editor of the journal, *Bioethics.*

As I write this, in November 1971, people are dying in East Bengal from lack of food, shelter, and medical care. The suffering and death that are occurring there now are not inevitable, not unavoidable in any fatalistic sense of the term. Constant poverty, a cyclone, and a civil war have turned at least nine million people into destitute refugees; nevertheless, it is not beyond the capacity of the richer nations to give enough assistance to reduce any further suffering to very small proportions. The decisions and actions of human beings can prevent this kind of suffering. Unfortunately, human beings have not made the necessary decisions. At the individual level, people have, with very few exceptions, not responded to the situation in any significant way. Generally speaking, people have not given large sums to relief funds; they have not written to their parliamentary representatives demanding increased government assistance; they have not demonstrated in the streets, held symbolic fasts, or done anything else directed toward providing the refugees with the means to satisfy their essential needs. At the government level, no government has given the sort of massive aid that would enable the refugees to survive for more than a few days. Britain, for instance, has given rather more than most countries. It has, to date, given £14,750,000. For comparative purposes, Britain's share of the nonrecoverable development costs of the Anglo-French Concorde project is already in excess of £275,000,000, and on present estimates will reach £440,000,000. The implication is that the British government values a supersonic transport more than thirty times as highly as it values the lives of the nine million refugees. Australia is another country which, on a per capita basis, is well up in the "aid to Bengal" table. Australia's aid, however, amounts to less than one-twelfth of the cost of Sydney's new opera house. The total amount given, from all sources, now stands at about £65,000,000. The estimated cost of keeping the refugees alive for one year is £464,000,000. Most of the refugees have now been in the camps for more than six months. The World Bank has said that India needs a minimum of £300,000,000 in assistance from other countries before the end of the year. It seems obvious that assistance on this scale will not be forthcoming. India will be forced to choose between letting the refugees starve or diverting funds from her own development program, which will mean that more of her own people will starve in the future.[1]

These are the essential facts about the present situation in Bengal. So far as it concerns us here, there is nothing unique about this situation except its magnitude. The Bengal emergency is just the latest and most acute of a series of major emergencies in various parts of the world, arising both from natural and from man-made causes. There are also many parts of the world in which people die from malnutrition and lack of food independent of any special emergency. I take Bengal as my example only because it is the present concern, and because the size of the problem has ensured that it has been given adequate publicity. Neither individuals nor governments can claim to be unaware of what is happening there.

What are the moral implications of a situation like this? In what follows, I shall argue that the way people in relatively affluent countries react to a situation like that in Bengal cannot be justified; indeed, the whole way we look at moral issues—our moral conceptual scheme—needs to be altered, and with it, the way of life that has come to be taken for granted in our society.

In arguing for this conclusion I will not, of course, claim to be morally neutral. I shall, however, try to argue for the moral position that I take, so that anyone who accepts certain assumptions, to be made explicit, will, I hope, accept my conclusion.

I begin with the assumption that suffering and death from lack of food, shelter, and medical care are bad. I think most people will agree about this, although one may reach the same view by different routes. I shall not argue for this view. People can hold all sorts of eccentric positions, and perhaps from some of them it would not follow that death by starvation is in itself bad. It is difficult, perhaps impossible, to refute such positions, and so for brevity I will henceforth take this assumption as accepted. Those who disagree need read no further.

My next point is this: if it is in our power to prevent something bad from happening, without thereby sacrificing anything of comparable moral importance, we ought, morally, to do it. By "without sacrificing anything of comparable moral importance" I mean without causing anything else comparably bad to happen, or doing something that is wrong in itself, or failing to promote some moral good, comparable in significance to the bad thing that we can prevent. This principle seems almost as uncontroversial as the last one. It requires us only to prevent what is bad, and not to promote what is good, and it requires this of us only when we can do it without sacrificing anything that is, from the moral point of view, comparably important. I could even, as far as the application of my argument to the Bengal emergency is concerned, qualify the point so as to make it: if it is in our power to prevent something very bad from happening, without thereby sacrificing anything morally significant, we ought, morally, to do it. An application of this principle would be as follows: if I am walking past a shallow pond and see a child drowning in it, I ought to wade in and pull the child out. This will mean getting my clothes muddy, but this is insignificant, while the death of the child would presumably be a very bad thing.

The uncontroversial appearance of the principle just stated is deceptive. If it were acted upon, even in its qualified form, our lives, our society, and our world would be fundamentally changed. For the principle takes, firstly, no account of proximity or distance. It makes no moral difference whether the person I can help is a neighbor's child ten yards from me or a Bengali whose name I shall never know, ten thousand miles away. Secondly, the principle makes no distinction between cases in which I am the only person who could possibly do anything and cases in which I am just one among millions in the same position.

I do not think I need to say much in defense of the refusal to take proximity and distance into account. The fact that a person is physically near to us, so that we have personal contact with him may make it more likely that we shall assist him, but this does not show that we ought to help him rather than another who happens to be further away. If we accept any principle of impartiality, universalizability, equality, or whatever, we cannot discriminate against someone merely because he is far away from us (or we are far away). Admittedly, it is possible that we are in a better position to judge what needs to be done to help a person near to us than one far away, and perhaps also to provide the assistance we judge to be necessary.

If this were the case, it would be a reason for helping those near to us first. This may once have been a justification for being more concerned with the poor in one's town than with famine victims in India. Unfortunately for those who like to keep their moral responsibilities limited, instant communication and swift transportation have changed the situation. From the moral point of view, the development of the world into a "global village" has made an important, though still unrecognized, difference to our moral situation. Expert observers and supervisors, sent out by famine relief organizations or permanently stationed in famine-prone areas, can direct our aid to a refugee in Bengal almost as effectively as we could get it to someone in our own block. There would seem, therefore, to be no possible justification for discriminating on geographical grounds.

There may be a greater need to defend the second implication of my principle—that the fact that there are millions of other people in the same position, in respect to the Bengali refugees, as I am, does not make the situation significantly different from a situation in which I am the only person who can prevent something very bad from occurring. Again, of course, I admit that there is a psychological difference between the cases; one feels less guilty about doing nothing if one can point to others, similarly placed, who have also done nothing. Yet this can make no real difference to our moral obligations.[2] Should I consider that I am less obliged to pull the drowning child out of the pond if on looking around I see other people, no further away than I am, who have also noticed the child but are doing nothing? One has only to ask this question to see the absurdity of the view that numbers lessen obligation. It is a view that is an ideal excuse for inactivity; unfortunately most of the major evils—poverty, overpopulation, pollution—are problems in which everyone is almost equally involved.

The view that numbers do make a difference can be made plausible if stated in this way: if everyone in circumstances like mine gave £5 to the Bengal Relief Fund, there would be enough to provide food, shelter, and medical care for the refugees; there is no reason why I should give more than anyone else in the same circumstances as I am; therefore I have no obligation to give more than £5. Each premise in this argument is true, and the argument looks sound. It may convince us, unless we notice that it is based on a hypothetical premise, although the conclusion is not stated hypothetically. The argument would be sound if the conclusion were: if everyone in circumstances such as mine were to give £5, I would have no obligation to give more than £5. If the conclusion were so stated, however, it would be obvious that the argument has no bearing on a situation in which it is not the case that everyone else gives £5. This, of course, is the actual situation. It is more or less certain that not everyone in circumstances like mine will give £5. So there will not be enough to provide the needed food, shelter, and medical care. Therefore by giving more than £5 I will prevent more suffering than I would if I gave just £5.

It might be thought that this argument has an absurd consequence. Since the situation appears to be that very few people are likely to give substantial amounts, it follows that I and everyone else in similar circumstances ought to give as much as possible, that is, at least up to the point at which by giving more one would begin to cause serious suffering for oneself and one's dependents—perhaps even beyond this point to the point of marginal utility, at which by giving more one would cause oneself and one's dependents as much suffering as one would prevent in Bengal. If everyone does this, however, there will be more than can be used for the benefit of the refugees, and some of the sacrifice will have been unnecessary. Thus, if everyone does what he ought to do, the result will not be as good as it would be if everyone did a little less than he ought to do, or if only some do all that they ought to do.

The paradox here arises only if we assume that the actions in question—sending money to the relief funds—are performed more or less simultaneously, and are also unexpected. For if it is to be expected that everyone is going to contribute something, then clearly each is not obliged to give as much as he would have been obliged to had others not been giving too. And if everyone is not acting more or less simultaneously, then those giving later will know how much more is needed, and will have no obligation to give more than is necessary to reach this amount. To say this is not to deny the principle that people in the same circumstances have the same obligations, but to point out that the fact that others have given, or may be expected to give, is a relevant circumstance: those giving after it has become known that many others are giving and those giving before are not in the same circumstances. So the seemingly absurd consequence of the principle I have put forward can occur only if people are in error about the actual circumstances—that is, if they think they are giving when others are not, but in fact they are giving when others are. The result of everyone doing what he really ought to do cannot be worse than the result of everyone doing less than he ought to do, although the result of everyone doing what he reasonably believes he ought to do could be.

If my argument so far has been sound, neither our distance from a preventable evil nor the number of other people who, in respect to that evil, are in the same situation as we are, lessens our obligation to mitigate or prevent that evil. I shall therefore take as established the principle I asserted earlier. As I have already said, I need to assert it only in its qualified form: if it is in our power to prevent something very bad from happening, without thereby sacrificing anything else morally significant, we ought, morally, to do it.

The outcome of this argument is that our traditional moral categories are upset. The traditional distinction between duty and charity cannot be drawn, or at least, not in the place we normally draw it. Giving money to the Bengal Relief Fund is regarded as an act of charity in our society. The bodies which collect money are known as "charities." These organizations see themselves in this way—if you send them a check, you will be thanked for your "generosity." Because giving money is regarded as an act of charity, it is not thought that there is anything wrong with not giving. The charitable man may be praised, but the man who is not charitable is not condemned. People do not feel in any way ashamed or guilty about spending money on new clothes or a new car instead of giving it to famine relief. (Indeed, the alternative does not occur to them.) This way of looking at the matter cannot be justified. When we buy new clothes not to keep ourselves warm but to look "well-dressed" we are not providing for any important need. We would not be sacrificing anything significant if we were to continue to wear our old clothes, and give the money to famine relief. By doing so, we would be preventing another person from starving. It follows from what I have said earlier that we ought to give money away, rather than spend it on clothes which we do not need to keep us warm. To do so is not charitable, or generous. Nor is it the kind of act which philosophers and theologians have called "supererogatory"—an act which it would be good to do, but not wrong not to do. On the contrary, we ought to give the money away, and it is wrong not to do so.

I am not maintaining that there are no acts which are charitable, or that there are no acts which it would be good to do but not wrong not to do. It may be possible to redraw the distinction between duty and charity in some other place. All I am arguing here is that the present way of drawing the distinction, which makes it an act of charity for a man living at the level of affluence which most people in the "developed nations" enjoy to give money to save someone else from starvation, cannot be supported. It is beyond the scope of my argument to consider whether the distinction should be redrawn or abolished altogether. There would be many other possible ways of drawing the distinction—for instance, one might decide that it is good to make other people as happy as possible, but not wrong not to do so.

Despite the limited nature of the revision in our moral conceptual scheme which I am proposing, the revision would, given the extent of both affluence and famine in the world today, have radical implications. These implications may lead to further objections, distinct from those I have already considered. I shall discuss two of these.

One objection to the position I have taken might be simply that it is too drastic a revision of our moral scheme. People do not ordinarily judge in the way I have suggested they should. Most people reserve their moral condemnation for those who violate some moral norm, such as the norm against taking another person's property. They do not condemn those who indulge in luxury instead of giving to famine relief. But given that I did not set out to present a morally neutral description of the way people make moral judgments, the way people do in fact judge has nothing to do with the validity of my conclusion. My conclusion follows from the principle which I advanced earlier, and unless that principle is rejected, or the arguments shown to be unsound, I think the conclusion must stand, however strange it appears.

It might, nevertheless, be interesting to consider why our society, and most other societies, do judge differently from the way I have suggested they should. In a well-known article, J. O. Urmson suggests that the imperatives of duty, which tell us what we must do, as distinct from what it would be good to do but not wrong not to do, function so as to prohibit behavior that is intolerable if men are to live together in society.[3] This may explain the origin and continued existence of the present division between acts of duty and acts of charity. Moral attitudes are shaped by the needs of society, and no doubt society needs people who will observe the rules that make social existence tolerable. From the point of view of a particular society, it is essential to prevent violations of norms against killing, stealing, and so on. It is quite inessential, however, to help people outside one's own society.

If this is an explanation of our common distinction between duty and supererogation, however, it is not a justification of it. The moral point of view requires us to look beyond the interests of our own society. Previously, as I have already mentioned, this may hardly have been feasible, but it is quite feasible now. From the moral point of view, the prevention of the starvation of millions of people outside our society must be considered at least as pressing as the upholding of property norms within our society.

It has been argued by some writers, among them Sidgwick and Urmson, that we need to have a basic moral code which is not too far beyond the capacities of the ordinary man, for otherwise there will be a general breakdown of compliance with the moral code. Crudely stated, this argument suggests that if we tell people that they ought to refrain from murder and give everything they do not really need to famine relief, they will do neither, whereas if we tell them that they ought to refrain from murder and that it is good to give to famine relief but not wrong not to do so, they will at least refrain from murder. The issue here is: Where should we draw the line between conduct that is required and conduct that is good although not required, so as to get the best possible result? This would seem to be an empirical question, although a very difficult one. One objection to the Sidgwick–Urmson line of argument is that it takes insufficient account of the effect that moral standards can have on the decisions we make. Given a society in which a wealthy man who gives 5 percent of his income to famine relief is regarded as most generous, it is not surprising that a proposal that we all ought to give away half our incomes will be thought to be absurdly unrealistic. In a society which held that no man should have more than enough while others have less than they need, such a proposal might seem narrow-minded. What it is possible for a man to do and what he is likely to do are both, I think, very greatly influenced by what people around are doing and expecting him to do. In any case, the possibility that by spreading the idea that we ought to be doing very much more than we are to relieve famine we shall bring about a general breakdown of moral behavior seems remote. If the stakes are an end to widespread starvation, it is worth the risk. Finally, it should be emphasized that these considerations are relevant only to the issue of what we should require from others, and not to what we ourselves ought to do.

The second objection to my attack on the present distinction between duty and charity is one which has from time to time been made against utilitarianism. It follows from some forms of utilitarian theory that we all ought, morally, to be working full time to increase the balance of happiness over misery. The position I have taken here would not lead to this conclusion in all circumstances, for if there were no bad occurrences that we could prevent without sacrificing something of comparable moral importance, my argument would have no application. Given the present conditions in many parts of the world, however, it does follow from my argument that we ought, morally, to be working full time to relieve great suffering of the sort that occurs as a result of famine or other disasters. Of course, mitigating circumstances can be adduced—for instance, that if we wear ourselves out through overwork, we shall be less effective than we would otherwise have been. Nevertheless, when all considerations of this sort have been taken into account, the conclusion remains: we ought to be preventing as much suffering as we can without sacrificing something else of comparable moral importance. This conclusion is one which we may be reluctant to face. I cannot see, though, why it should be regarded as a criticism of the position for which I have argued, rather than a criticism of our ordinary standards of behavior. Since most people are self-interested to some degree, very few of us are likely to do everything that we ought to do. It would, however, hardly be honest to take this as evidence that it is not the case that we ought to do it.

It may still be thought that my conclusions are so wildly out of line with what everyone else thinks and has always thought that there must be something wrong with the argument somewhere. In order to show that my conclusions, while certainly contrary to contemporary Western moral standards, would not have seemed so extraordinary at other times and in other places, I would like to quote a passage from a writer not normally thought of as a way-out radical, Thomas Aquinas.

> Now, according to the natural order instituted by divine providence, material goods are provided for the satisfaction of human needs. Therefore the division and appropriation of property, which proceeds from human law, must not hinder the satisfaction of man's necessity from such goods. Equally, whatever a man has in superabundance is owed, of natural right, to the poor for their sustenance. So Ambrosius says, and it is also to be found in the Decretum Gratiani: "The bread which you withhold belongs to the hungry; the clothing you shut away, to the naked; and the money you bury in the earth is the redemption and freedom of the penniless."[4]

I now want to consider a number of points, more practical than philosophical, which are relevant to the application of the moral conclusion we have reached. These points challenge not the idea that we ought to be doing all we can to prevent starvation, but the idea that giving away a great deal of money is the best means to this end.

It is sometimes said that overseas aid should be a government responsibility, and that therefore one ought not to give to privately run charities. Giving privately, it is said, allows the government and the noncontributing members of society to escape their responsibilities.

This argument seems to assume that the more people there are who give to privately organized famine relief funds, the less likely it is that the government will take over full responsibility for such aid. This assumption is unsupported, and does not strike me as at all plausible. The opposite view—that if no one gives voluntarily, a government will assume that its citizens are uninterested in famine relief and would not wish to be forced into giving aid—seems more plausible. In any case, unless there were a definite probability that by refusing to give one would be helping to bring about massive government assistance, people who do refuse to make voluntary contributions are refusing to prevent a certain amount of suffering without being able to point to any tangible beneficial consequence of their refusal. So the onus of showing how their refusal will bring about government action is on those who refuse to give.

I do not, of course, want to dispute the contention that governments of affluent nations should be giving many times the amount of genuine, no-strings-attached aid that they are giving now. I agree, too, that giving privately is not enough, and that we ought to be campaigning actively for entirely new standards for both public and private contributions to famine relief. Indeed, I would sympathize with someone who thought that campaigning was more important than giving oneself, although I doubt whether preaching what one does not practice would be very effective. Unfortunately, for many people the idea that "it's the government's responsibility" is a reason for not giving which does not appear to entail any political action either.

Another, more serious reason for not giving to famine relief funds is that until there is effective population control, relieving famine merely postpones starvation. If we save the Bengal refugees now, others, perhaps the children of these refugees, will face starvation in a few years' time. In support of this, one may cite the now well-known facts about the population explosion and the relatively limited scope for expanded production.

This point, like the previous one, is an argument against relieving suffering that is happening now, because of a belief about what might happen in the future; it is unlike the previous point in that very good evidence can be adduced in support of this belief about the future. I will not go into the evidence here. I accept that the earth cannot support indefinitely a population rising at the present rate. This certainly poses a problem for anyone who thinks it important to prevent famine. Again, however, one could accept the argument without drawing the conclusion that it absolves one from any obligation to do anything to prevent famine. The conclusion that should be drawn is that the best means of preventing famine, in the long run, is population control. It would then follow from the position reached earlier that one ought to be doing all one can to promote population control (unless one held that all forms of population control were wrong in themselves, or would have significantly bad consequences). Since there are organizations working specifically for population control, one would then support them rather than more orthodox methods of preventing famine.

A third point raised by the conclusion reached earlier relates to the question of just how much we all ought to be giving away. One possibility, which has already been mentioned, is that we ought to give until we reach the level of marginal utility—that is, the level at which, by giving more, I would cause as much suffering to myself or my dependents as I would relieve by my gift. This would mean, of course, that one would reduce oneself to very near the material circumstances of a Bengali refugee. It will be recalled that earlier I put forward both a strong and a moderate version of the principle of preventing bad occurrences. The strong version, which required us to prevent bad things from happening unless in doing so we would be sacrificing something of comparable moral significance, does seem to require reducing ourselves to the level of marginal utility. I should also say that the strong version seems to me to be the correct one. I proposed the more moderate version—that we should prevent bad occurrences unless, to do so, we had to sacrifice something morally significant—only in order to show that even on this surely undeniable principle a great change in our way of life is required. On the more moderate principle, it may not follow that we ought to reduce ourselves to the level of marginal utility, for one might hold that to reduce oneself and one's family to this level is to cause something significantly bad to happen. Whether this is so I shall not discuss, since, as I have said, I can see no good reason for holding the moderate version of the principle rather than the strong version. Even if we accepted the principle only in its moderate form, however, it should be clear that we would have to give away enough to ensure that the consumer society, dependent as it is on people spending on trivia rather than giving to famine relief, would slow down and perhaps disappear entirely. There are several reasons why this would be desirable in itself. The value and necessity of economic growth are now being questioned not only by conservationists, but by economists as well.[5] There is no doubt, too, that the consumer society has had a distorting effect on the goals and purposes of its members. Yet looking at the matter purely from the point of view of overseas aid, there must be a limit to the extent to which we should deliberately slow down our economy; for it might be the case that if we gave away, say, 40 percent of our Gross National Product, we would slow down the economy so much that in absolute terms we would be giving less than if we gave 25 percent of the much larger GNP that we would have if we limited our contribution to this smaller percentage.

I mention this only as an indication of the sort of factor that one would have to take into account in working out an ideal. Since Western societies generally consider one percent of the GNP an acceptable level for overseas aid, the matter is entirely academic. Nor does it affect the question of how much an individual should give in a society in which very few are giving substantial amounts.

It is sometimes said, though less often now than it used to be, that philosophers have no special role to play in public affairs, since most public issues depend primarily on an assessment of facts. On questions of fact, it is said, philosophers as such have no special expertise, and so it has been possible to engage in philosophy without committing oneself to any position on major public issues. No doubt there are some issues of social policy and foreign policy about which it can truly be said that a really expert assessment of the facts is required before taking sides or acting, but the issue of famine is surely not one of these. The facts about the existence of suffering are beyond dispute. Nor, I think, is it disputed that we can do something about it, either through orthodox methods of famine relief or through population control or both. This is therefore an issue on which philosophers are competent to take a position. The issue is one which faces everyone who has more money than he needs to support himself and his dependents, or who is in a position to take some sort of political action. These categories must include practically every teacher and student of philosophy in the universities of the Western world. If philosophy is to deal with matters that are relevant to both teachers and students, this is an issue that philosophers should discuss.

Discussion, though, is not enough. What is the point of relating philosophy to public (and personal) affairs if we do not take our conclusions seriously? In this instance, taking our conclusion seriously means acting on it. The philosopher will not find it any easier than anyone else to alter his attitudes and way of life to the extent that, if I am right, is involved in doing everything that we ought to be doing. At the very least, though, one can make a start. The philosopher who does so will have to sacrifice some of the benefits of the consumer society, but he can find compensation in the satisfaction of a way of life in which theory and practice, if not yet in harmony, are at least coming together.

NOTES

1. There was also a third possibility: that India would go to war to enable the refugees to return to their lands. Since I wrote this paper, India has taken this way out. The situation is no longer that described earlier, but this does not affect my argument, as the next paragraph indicates.

2. In view of the special sense philosophers often give to the term, I should say that I use "obligation" simply as the abstract noun derived from "ought," so that "I have an obligation to" means no more, and no less, than "I ought to." This usage is in accordance with the definition of "ought" given by the Shorter Oxford English

Dictionary: "the general verb to express duty or obligation." I do not think any issue of substance hangs on the way the term is used; sentences in which I use "obligation" could all be rewritten, although somewhat clumsily, as sentences in which a clause containing "ought" replaces the term "obligation."

3. J. O. Urmson, "Saints and Heroes," *Essays in Moral Philosophy*, Abraham I. Melden, ed. Seattle: University of Washington Press, 1958, p. 214. For a related but significantly different view see also Henry Sidgwick, *The Methods of Ethics*, 7th ed. London: Dover Press, 1907, pp. 220–221, 492–493.

4. Summa Theologica, II-II, Question 66, Article 7, in Aquinas, *Selected Political Writings*, ed. A. P. d'Entreves, ed. trans. J. G. Dawson. Oxford: Basil Blackwell, 1948, p. 171.

5. See, for instance, John Kenneth Galbraith, *The New Industrial State*. Boston: Houghton Mifflin, 1967; and E. J. Mishan, *The Costs of Economic Growth*. New York: Praeger, 1967.

Rights and the Duty
to Bring Aid*

JOHN ARTHUR

John Arthur is Professor of Philosophy and Director of the
Program in Philosophy, Politics, and Law, at the State University
of New York at Binghamton. He is the author of *The Unfinished
Constitution* and *Words that Bind: Judicial Review and the
Grounds of Modern Constitutional Theory*.

There is no doubt that the large and growing incidence of world
hunger constitutes a major problem, both moral and practical, for
the fortunate few who have surpluses of cheap food. Our habits
regarding meat consumption exemplify the magnitude of the moral
issue. Americans now consume about two and one-half times the
meat they did in 1950 (currently about 125 lb per capita per year).
Yet, meat is extremely inefficient as a source of food. Only a small
portion of the total calories consumed by the animal remains to be
eaten in the meat. As much as 95 percent of the food is lost by feeding and eating cattle rather than producing the grain for direct
human consumption. Thus, the same amount of food consumed by
Americans largely indirectly in meat form could feed one and a half
billion persons on a (relatively meatless) Chinese diet. Much, if not
all, of the world's food crisis could be resolved if Americans were simply to change their eating habits by moving toward direct consumption of grain and at the same time providing the surpluses for the
hungry. Given this, plus the serious moral problems associated with
animal suffering,[1] the overall case for vegetarianism seems strong.

I want to discuss here only one of these two related problems,
the obligations of the affluent few to starving people. I begin by considering a recent article on the subject by Peter Singer, entitled
"Famine, Affluence, and Morality" (reprinted in this volume).[2] I argue
that Singer fails to establish the claim that such an obligation exists.
This is the case for both the strong and weak interpretations of his
view. I then go on to show that the role of rights needs to be given
greater weight than utilitarian theories like Singer's allow. The rights

*Aiken, William and Hugh LaFollette, (ed. by), *World Hunger and
Moral Obligation*, © by Prentice-Hall, 1977, pp. 37-48.

of both the affluent and the starving are shown to be morally significant but not in themselves decisive, since obligations of benevolence
can and often do override rights of others (e.g., property rights).
Finally, I argue that under specific conditions the affluent are obligated not to exercise their rights to consume at the expense of others'
lives.

II

Singer's argument is in two stages. First, he argues that two general moral principles are and ought to be accepted. Then he claims
that the principles imply an obligation to eliminate starvation. The
first principle is simply that "suffering and death from lack of food,
shelter, and medical care are bad."[3] This principle seems obviously
true and I will have little to say about it. Some may be inclined to
think that the existence of an evil in itself places an obligation on
others, but that is, of course, the problem which Singer addresses. I
take it that he is not begging the question in this obvious way and
will argue from the existence of evil to the obligation of others to
eliminate it. But how, exactly, does he establish the connection? It is
the second principle which he thinks shows that connection.

The necessary link is provided by either of two versions of this
principle. The first (strong) formulation which Singer offers of the
second principle is as follows:

> if it is in our power to prevent something bad from happening,
> without thereby sacrificing anything of comparable moral impor-
> tance, we ought, morally, to do it.[4]

The weaker principle simply substitutes for "comparable moral
importance" the phrase "any moral significance." He goes on to
develop these notions, saying that:

> By 'without sacrificing anything of comparable moral impor-
> tance' I mean without causing anything else comparably bad to
> happen, or doing something that is wrong in itself, or failing to
> promote some moral good, comparable in significance to the bad
> thing we can prevent.[5]

These remarks can be interpreted for the weaker principle by simply
eliminating "comparable" in the statement.

One question is, of course, whether either of these two principles ought to be accepted. There are two ways in which this could be established. First, they could be shown, by philosophical argument, to follow from reasonably well established premises or from a general theory. Second, they might be justified because they are principles that underlie particular moral judgments the truth of which is accepted. Singer doesn't do either of these explicitly, although he seems to have the second in mind. He first speaks of what he takes to be the "uncontroversial appearance" of the principles. He then applies the principles to a similar case in which a drowning child requires help. Singer argues, in essence, that since the drowning is bad and it can be avoided without sacrificing something of moral significance, it is obligatory that the child be saved. He claims further that both the strong and weak versions are sufficient to establish the duty. Dirtying one's clothes, for example, is not of "moral significance" and so does not justify failure to act. The last part of his paper is devoted to the claim that the analogy between the case of the child and starving people is apt in that geographical distance and others' willingness to act are not acceptable excuses for inaction.

III

My concern here is not with these latter issues. Rather, I want to focus on the two versions of the second principle, discussing each in terms of (1) whether it is plausible, and (2) if true, whether it establishes the duty to provide aid. I will deal with the weak version first, arguing that it fails at step (2) in the argument.

This version reads, "if it is in our power to prevent something bad from happening without thereby sacrificing anything morally significant we ought morally to do it." Singer later claims that:

> Even if we accept the principle in its moderate form, however, it should be clear that we would have to give away enough to ensure that the consumer society, dependent as it is on people spending on trivia rather than giving to famine relief, would slow down and perhaps disappear entirely.[6]

The crucial idea of "morally significant" is left largely unanalyzed. Two examples are given: dirtying one's clothes and being "well dressed." Both are taken to be morally insignificant.

It could perhaps be argued against Singer that these things are morally significant. Both, for example, would be cases of decreasing aesthetic value, and if you think aesthetic values are intrinsic you might well dispute the claim that being "well dressed" is without moral significance. There is, however, a more serious objection to be raised. To see this, we need to distinguish between the possible value of the fact of being "well dressed" and the value of the enjoyment some persons receive and create by being "well dressed" (and, of course, the unhappiness avoided by being "badly dressed").

That such enjoyment and unhappiness are of some moral significance can be seen by the following case. Suppose it were possible that, by simply singing a chorus of "Dixie" you could eliminate all the unhappiness and embarrassment that some people experience at being badly dressed. Surely, doing that would be an act of moral significance. It would be good for you to do so, perhaps even wrong not to. Similarly, throwing mud on people's clothes, though not a great wrong, is surely not "without any moral significance."

It seems then, that the weak principle (while perhaps true) does not generally establish a duty to provide aid to starving people. Whether it does in specific instances depends on the nature of the cost to the person providing the aid. If either the loss to the giver is in itself valuable or the loss results in increased unhappiness or decreased happiness to someone, then the principle does not require that the burden be accepted.

(It is interesting to ask just how much giving would be required by this principle. If we can assume that givers would benefit in some minimal way by giving—and that they are reasonable—then perhaps the best answer is that the level of giving required is the level that is actually given. Otherwise, why would people not give more if there is no value to them in things they choose to keep?)

In addition to the moral significance of the costs that I just described, there is a further problem which will become particularly significant in considering the strong principle. For many people it is part of their moral sense that they and others have a special relationship to their own goals or projects. That is, in making one's choices, a person may properly weigh the outcome that one desires more heavily than the goals that others may have. Often this is expressed as a right or entitlement.[7] Thus, for example, if P acquires some good (x) in a just social arrangement without violating others' rights, then P has a special title to x that P is entitled to weigh against the desires of others. P need not, in determining whether he ought to give x to another, overlook the fact that x is his; he acquired it fairly, and so has special say in what happens to it. If this is correct, it is a fact of some moral significance and thus would also block the inference from the weak principle to the obligation to give what one has to others. I will pursue this line of argument in the following section while considering the strong version of the principle.

IV

Many people, especially those inclined toward utilitarianism, would probably accept the preceding, believing that it is the stronger of the two principles that should be used. "After all," they might argue, "the real issue is the great disparity between the amount of good which could be produced by resources of the rich if applied to problems of starvation as against the small amount of good produced by the resources if spent on second cars and houses, fancy clothes and so on." I will assume that the facts are just as the claim suggests. That is, I will assume that it can not be plausibly argued that there are, for example, artistic or cultural values which (1) would be lost by such redistribution of wealth and (2) are equal in value to the starvation which would be eliminated. Thus, if the strong principle is true, then it (unlike the weak version) would require radical changes in our common understanding of the duties of the wealthy to starving people.

But is it true, as Singer suggests, that "if it is in our power to prevent something bad from happening without thereby sacrificing something of comparable moral significance we ought morally to do it?" Here the problem with the meaning of "moral significance" is even more acute than in the weak version. All that was required for the weak principle was that we be able to distinguish courses of action that have moral significance from those that do not. Here, however, the moral significance of alternative acts must be both recognized and weighed. And how is this to be done, according to Singer? Unfortunately, he provides little help here, though this is crucial in evaluating his argument.

I will discuss one obvious interpretation of "comparable moral significance," argue it is inadequate, and then suggest what I take to be some of the factors an adequate theory would consider.

Assuming that giving aid is not "bad in itself," the only other facts which Singer sees as morally significant in evaluating obligations are the good or bad consequences of actions. Singer's strong version obviously resembles the act utilitarian principle. With respect to starvation, this interpretation is open to the objection raised at the end of part III, since it takes no account of a variety of important factors, such as the apparent right to give added weight to one's own choices and interests, and to ownership. I now wish to look at this claim in more detail.

Consider the following examples of moral problems which I take to be fairly common. One obvious means by which you could aid others is with your body. Many of your extra organs (eye, kidney) could be given to another with the result that there is more good than if you kept both. You wouldn't see as well or live as long, perhaps, but that is not of comparable significance to the benefit others would receive. Yet, surely the fact that it is your eye and you need it is not insignificant. Perhaps there could be cases where one is obligated to sacrifice one's health or sight, but what seems clear is that this is not true in every case where (slightly) more good would come of your doing so. Second, suppose a woman has a choice between remaining with her husband or leaving. As best she can determine, the morally relevant factors do not indicate which she should do (the consequences of each seem about equally good and there is no question of broken promises, deception, or whatever). But, suppose in addition to these facts, it is the case that by remaining with her husband the woman will be unable to pursue important aspects of the plan of life she has set for herself. Perhaps by remaining she will be forced to sacrifice a career which she wishes to pursue. If the only facts that are of moral significance are the consequences of her choice, then she ought, presumably, to flip a coin (assuming there is some feature of her staying that is of equal importance to the unhappiness at the loss of the career she will experience). Surely, though, the fact that some goals are ones she chooses for herself (assuming she doesn't violate the others' rights) is of significance. It is, after all, her life and her future and she is entitled to treat it that way. In neither of these cases is the person required to accept as equal to his or her own goals and well-being the welfare of even his or her family, much less the whole world. The fact that others may benefit even slightly more from their pursuing another course is not in itself sufficient to show they ought to act other than they choose. Servility, though perhaps not a vice, is certainly not an obligation that all must fulfill.[8]

This goes part way, I think, in explaining the importance we place on allowing people maximal latitude in pursuing their goals. Rights or entitlements to things that are our own reflect important facts about people. Each of us has only one life and it is uniquely valuable to each of us. Your choices do not constitute my life, nor do mine yours. The purely utilitarian interpretation of "moral significance" provides for assigning no special weight to the goals and interests of individuals in making their choices. It provides no basis for saying that though there may be greater total good done by one course, still a person could be entitled for some reason to pursue another.

It seems, then, that determining whether giving aid to starving persons would be sacrificing something of comparable moral significance demands weighing the fact that the persons are entitled to give special weight to their own interests where their future or (fairly acquired) property is at issue. Exactly how much weight may be given is a question that I will consider shortly. The point here is that the question of the extent of the obligation to eliminate starvation has not been answered. My argument was that however "moral significance" is best understood, it is far too simple to suggest that only the total good produced is relevant. If providing quality education for one's children is a goal, then (assuming the resources were acquired fairly) the fact that it is a goal itself provides additional weight against other ways the resources might be used, including the one that maximizes the total good. Further, if the resources to be used for the purpose are legitimately owned, then that too is something that the parent is entitled to consider.

Returning to the case of the drowning child, the same point may be made. Suppose it is an important part of a person's way of life that he not interfere. Perhaps the passer-by believes God's will is being manifested in this particular incident and strongly values non-interference with God's working out of His plan. Surely, this is especially relevant to the question of whether the person is obligated to intervene, even when the greatest good would be promoted by intervention. When saying that a person is obligated to act in some way, the significance to the person of the act must not only be considered along with all the other features of the act, but is also of special moral significance in determining that person's duty. More, however, needs to be said here.

Suppose, for instance, that the case were like this: A passer-by sees a child drowning but fails to help, not for the sake of another important goal but rather out of lack of interest. Such situations are not at all uncommon, as when people fail to report violent crimes they observe in progress. I assume that anyone who fails to act in such circumstances is acting wrongly. As with the case of the utilitarian principle discussed earlier, the drowning child also represents a limiting case. In the former, no significance is assigned to the woman's choice by virtue of its being hers. Here, however, the interests of others are not weighed. An acceptable principle of benevolence would fall between the two limiting cases. The relative moral significance of alternative acts could then be determined by applying the principle, distinguishing acts which are obligatory from charitable ones.

In summary, I have argued that neither the strong nor the weak principle advanced by Singer provides an adequate solution to the issue of affluence and hunger. The essential problem is with his notion of "moral significance." I argued that the weak principle fails to show any obligations, given the normal conception of factors which possess such significance. I then argued that the strong principle (which is close to act utilitarianism) is mistaken. The basic objection to this principle is that it fails to take account of certain aspects of the situation which must be considered in any adequate formulation of the principle.

V

As I suggested earlier, a fully adequate formulation of the principle of benevolence depends on a general theory of right. Such a theory would not only include a principle of benevolence but also give account of the whole range of rights and duties and a means to weigh conflicting claims. In this section, I discuss some of the various problems associated with benevolence, obligation, and rights. In the final section, I offer what I believe to be an adequate principle of benevolence.

One view, which has been criticized recently by Judith Thomson,[9] suggests that whenever there is a duty or obligation there must be a corresponding right. I presume we want to say that in some cases (e.g., the drowning child) there is an obligation to benevolence, but does this also mean that the child has a right to be aided? Perhaps there is only a semantic point here regarding "right," but perhaps also there is a deeper disagreement.

I suggest that, whether we call it a "right" or not, there are important differences between obligations based on benevolence and other obligations. Two differences are significant. First, the person who has the obligation to save the drowning child did not do anything that created the situation. But, compare this case with a similar one of a lifeguard who fails to save someone. Here there is a clear sense in which the drowning victim may claim a right to have another do his utmost to save him. An agreement was reached whereby the lifeguard accepted the responsibility for the victim's welfare. The guard, in a sense, took on the goals of the swimmers as his own. To fail to aid is a special sort of injustice that the passer-by does not do. It seems clearly appropriate to speak of the lifeguard's failure to act as a case of a right being violated.

A second important point regarding the drowning child example and rights is that the passer-by is not taking positive steps in reference to the child. This can be contrasted with an action that might be taken to drown a child who would not otherwise die. Here, again, it is appropriate to describe this act as a violation of a right (to life). Other violations of rights also seem to require that one act, not merely fail to take action—for example, property rights (theft) and privacy rights (listening without leave). The drowning child and starvation cases are wrong not because of acts but the failure to act.

Thus, there are important differences between duties of benevolence and others where a right is obviously at issue. Cases of failing to aid are not (unlike right violations) either instances of positive actions that are taken or ones in which the rich or the passer-by has taken responsibility by a previous act. It does not follow from this, however, that strong obligations are not present to save other persons. Obviously, one ought to aid a drowning child (at least) in cases where there is no serious risk or cost to the passer-by. This is true even though there is no obvious right that the child has to be aided.

Furthermore, if saving a drowning child requires using someone's boat without their permission (a violation of property right), then it still ought to be done. Duties to bring aid can override duties not to violate rights. The best thing to say here is that, depending on the circumstances, duties to aid and not to violate rights can each outweigh the other. Where actions involve both violation of rights and failing to meet duties to aid (the lifeguard's failing to save), the obligation is stronger than either would be by itself. Describing the situation in this way implies that although there is a sense in which the boat owner, the affluent spender, and the passer-by have a right to fail to act, still they are obligated not to exercise that right because there is a stronger duty to give aid.

Some may be inclined to say, against this, that in fact the passer-by does not have such a right not to help. But this claim is ambiguous. If what is meant is that they ought to help, then I agree. There is, however, still a point in saying owners of food have the right to use the food as they see fit. It serves to emphasize that there is a moral difference between these cases and ones where the object of need is not legitimately owned by anyone (as, for example, if it's not another's boat but a log that the drowning child needs). To say that the property right is lost where the principle of benevolence overrides is to hide this difference, though it is morally significant.

Other people might be inclined to say about these situations that the point of saying someone has a right to their food, time, boat, or whatever is that others ought not to intervene to force them to bring aid. A person defending this view might accept my claim that in fact the person ought to help. It might then be argued that because they are not violating a right of another (to be saved) and they have a (property) right to the good, others can't, through state authority, force them to bring aid.

This claim obviously raises a variety of questions in legal and political philosophy, and is outside the scope of the present paper. My position does not preclude good samaritan laws, nor are they implied. This is a further question which requires further argument. That one has a moral right to *x*, but is obligated for other reasons not to exercise the right, leaves open the issue of whether others either can or should make that person fulfill the obligation.

If what I have said is correct, two general points should be made about starvation. First, even though it may be that the affluent have a right to use resources to pursue their own goals, and not provide aid, they may also be strongly obligated not to exercise the right. This is because, in the circumstances, the duty to benevolence is overriding. The existence and extent of such an obligation can be determined only by discovering the relative weight of these conflicting principles. In the final section, I consider how this should be done.

Second, even if it is also true that the passer-by and the affluent do not violate a right of another in failing to help, it may still be the case that they strongly ought not do so. Of course, their behavior could also be even worse than it is (by drowning the child or sending poisoned food to the hungry and thus violating their rights). All that shows, however, is that the failure to help is not the most morally objectionable course that can be imagined in the circumstances. This point hardly constitutes justification for failing to act.

VI

I argued earlier that neither Singer's weak principle nor the utilitarian one is what we are after. The former would imply (wrongly) little or no duty of benevolence, and the latter does not take seriously enough the rights and interests of the affluent. What is needed is a principle which we may use to determine the circumstances in which the needs of others create a duty to bring aid that is more stringent than the rights of the affluent to pursue their own interests and use their property as they desire.

The following principle, while similar to the utilitarian one, seems to be most adequate: "If it is in our power to prevent death of an innocent without sacrificing anything of substantial significance then we ought morally to do it." The problem, of course, is to determine exactly what is meant by "substantial significance." I assume there are no duties present that arise out of others' rights, as, for example, those of one's children to be provided for. Considerations of that sort would lead beyond the present paper. My concern here is limited to instances in which there is a question of bringing aid (where no obvious right to the aid is present) or using resources for other (preferred) ends.

There are two questions which are important in deciding whether what is being given up by the affluent is of substantial significance. First, we might specify objectively the needs that people have, and grant that the duty to bring aid is not present unless these needs have already been met. Included among the needs which are of substantial significance would be those things without which a person cannot continue to function physically, for example, food, clothing, health care, housing, and sufficient training to provide these for oneself.

It also, however, seems reasonable that certain psychological facts ought to be weighed before a person is obligated to help others meet their needs. For example, if you cannot have an even modestly happy life without some further good, then surely that, too, is something to which you are entitled. This suggests a second, subjective standard that should also be employed to determine whether something is of no substantial significance and so ought not be consumed at the expense of others' basic needs. The best way to put this, I believe, is to say that "if the lack of x would not affect the long-term happiness of a person, then x is of no substantial significance." By "long-term happiness" I mean to include anything which, if not acquired, will result in unhappiness over an extended period of one's life, not just something the lack of which is a source of momentary loss but soon forgotten. Thus, in a normal case, dirtying one's clothes to save a drowning child is of no substantial significance and so the duty of benevolence is overriding. If, however, selling some possession for famine relief would mean the person's life really is (for a long period) less happy, then the possessions are of substantial significance and so the person is not wrong in exercising the right of ownership instead of providing aid. If the possessions had been sold, it would have been an act of charity, not fulfillment of a duty. The same analysis can be provided for other choices we make, for example, how our time is spent and whether to donate organs. If doing so would result in your not seeing well and this would make your life less happy over time, then you are not obligated to do so.

If what I have said is correct, then duties of benevolence increase as one's dependence on possessions for living a happy life decreases. If a person's long-term happiness does not depend on (second?) cars and fancy clothes, then that person ought not to purchase those goods at the expense of others' basic needs being unfulfilled. Thus, depending on the psychological nature of persons, their duties of benevolence will vary.

The question of the actual effect of not buying a new car, house, clothes, or whatever on one's long-term happiness is of course a difficult one. My own feeling is that if the principle were to be applied honestly, those of us who are relatively affluent would discover that a substantial part of the resources and time we expend should be used to bring aid. The extent of the obligation must, finally, be determined by asking whether the lack of some good really would result in a need not being met or in a less happy life for its owner, and that is a question between each of us and our conscience.

In summary, I have argued that Singer's utilitarian principle is inadequate to establish the claim that acts to eliminate starvation are obligatory, but that such an obligation still exists. The rights of both the affluent and the hungry are considered, and a principle is defended which clarifies the circumstances in which it is a duty and not merely charitable to provide aid to others whose basic needs are not being met.

NOTES

1. Peter Singer, Animal Liberation. New York: New York Review of Books/Random House, 1975.
2. Peter Singer, "Famine, Affluence, and Morality," Philosophy and Public Affairs, I, no. 3 (Spring 1972).
3. Ibid., p. 28 (in this volume).
4. Ibid.
5. Ibid. I assume "importance" and "significance" are synonymous.
6. Ibid., p. 36 (in this volume).
7. In a recent book (*Anarchy, State, and Utopia*, New York: Basic Books, 1974), Robert Nozick argues that such rights are extensive against state authority.
8. For an argument that servility is wrong, see Thomas Hill, "Servility and Self-Respect," *The Monist*, VII, no. 4 (January 1973).
9. Judith Jarvis Thomson, "The Right to Privacy," *Philosophy and Public Affairs*, IV, no. 4 (Summer 1975).

The Life-Saving Analogy

GARRETT CULLITY

Garrett Cullity teaches in the Department of Moral Philosophy of the University of St. Andrews. He is currently working on a book, *The Moral Demands of Affluence.*

"It is morally wrong for affluent people not to help the chronically poor." Many people read this remark in a way that allows them to agree with it, while believing that they're not personally doing anything wrong—perhaps even that no individual is. They read it as maintaining that we are collectively acting wrongly. But on a second reading, it issues a direct personal challenge: It is wrong for affluent *individuals* not to help the world's poor, in failing to contribute their own time and money to voluntary international aid agencies. In this essay, I discuss the most prominent argument for this personal challenge.

To argue that individual noncontribution to aid agencies[1] is wrong, you need to identify a morally significant relation in which each affluent individual stands to destitute people. Your argument can take one of two forms. Let's call it a *derivative* argument if it seeks to derive this relation (one between affluent *individuals* and the destitute) from a morally significant relation in which affluent people *collectively* stand to the destitute. *Nonderivative* arguments, by contrast, seek to establish the existence of a morally significant relation between affluent individuals and the destitute more directly, without mediating the relation through group membership in this way.

One method available to both derivative and nonderivative arguments is to argue by analogy. This method begins by identifying a relation that is clearly morally significant, then argues that, since the relation of the affluent to the destitute is relevantly similar, we should attribute the same moral significance to it. Various analogies are used by different writers in this way: according to the most forceful of them, noncontribution to aid agencies is like failing to take some simple measure to save a life threatened right in front of you.[2] This is the "Life-Saving Analogy."

Arguments that invoke the Life-Saving Analogy to support the wrongness of individual noncontribution I shall call Life-Saving Arguments. These differ, depending on the moral relation which the analogy is being used to establish. Some of them maintain that I *violate the threatened person's right* to be saved, I *infringe a duty* to save him, or both.[3] The best-known Life-Saving Argument, though—Peter Singer's—attributes moral significance to a simpler relation.[4] If you could easily save a stranger's life—you could save a drowning child, say, by wading into a pond—then failing to do so would be seriously wrong. And according to Singer, this shows that the following relation is morally significant: *being able to avert a very great harm to a person* (in this case, the loss of his life) *at small personal cost*. Any plausible normative ethical theory, he maintains, must agree. But every affluent individual stands in this relation towards those destitute people whose lives are threatened by illness or hunger: each of us can help them, at small personal cost, through the agency of aid organizations.[5] Undoubtedly, there are differences between the two cases: we could sum them up by saying that in his example, you could save a life *directly*, whereas with the distant poor you can do so only indirectly. But unless those differences are *morally relevant*, noncontribution to aid agencies remains as seriously wrong as failing to save a life directly.

Now the most fundamental kind of objection to Life-Saving Arguments attacks the method of arguing by analogy itself. This method begins with one kind of situation where it seems "intuitively" (i.e., pretheoretically) obvious that inaction is morally wrong, and then maintains that unless a moral disanalogy can be found, inaction must be regarded as equally wrong in a second kind of situation. But what prevents us from arguing in the reverse direction? It seems intuitively obvious to most people that noncontribution to aid agencies is not seriously morally wrong: why not argue that unless there are morally relevant differences, refusing to save a life directly is not seriously wrong? Alternatively, why not argue that since it seems intuitively obvious to most people that inaction is seriously wrong in one case but not the other, there *must* be a moral disanalogy? The essence of the objection is this: if you appeal to one set of widespread moral intuitions in order to challenge another, what entitles you to be more confident about the first than the second?

This first, methodological challenge is a serious one, but I have argued elsewhere that it can be met.[6] A different kind of objection accepts the method of argument by analogy itself, but attacks the Life-Saving Analogy in particular. One familiar objection of this kind maintains that aid agencies confer no net benefit on the poor, and perhaps even impose a net cost: contributing to aid agencies, far from being like saving a life, is more like exacerbating the threat.[7]

But I shall concentrate here on two less familiar objections. The first questions whether, even if aid agencies do confer a net benefit on the very poor, the effect of my contributions of time and money to those agencies will be the saving of life. And the second questions whether one can begin (as Singer does) with a situation involving a single threat to life, and draw his conclusions concerning a situation involving an enormous number of potential beneficiaries of our help.

Why concentrate on these two objections? One reason is that they challenge more than just Life-Saving Arguments. We shall find that the first objection threatens *any* argument for the wrongness of individual noncontribution, derivative or nonderivative, and whether arguing by analogy or not; and that the issue raised by the second affects all nonderivative arguments too. The other reason is that both objections are good ones: in its simple form, the Life-Saving Argument must be rejected.

I: Saving Life

Singer's argument by analogy, as I read it, maintains that an affluent person's contributions to aid agencies will avert threats to people's lives.[8] However, this claim is false. The reason for this is not that the net effect of the activity of aid agencies fails to benefit the very poor. (I think a clear case can be mounted for opposing such a view.)[9] Rather, there are two better reasons.

Disaster Prevention and Disaster Relief

The first is simply that most nongovernment agencies are now primarily concerned with preventing future harm to poor people and improving their lives, rather than conducting emergency relief operations. To prevent the perpetuation of food scarcity, aid agencies have been concerned since the 1960s not simply to provide hungry people with food, but to implement programmes aiming to reduce communities' vulnerability to further crop failures, and to foster improvements in basic medicine and education. Many nongovernment agencies do seek to supplement governmental emergency relief operations, but this is becoming a progressively smaller part of their activities. Most of what they do, therefore, amounts not to providing life-saving aid, but rather preventing the need for it. It is not so much saving a drowning person as funding a swimming education program.

Clearly, however, this first objection does not apply to the disaster relief activities to which some aid agencies do devote themselves entirely, and many others in part. Here, a second objection applies.

Spreading the Effect of my Donation

Suppose that, in response to a distant food crisis, I donate enough money to an aid agency to sustain one person for its likely duration. What will the effect of my donation be? Hopefully, it will enable the agency to buy more food.[10] But the extra food bought with my money will not be used (nor would it be proper for it to be used) to feed one extra person. It will be sent to a food distribution camp, and shared among the hungry people there. Had I refrained from making my donation, no one would have failed to receive food: the available food would have been spread a little more thinly across everyone. And only very slightly more thinly. If there are a thousand people in the camp, their each receiving a thousandth of a food ration more or less each day will not make much difference. Indeed, the effect of this increment of food on a person's hunger and health is likely to be imperceptible. (Even for those people whose bodies have a fairly definite threshold with regard to malnutrition—so that at a certain level of food intake, reducing it only slightly will put them suddenly in a precarious state—it is unlikely to be my noncontribution which makes this difference, rather than, for instance, the method of food allocation at the camp.)

This is not to deny that contributors to aid agencies collectively make a significant difference to the destitute. But I do not make such a difference. Any hungry person should be quite indifferent to whether I donate or not. Indeed, notwithstanding my far greater wealth, I probably lose more by making such donations than anyone gains from them. Let us call this the imperceptibility objection.[11]

The challenge to the Life-Saving Argument is plain. Its analogy, it seems, should be revised as follows: I'm invited to contribute to a fund for employing lifeguards to patrol a certain stretch of water, but am told that my donation won't make the difference between anyone's living and dying. Surely my refusal seems intuitively less wrong than failing to rescue a person drowning right next to me.

Generalizing the Imperceptibility Objection

The imperceptibility objection, therefore, threatens the Life-Saving Argument. But next, notice that it challenges all other arguments for the same conclusion.

At the outset, I divided arguments for the wrongness of individual noncontribution to aid agencies into two categories. Derivative arguments derive the claim that there is a morally significant relation between affluent individuals and the destitute from the claim that the affluent collectively stand in a morally significant relation to the destitute; nonderivative arguments do not.

So far, we have been considering one kind of nonderivative argument: an argument by analogy for attributing moral significance to the relation of *being able to avert a very great harm at relatively small cost to yourself*. The imperceptibility objection has shown that the affluent do not stand in this relation even to the starving. Therefore, whether they argue by analogy or not, nonderivative arguments seeking to establish *this* relation fail. But the difficulties can be extended to the other relations which nonderivative arguments seek to establish—a right not to be hungry, for instance, or a duty of beneficence borne by the fortunate towards the needy. If my contributions to an aid agency will not themselves substantially help anyone, how can my not making them violate such a right, or abrogate such a duty?

It is tempting to think that derivative arguments escape these problems. After all, the imperceptibility objection does not impugn our ability *collectively* to avert great harm to the destitute at relatively small cost. The difficulty, though, is to spell out the derivation of *individual* moral wrongness from this or any other collective relation to the destitute. The most natural route for such a derivation would be this: given a group which collectively acts wrongly in failing to achieve a certain result, any member of the group who fails to contribute to achieving that result is individually acting wrongly. But the imperceptibility objection has blocked this route: my donating money to an aid agency will not, in any straightforward sense, contribute to feeding the hungry. If I donate it they will be no less hungry than if I don't.

It might seem that what is needed here is a universalization argument: what makes my individual noncontribution wrong is that if everyone acted in the same way, the destitute would be left unassisted. However, for a start, this pattern of argument seems to run into clear counterexamples. Suppose we ought collectively to build a fence to protect a vulnerable fellow villager and each of us owns ten fenceposts. If few others are doing anything, surely I'm not morally bound to erect my ten posts anyway? And more seriously, consider *why* this is a counterexample. What is ridiculous about my unilaterally erecting the posts is that this personally troublesome action makes no contribution to the end of protecting the villager. But as we have seen, there is a clear sense in which my donating money to an aid agency makes no contribution to the end of helping the destitute—it makes no difference to them whether or not I do it— although it makes a difference to me.

   The imperceptibility objection, then, challenges *all* arguments for the wrongness of individual noncontribution. However, there is a reply to it.[12]

The Argument from Transitivity

Consider a famine relief scheme which operates as follows: each donation is used to buy a particular parcel of food, which is allocated to a particular needy individual. No such scheme exists,[13] but if it did, it would clearly circumvent the imperceptibility objection—my contribution would make a perceptible difference to the scheme's beneficiaries. A Life-Saving Argument for the wrongness of failing to contribute to *this* sort of scheme remains unchallenged. The failure to contribute *would* be a failure to avert threats to life.

   But there is a good reason why such schemes do not exist. It would be perverse to adopt the earmarking policy in preference to the actual one, of using donations collectively to fund a food supply shared among the occupants of a food distribution camp. The earmarking policy would be perverse (quite apart from considerations of unfairness) because of its inefficiency—which is to say that more people would suffer more greatly under this policy than under the actual one. If so, it is clear what I morally ought to do if I could decide whether aid agencies were to conform to the earmarking model or the existing one. People would be left perceptibly worse off by the earmarking policy; therefore there is a clear reason for anyone concerned about other people's welfare to choose the nonearmarking policy, and none favoring the alternative. Again, the imperceptibility objection is no objection to this.

   But I don't have any such power; so how does this help to address the imperceptibility objection? To see the counterargument, we need to think about the transitivity of judgments of moral wrongness. Consider, first, inferences of the following form:

1. Given only alternatives A and B, it would be uniquely wrong to choose A.
2. Given only alternatives B and C, it would be uniquely wrong to choose B.
3. Therefore given only alternatives A and C, it would be uniquely wrong to choose A.

When I say that doing something would be "uniquely wrong" given a certain set of alternatives, what I mean is that it is the only thing that would be wrong given those alternatives. (That is, if there can be cases where all your alternatives are wrong, this is not one of them.) With this clarification, this form of inference is easily supported. If, given only two alternatives, choosing one would be uniquely wrong, then it would be worse to choose it; and "worse than" is a paradigm of a transitive relation. If A is worse than B, and B is worse than C, then A must be worse than C.

But now consider a second kind of inference:

1. Given only alternatives A and B, it would be uniquely wrong to choose A.
2. If one had to choose between being given only alternatives A and B, and being given only alternatives A and C, it would be uniquely wrong to choose to be given only alternatives A and B.
3. Therefore given only alternatives A and C, it would be uniquely wrong to choose A.

Let's apply the same line of thought here. According to premise (2), choosing to be put in a first situation (where one must choose between A and B) would be worse than choosing to be put in a second (where one must choose between A and C). And premise (1) tells us, as before, that choosing A would be worse than choosing B. Suppose for a moment that choosing A were not worse than choosing C. If so, (2) would tell us that choosing the first situation, where the best one could do is to choose B, would be *worse* than choosing the second, where one could not do better than to choose A. But this implies, given premise (1), that choosing to be able to choose the better of two alternatives would be worse than choosing to be able to choose the worse of the two. And this is false. Therefore the supposition must be false: A must be worse than C. So the conclusion, (3), must be true if the premises are true.

The second form of inference, then, is also valid. And if so, an argument of this form refutes the imperceptibility objection. For A, read "spending all my money on myself"; for B, "contributing some money to an aid agency of the earmarking kind"; and for C, "contributing some money to an aid agency of the existing, nonearmarking kind." We saw earlier that it would be uniquely wrong to keep one's money to oneself, rather than contributing to an earmarking agency, if these were one's only alternatives. But we also saw that it would be uniquely wrong to choose to have earmarking agencies rather than nonearmarking ones, were one given that choice. If so, it must be wrong to keep one's money to oneself instead of contributing to a nonearmarking agency.

This deals with the second, imperceptibility objection to the claim that my contributions to aid agencies save lives. But notice that the same strategy of argument also succeeds against the first— the objection that those aid agencies are primarily working to prevent threats to life instead. For again, given a choice between preventing such threats from arising and averting them once they have arisen, it would be uniquely wrong not to choose the former. However, if averting present poverty-related threats to life were the only option, failing to do so would be uniquely wrong, thanks to the life-saving analogy. The transitivity of moral wrongness again implies that where the preventive option is also available, refusing to take either can hardly be less wrong.

So far, I have considered two reasons for believing that an affluent individual's contributions to aid agencies are unlikely to avert a threat to anyone's life. Many voluntary aid agencies are more concerned with preventing future threats than addressing present ones, and the effects of my contributions will be spread over many people rather than concentrated on a few. In reply, I have not denied any of this. Noncontribution to aid agencies is not a failure to save life. However, I have shown that noncontribution remains morally *analogous* to the failure to save life: a Life-Saving Argument remains intact. If we consider any contribution large enough to have saved someone's life through an earmarking agency (and it seems that we're talking of something like $30 here),[14] then even if it will not actually save anyone's life, the argument from transitivity shows that failing to make it is as wrong as failing to save life. Any alternative nonderivative or derivative argument can handle the imperceptibility objection in the same way.

II: Saving Lives

I have examined a first challenge to the Life-Saving Analogy between noncontribution to aid agencies and the direct and unextenuated failure to save a life. The effect of my contributions of time and money to those agencies will almost certainly not be the saving of life. However, this point has been met, leaving a Life-Saving Argument intact. Now for a second disanalogy. It affects, not *whether* the Life-Saving Analogy supports a conclusion concerning the wrongness of individual noncontribution, but rather the strength of that conclusion.

So far, we have simply been discussing the conclusion that noncontribution to aid agencies is as wrong as letting someone die in front of you. This, I think, is a striking conclusion. However, it is compatible with holding that no one who has made one donation to an aid agency acts wrongly in stopping there. A Life-Saving Argument which claimed only this would perhaps be criticizing relatively few affluent people.

Singer goes much further. His full conclusion is that "we ought to give until we reach the level of marginal utility—that is, the level at which, by giving more, I would cause as much suffering to myself or my dependants as I would relieve by my gift. This would mean, of course, that one would reduce oneself to very near the material circumstances of a Bengali refugee."[15] How does he arrive at this extremely demanding claim?

Iteration

Singer's thought is evidently this: the Life-Saving Analogy can be iterated. Suppose that, confronted by two drowning children, I can only be bothered to save one. No doubt, more can be said morally for me than someone who saved neither, but my failure to save the second child remains morally wrong, and for the same reason as before: the cost of helping is trifling compared to what's at stake for him. The Life-Saving Analogy then instructs us to say the same about someone who refuses to make a second contribution to an aid agency. And the same goes for every successive contribution. Not making it will be wrong provided only that, *considered in isolation* (that is, apart from any contributions I have already made), not making it remains comparable to the direct and unextenuated failure to save a life.

It is sometimes maintained that the most that can be morally demanded[16] of any of us towards helping the destitute is that one do one's share. "Why must I sacrifice nearly all of my own interests and projects to relieve this suffering when my being required to sacrifice this much is only the result of the indifference of nearly everyone else, and of their failure to help at all[?] This imposes an unfairly large sacrifice and burden on me. What morality requires is a fair distribution, to all those capable of sharing it, of the burden of helping those in need."[17] However, the counterargument is clear.[18] To the example of the two drowning children, add a second bystander. If the other bystander walks off and leaves me to deal with both of them, then no doubt this is contemptible. However, this surely does not allow me to save the first child and abandon the second, in accordance with my share of the required help. The underlying point is simply that, when an accusation of immoral callousness is made against someone who won't avert threats to other people's lives, protestations concerning one's share of the cost are irrelevant. Given the Life-Saving Analogy, the corresponding claim concerning world poverty—that morality demands only doing one's share towards alleviating it, even when one knows that others are not doing theirs—is no more credible.

Now there is one way in which, even on the iterative reading of the Life-Saving Argument, whether further contributions to aid agencies are morally demanded of me will depend on my previous contributions. The greater my contributions to aid agencies, the poorer I'll become, and as I become poorer, donating the same amount of money will become a progressively greater sacrifice. Eventually, that sacrifice might become too severe to demand it of me even to save a life directly. How severe is that? The common view seems to be that if saving someone's life would mean endangering my own, suffering a serious and permanent physical injury, or something comparable, and *this* deters me, then my inaction would not be wrong—rather, saving the life would have been heroic. If this is right, then once the sacrifice in making a further $30 donation has become *this* severe, my subsequent noncontribution will no longer be wrong. On the iterative reading, then, I will be morally required to keep giving money until either I reach this point, or there are no more destitute people to help. And the latter condition is unlikely to be met soon.[19]

Thus, on this iterative interpretation of the Life-Saving Argument, its full conclusion is the following:

The Iterative Conclusion

> Ceasing to contribute to aid agencies will only be permissible when I have become so poor that making any further $30 contribution (one large enough to be comparable to averting a threat to someone's life) would itself be such a great sacrifice that it would not be wrong to let someone die in front of me at that cost.

The conventional view of how great that sacrifice must be has just been described. To be sure, this view has been attacked as unjustifiably lenient—Singer evidently thinks so, in concluding that we ought to reduce ourselves to the level below which we would cause more suffering to ourselves than we would relieve in our beneficiaries.[20] But notice that, even on the conventional view of the magnitude of a heroic sacrifice, the Iterative Conclusion generates severe demands. For even on the conventional view, it demands that I reduce myself to the level below which giving up another $30 would be the same as submitting myself to a serious and permanent physical injury. And surely I can only claim to have reached this point by becoming very poor indeed.

Aggregation

We wanted to know when the Life-Saving Argument will allow us to *stop* contributing to aid agencies. The Iterative Conclusion seems a persuasive answer. Its persuasiveness comes from its simplicity: if noncontribution is morally comparable to not saving a life directly, and if the grounds for the wrongness of not saving a life are iterative, then the grounds for the wrongness of noncontribution must also be iterative.

But isn't there a way of answering our question which is simpler still? According to the Life-Saving Argument, noncontribution is morally comparable to not saving lives directly; we want to know when we may permissibly stop contributing; so why not simply ask: when may we permissibly stop saving lives directly? And putting the matter this way reveals that the Life-Saving Analogy with which we have been working can be improved. A potential contributor to aid agencies is more closely analogous to someone confronted by a great many drowning people than to someone confronted by one. So why not simply examine our intuitions concerning the more closely analogous case? Suppose, then, that what I come across is not a pond containing one or two drowning children, but the nightmarish scene of a lake, or even a sea, teeming with them. And suppose (to complete the analogy) that many other people could help to save them, but relatively few are doing so. But now, it is surely far from intuitively obvious that it would be wrong of me not to spend practically every waking moment saving lives. This is what the iterative approach would require: I may only stop when the five minutes necessary to save one further individual would itself be a severe sacrifice. But if there is any intuitive response to such a case, it is surely not this. No doubt, saving no one would be wrong, but would it be obviously wrong, say, to spend my mornings pulling people out of the water and my afternoons pursuing my own life?

It might seem that if intuition says this, intuition must be confused. If we think that the case against abandoning the second of two drowning children is the same as the case against abandoning the first, how can we resist the demanding conclusion concerning the case where many lives are threatened? If the moral considerations relating to a second victim simply iterate those relating to the first, they must be iterated for every subsequent victim as well.

However, there need be no confusion. For we needn't explain the wrongness of abandoning the second of two drowning children in terms of iteration. The iterative approach uses the following method to derive a conclusion concerning what an agent is morally required to do when presented with more than one person in extreme need: begin with what you would have been required to do for a single needy person, then iterate this for every other. But there is an alternative approach to such situations: begin instead by assessing the magnitude of the overall collective need of the people who could be helped, then ask directly what overall sacrifice can be morally demanded of you in response to that collective need. This aggregative approach, to be sure, does not as such preclude conclusions as strong as or even stronger than those generated by the iterative approach. But versions of it do yield weaker conclusions; and we saw some intuitive support for one of them in considering the imagined case of a sea of drowning children. According to such aggregative approaches, I may permissibly stop saving lives on the ground that I have given up as much as is demanded of me on their collective behalf, even though the sacrifice involved in saving one more life remains small. And on such an approach, the judgments about the two drowning children and the sea of drowning children can be reconciled. The complaint against someone who saves only one of two drowning children will not concern the trifling cost of saving the second child, but the trifling cost of saving *both* lives. This removes the obstacle to agreeing that the failure to save the second child is wrong, while rejecting the extreme demands generated by the iterative approach. The two intuitions are not contradictory after all.

The aggregative approach draws a different conclusion from the Life-Saving Argument. We can state it thus:

The Aggregative Conclusion

> Ceasing to contribute to aid agencies will only be permissible when I have become so poor that any further contribution would make my *total* sacrifice greater than can be demanded of me to save other people's lives.

This formulation leaves it open just how the magnitude of the sacrifice which can be demanded of me relates to the number of lives to be saved. According to the very weakest version of the aggregative approach, this magnitude is constant, irrespective of the number of lives in question: I'm not required to sacrifice more for a hundred people than I am for one. However, only the weakest version claims this. There is a range of aggregative approaches which are progressively more demanding than this weakest version, but whose conclusions remain weaker than the Iterative Conclusion.

Generalizing the Issue Between the Two

This gives us the Life-Saving Analogy's second challenge. A potential contributor to an aid agency is more like someone confronted by many drowning people than someone confronted by one, and this appears to support a weaker, Aggregative Conclusion rather than the stronger, Iterative Conclusion sought by Singer. In discussing the first challenge—that my contributions to aid agencies will not save life—I showed that it threatened not only the Life-Saving Argument, but all other arguments for the wrongness of individual noncontribution as well. Does the issue between the Aggregative and Iterative Conclusions also generalize to those other arguments, affecting this time not their validity as such, but the strength of their conclusions?

Yes: but this time, not all of them. Nonderivative arguments do all seem to confront this issue. Recall that they assert a morally significant relation between an affluent individual such as myself and the destitute which makes my noncontribution to aid agencies wrong, and which is not derived from a morally significant relation between the affluent collectively and the destitute. Now either the asserted relation holds between me and destitute individuals, or it holds between me and the destitute taken collectively. If the former, then it is hard to see how the moral relation—whether it concerns rights, duties, or potential benefaction—can fail to be the same in respect of *each* destitute person. But then I stand to each of them in my relation whose moral significance suffices to make a noncontribution to aid agencies wrong; if so, the route to an extremely demanding conclusion by iteration lies open. If the latter, then it is hard to see how my making a contribution which is morally comparable to saving only one life can fulfill any duty I owe to the destitute collectively, satisfy their collective right to be helped, or meet the demand incurred through any other moral relation I bear to them collectively; again, the case for iteration seems clear.

With derivative arguments, however, the situation is different. They derive the wrongness of my noncontribution from my membership of an affluent group which bears a collective responsibility to help the destitute. It is easy to see how the derivative individual demand could simply be to do my share towards the group's discharging that responsibility.

(However, we have seen the implausibility of requiring me only to do my share if a second bystander leaves me to deal with two drowning children—which is to say that it's implausible to derive the moral demand on me in this case from a collective responsibility. If the Life-Saving Analogy can be upheld, as I claim, then the attempt to derive the wrongness of noncontribution from collective responsibility is equally implausible.)

Adjudicating Between the Two

I have suggested that intuition favors the Aggregative over the Iterative Conclusion. When considering someone confronted directly by many threatened lives, we do not readily draw the severely demanding analogue of the Iterative Conclusion. But how strong a source of support for the Aggregative Conclusion is this intuitive judgment?

It is certainly a serious blow to any argument for the Iterative Conclusion which uses Singer's methodology. As we noted at the outset, he begins with a case where the moral status of inaction seems intuitively obvious, then argues that unless a morally relevant disanalogy can be established, we should accord the same moral status to noncontribution to aid agencies. This methodology would seem committed to following our intuitive judgments about the more closely analogous case, and drawing the weaker conclusion. Of course, nothing privileges these intuitive judgments—especially when they concern such a quickly described and far-fetched situation. However, as I have already suggested, the Life-Saving Analogy itself cannot support such an attack. One may try arguing that since not saving a first person at small cost is wrong, and there is no good reason against saying the same for any subsequent threatened person, the weaker conclusion must be mistaken; but this begs the question. According to the aggregative approach, the point about a lone threatened person is not that *that person* can be saved at small cost, but that the entire number of threatened people can be.

Thus, the Aggregative Conclusion is not refuted by the Life-Saving Argument itself. There is, however, a strong and simple challenge to it, of the following form. Why should my failure to save the hundred-and-first, or the thousand-and-first person be any more excusable than my failure to save the first, if the cost remains trifling compared to what is at stake for that person? My having already saved a thousand lives does nothing to alter the fact that I could save *this* person at an insignificant cost. Intuition is telling me, in effect, to lump all the threatened people together, and assess my sacrifice in relation to this collective entity; but this ignores the very real plight of the individuals conglomerated in this way.

This is hardly the end of the story. It is easy to think of replies offered by various normative ethical theories. An indirect consequentialist may appeal to the beneficial consequences of setting ourselves achievable moral standards.[21] Theories of a contractualist kind may support a resuscitation of the requirement that each of us does one's moral share.[22] And some virtue theorists will want to argue as follows: my having already saved a thousand lives may not alter the fact that the person in front of me could be saved at an insignificant cost, but it does help to show that I am not a callous person, and therefore (since the moral assessment of actions derives from that of agents) that my leaving the thousand-and-first person is not wrong. What is difficult, though, is to see how to resolve the issue between the Aggregative and Iterative Conclusions without examining the plausibility of such general normative theories.[23] So I'll have to leave it unresolved here.

Conclusion

I have concentrated on one kind of argument for the wrongness of affluent individuals' not contributing money to voluntary international aid agencies: one which draws an analogy between failing to contribute money to aid agencies and failing to make some small effort to save a life threatened right in front of you. However, in examining two different attacks on this analogy, I have shown that both raise challenges of wider significance. The first attack established that the effect of my contributions to aid agencies will almost certainly not be the saving of anyone's life. This threatened to undermine *all* arguments for the wrongness of individual noncontribution. However, my reply, appealing to relations of transitivity between our moral judgements, left a Life-Saving Argument intact.

The second attack opposed the attempt to use an analogy concerning a threat to a single life to support an extremely demanding conclusion concerning threats to many lives. This challenge concerned not the validity of the argument as such, but the strength of its conclusion; again, we found the issues here to be of wider significance, applying to all nonderivative arguments.

Whether the second attack succeeds is unclear. Even if it does, though, the Life-Saving Analogy still supports the aggregative conclusion. At its very weakest, this claims that you are morally required to keep contributing your time and money to aid agencies, until you have become so poor that any further contribution would make your total sacrifice so great that it would not be wrong to let someone die in front of you at that cost. This is still a much stronger standard than most of us are prepared to live up to.

NOTES

1. I use "aid agencies" throughout to refer to voluntary, nongovernment, international aid agencies. "Noncontribution" will always refer to affluent individuals' failure to contribute time and money to aid agencies of this kind.
2. For other arguments by analogy, see Nagel (1977: 58) and Brown (1977: 71), where the analogy concerns property-ownership, and Gorovitz (1977: 132–133, 141), where it concerns bigotry.
3. See e.g., O'Neill (1975).

4. Singer (1972). For a similar argument for an even stronger conclusion, see Rachels (1979).

5. At the time of writing, the last year for which Oxfam was able to supply me with an estimate of the cost of sustaining the lives of its beneficiaries was 1991. In that year, it claimed that £23 would feed one person for 6 months in Ethiopia, Mozambique, Sudan, Angola, Malawi and Liberia—that is, about a dollar-and-a-half per week.

6. See Cullity (1994).

7. See e.g., Hardin (1974) and (1983), Lucas and Ogletree (1976) (especially the contributions by Fletcher, Englehardt and Hardin), Paddock and Paddock (1967), Ehrlich (1971), and Meadows et al. (1972).

8. Another reading is possible. Singer's conclusion is clearly that *individual* noncontribution is wrong, but he might be read as offering a derivative argument for it—as inferring it from our *collective* ability to avert very great harm to the destitute at a relatively insignificant cost. However, the difficulties for the inference from collective to individual wrongness will be discussed later.

9. The extensive literature supporting this case includes Sen (1981), Drèze and Sen (1989) and (1990), Meier (1984), Singer et al. (1987), and Maskrey (1989).

10. I say "hopefully" because a donation of $20 to $30 is actually rather unlikely to do this. World food trade is conducted in tons, and at 1993 prices of $123, $137, and $250 for a ton of wheat, cassava or rice, the likelihood that *my* donation will make the difference between an aid agency's buying an extra ton and not doing so is small. (FAO 1994: 76, 85, 74.) However, this point by itself does not undermine the Life-Saving Analogy: if I know that spending a small amount of money has a 10 percent chance of saving several lives, it still seems wrong to refuse.

11. For versions of this objection, see Whelan (1991: 158–161), and Goodin (1985: 162–163). However, neither concludes that contributing nothing to aid agencies is morally acceptable, and it is unclear why not. Why should noncontribution be wrong if it makes no difference to anyone whether or not I contribute?

12. For a different response to the imperceptibility objection, see Glover (1975) and Parfit (1984: 75–86). They try to show that it has consequences that even its proponents will find counterintuitive.

13. Child-sponsorship schemes for the relief of poverty do, although most of these target aid at an entire community rather than a single child or family.

14. See note 5.

15. Singer (1972: 241).

16. What I mean in saying that an action is morally demanded is simply that it would be morally wrong not to perform it.

17. Brock (1991: 912), who calls this the "Why me?" objection. See Kagan (1991: 924–925) for a reply.

18. This observation is not new. See Feinberg (1970: 244); Bennett (1981: 84); Fishkin (1982: Ch.10); Barry (1982: 222); Goodin (1985: 134–144).

19. The World Bank estimated in 1990 that over a billion people had an annual income of less than $370, and that 630 million had less than $275 (in 1985 "purchasing parity power" U.S. dollars). The $275 to $370 range spans its estimated poverty lines—the incomes required to sustain a minimum standard of nutrition and other basic necessities, as well as the estimated cost of "participating in the everyday life of society"—for a number of countries among those with the lowest average incomes: Bangladesh, Egypt, India, Indonesia, Kenya, Morocco, and Tanzania. See The World Bank (1990: 26–27).

20. See Singer (1972: 241). For a detailed challenge to the conventional view concerning heroic sacrifices, see Kagan (1989).

21. See Hooker (1991).

22. See Murphy (1993: 290–292), who seeks to distinguish affluent people's relation to the destitute from that of two bystanders to two drowning people.

23. Difficult, but not impossible, it seems to me. Defending a nontheoretical resolution of the issue between the aggregative and iterative conclusions requires much more space than I have here, though.

REFERENCES

Barry, Brian, 1982. "Humanity and Justice in Global Perspective," Nomos 24:219–252.

Bennett, Jonathan, 1981. "Morality and Consequences," S.M. McMurrin, ed. *The Tanner Lectures on Human Values 2*. Cambridge: Cambridge University Press; pp. 45–116.

Brock, Dan W., 1991. "Defending Moral Options," *Philosophy and Phenomenological Research* 51:909–913.

Brown, Peter G., 1977. "Food as National Property," Brown, Peter, and Shue Henry, eds. *Food Policy: The Responsibility of the United States in the Life and Death Choices*. New York: The Free Press, pp. 65–78.

Cullity, Garrett, 1994. "International Aid and the Scope of Kindness," *Ethics* 105:99–127.

Drèze, Jean, and Sen, Amartya, 1989. *Hunger and Public Action*. Oxford: Clarendon Press.

Drèze, Jean, and Sen, Amartya, eds. 1990. *The Political Economy of Hunger*. vol. 2: *Famine Prevention*. Oxford: Clarendon Press.

Ehrlich, Paul, 1971. *The Population Bomb*. New York: Ballantine Books.

Feinberg, Joel, 1970. *Doing and Deserving.* Princeton, NJ: Princeton University Press.

Fishkin, James S., 1982. *The Limits of Obligation.* New Haven, CT: Yale University Press.

Food and Agricultural Organization (FAO) 1994. *Commodity Review and Outlook 1993–94.* Rome: FAO.

Glover, Jonathan, 1975. "It Makes No Difference Whether or Not I Do It," *Proceedings of the Aristotelian Society.* (Suppl.) 49:171–90.

Goodin, Robert E., 1985. *Protecting the Vulnerable: A Reanalysis of Our Social Responsibilities.* Chicago: University of Chicago Press.

Gorovitz, Samuel, 1977. "Bigotry, Loyalty, and Malnutrition," Brown, Peter, and Shue, Henry, eds. *Food Policy: The Responsibility of the United States in the Life and Death Choices.* New York: The Free Press, pp. 129–142.

Hardin, Garrett, 1974. "Lifeboat Ethics: The Case Against Helping the Poor," *Psychology Today;* reprinted in James Rachels, ed. *Moral Problems,* 3rd edn. New York: Harper and Row, 1979, pp.279-291.

Hardin, Garrett, 1983. "Living on a Lifeboat," in Jan Narveson, ed. *Moral Issues,* Toronto; Oxford University Press, pp. 166-178.

Hooker, Brad, 1991. "Rule-Consequentialism and Demandingness: A Reply to Carson," *Mind* 100:270–276.

Kagan, S., 1989. *The Limits of Morality.* Oxford: Clarendon Press.

Kagan, S., 1991. "Replies to My Critics," *Philosophy and Phenomenological Research* 51:919–928.

Lucas, George R., Jr., and Ogletree, Thomas W., eds. 1976. *Lifeboat Ethics: The Moral Dilemmas of World Hunger.* New York: Harper & Row.

Maskrey, Andrew, 1989. *Disaster Mitigation: A Community-Based Approach.* Oxford: Oxfam Publications.

Meadows, Donella H., Meadows, Dennis L., Randers, Jorgen, and Behrens, William W., III, 1972. *The Limits of Growth: A Report for the Club of Rome's Project on the Predicament of Mankind.* London: Pan Books.

Meier, Gerald M., 1984. *Emerging from Poverty.* New York: Oxford University Press.

Murphy, Liam B., 1993. "The Demands of Beneficence," *Philosophy and Public Affairs* 22:267–292.

Nagel, Thomas, 1977. "Poverty and Food: Why Charity Is Not Enough," Brown, Peter, and Shue, Henry, eds. *Food Policy: The Responsibility of the United States in the Life and Death Choices.* New York: The Free Press, pp. 54–62.

O'Neill, Onora, 1975. "Lifeboat Earth," *Philosophy and Public Affairs.* 4:273–292.

Paddock, Paul, and Paddock, William, 1967. *Famine—1975!* Boston: Little, Brown & Co.

Parfit, Derek, 1984. *Reasons and Persons.* Oxford: Clarendon Press.

Rachels, James, 1979. "Killing and Starving to Death," *Philosophy* 54:159–171.

Sen, Amartya, 1981. *Poverty and Famines: An Essay on Entitlement and Deprivation.* Oxford: Clarendon Press.

Singer, H., Wood, J., and Jennings, T., 1987. *Food Aid: The Challenge and the Opportunity* Oxford: Clarendon Press.

Singer, Peter, 1972. "Famine, Affluence and Morality," *Philosophy and Public Affairs* 1:229–243.

Whelan, John M. Jr., 1991. "Famine and Charity," *The Southern Journal of Philosophy* 29:149–166.

The World Bank, 1990. *World Development Report 1990: Poverty.* New York: Oxford University Press.

Suffer the Little Children

HUGH LAFOLLETTE AND LARRY MAY

Hugh LaFollette teaches philosophy at East Tennessee State University. His book *Persons and Personal Relationships* was recently published by Blackwell. His book *Brute Science* (co-authored with Niall Shanks) will be published by Routledge next year.

Larry May is professor of philosophy at Washington University in St. Louis. He has authored three books: *The Morality of Groups*, (Notre Dame), *Sharing Responsibility* (Chicago), and *The Socially Responsive Self* (just completed). He has also co-edited five books and published numerous articles.

Children are the real victims of world hunger: at least 70 percent of the malnourished people of the world are children. By best estimates forty thousand children a day die of starvation (FAO 1989: 5). Children do not have the ability to forage for themselves, and their nutritional needs are exceptionally high. Hence, they are unable to survive for long on their own, especially in lean times. Moreover, they are especially susceptible to diseases and conditions that are the staple of undernourished people: simple infections and simple diarrhea (UNICEF 1993: 22). Unless others provide adequate food, water, and care, children will suffer and die (WHO 1974: 677, 679). This fact must frame any moral discussions of the problem.

And so it does—at least prephilosophically. When most of us first see pictures of seriously undernourished children, we want to help them, we have a sense of responsibility to them, we feel sympathy toward them (Hume 1978: 368–371). Even those who think we need not or should not help the starving take this initial response seriously: they go to great pains to show that this sympathetic response should be constrained. They typically claim that assisting the hungry will demand too much of us, or that assistance would be useless and probably detrimental. The efforts of objectors to undermine this natural sympathetic reaction would be pointless unless they saw its psychological force.

We want to explain and bolster this sympathetic reaction—this conviction that those of us in a position to help are responsible to the malnourished and starving children of the world. We contend that we have this responsibility to starving children unless there are compelling reasons that show that this sympathetic reaction is morally inappropriate (Hume 1978: 582). This requires, among other things, that we seek some "steady and general point of view" from which to rebut standard attempts to explain away this instinctive sympathetic response. By showing that assistance is neither too demanding nor futile, we think more people will be more inclined to act on that prephilosophical sense of responsibility. And, by philosophically championing that sense of responsibility, we will make most people feel more justified in so acting.

Vulnerability and Innocence

Our initial sense of responsibility to the starving and malnourished children of the world is intricately tied to their being paradigmatically vulnerable and innocent. They are paradigmatically vulnerable because they do not have the wherewithal to care for themselves; they must rely on others to care for them. All children are directly dependent on their parents or guardians, while children whose parents cannot provide them food—either because of famine or economic arrangements—are also indirectly dependent on others: relief agencies or (their own or foreign) governments. Children are paradigmatically innocent since they are neither causally nor morally responsible for their plight. They did not cause drought, parched land, soil erosion, and overpopulation; nor are they responsible for social, political, and economic arrangements which make it more difficult for their parents to obtain food. If anyone were ever an innocent victim, the children who suffer and die from hunger are.

Infants are especially vulnerable. They temporarily lack the capacities that would empower them to acquire the necessities of life. Thus, they are completely dependent on others for sustenance. This partly explains our urge to help infants in need. James Q. Wilson claims that our instinctive reaction to the cry of a newborn child is demonstrated quite early in life.

> As early as ten months of age, toddlers react visibly to signs of distress in others, often becoming agitated; when they are one and a half years old they seek to do something to alleviate the other's distress; by the time they are two years old they verbally sympathize ... and look for help (Wilson 1993: 139–40).

Although this response may be partly explained by early training, available evidence suggests that humans have an "innate sensitivity to the feelings of others" (Wilson 1993: 140). Indeed, Hans Jonas claims the parent-child relationship is the "archetype of responsibility," where the cry of the newborn baby is an ontic imperative "in which the plain factual 'is' evidently coincides with an 'ought'" (1983: 30).

This urge to respond to the infant in need is, we think, the appropriate starting point for discussion. But we should also explain how this natural response generates or is somehow connected to moral responsibility.

The Purpose of Morality

The focus of everyday moral discussion about world hunger is on the children who are its victims. Yet the centrality of children is often lost in more abstract debates about rights, obligations, duties, development, and governmental sovereignty. We do not want to belittle either the cogency or the conclusions of those arguments. Rather, we propose a different way of conceptualizing this problem. Although it may be intellectually satisfying to determine whether children have a right to be fed or whether we have an obligation to assist them, if those arguments do not move us to action, then it is of little use—at least to the children in need. So we are especially interested in philosophical arguments which are more likely to motivate people to act. We think arguments that keep the spotlight on starving children are more likely to have that effect.

Moreover, by thinking about hunger in these ways we can better understand and respond to those who claim we have no obligation to assist the starving. We suspect that when all the rhetoric of rights, obligations, and population control are swept away, what most objectors fear is that asking people to assist the starving and undernourished is to ask too much. Morality or no, people are unlikely to act in ways they think require them to substantially sacrifice their personal interests. Thus, as long as most people think helping others demands too much, they are unlikely to provide help.

John Arthur's critique of Peter Singer (both essays reprinted here), highlights just this concern. Arthur objects to moral rules which require people to abandon important things to which they have a right.

> Rights or entitlements to things that are our own reflect important facts about people. Each of us has only one life and it is uniquely valuable to each of us. Your choices do not constitute my life, nor do mine yours.... It seems, then, that in determining whether to

give aid to starving persons ... [agents must assign] special weight
to their own interests (Arthur 1977: 43).

Thus, people need not assist others if it requires abandoning
something of substantial moral significance. Since what we mean by
"substantial moral significance" has an ineliminable subjective element (Arthur 47), some individuals may conclude that sending *any*
money to feed the starving children would be to ask too much of them.
Arthur thereby captures a significant element of most people's worries
about assisting the needy. The concern for our own projects and interests is thought to justify completely repressing, or at least constraining, our natural sympathies for children in need.

At bottom, we suspect that what is at issue is the proper conception and scope of morality. Some philosophers have argued that
morality should not be exceedingly demanding; indeed, one of the
stock criticisms of utilitarianism is that it is far too demanding. On
the other hand, some theorists, including more than a few utilitarians, have bitten the proverbial bullet and claimed that morality is
indeed demanding, and that its demandingness in no way counts
against its cogency (Parfit 1984; Kegan 1988; Cullity, this volume). On
the former view, morality should set expectations which all but the
most weak-willed and self-centered person can satisfy; on the latter
view, morality makes demands that are beyond the reach of most, if
not all, of us.

We wish to take the middle ground and suggest that morality is
a delicate balancing act between Milquetoast expectations which
merely sanctify what people already do, and expectations which are
excessively demanding and, thus, are psychologically impossible—or
at least highly improbable. Our view is that the purpose of morality is
not to establish an edifice that people fear, but to set expectations that
are likely to improve us, and—more relevant to the current issue—to
improve the lot of those we might assist. Morality would thus be like
any goal which enables us to grow and mature: they must be within
reach, yet not easily reachable (LaFollette 1989: 503–506). Of course,
what is within reach changes over time; and what is psychologically
probable depends, in no small measure, on our beliefs about what is
morally expected of us. So by expecting ourselves to do more and to
be more than we currently do and are, we effectively stimulate ourselves to grow and improve. But all that is part of the balancing act of
which we speak.

Thus, we frame the moral question in the following way: What
should responsible people do? Our initial sympathetic response is to
help the starving children. Are there any compelling reasons to think
our compassion should, from some "steady and general point of view,"

be squelched? We think the answer is "No." Are there additional reasons that bolster this initial reaction? We think the answer is "Yes." In short, we think our initial conviction that we are responsible to malnourished children is not only undefeated, it is also rationally justified.

Moral Responsibility

We "instinctively" respond to the needs of starving and malnourished children. But are we, in fact, morally responsible for their plight? There are, of course, two different questions intermingled here: (1) Are we *causally* responsible *for* their condition—did we, individually or collectively, cause their hunger or create the environment which made their hunger and malnourishment more likely? (2) Are we *morally* responsible *to* these children, whether or not we are causally responsible for the conditions that make them hungry?

It is a commonplace of moral argument that people are morally responsible to those to whom they cause harm. If I run a stoplight and hit your auto, then I must pay any medical bills and either repair or replace your auto. If I trip you, causing you to break your arm, then I am expected to carry any resulting financial burden. The principle here is that we should respond to those whose cry for help results from our actions. If others are contributing causes to the harm, we may be jointly responsible to you (Hart and Honore 1959: 188–229). Or, if my action was itself caused by the actions of some other agent—for example, if someone shoved me into you—then this other person is both causally and morally responsible for the harm. But, barring such conditions, a person is morally responsible for harms he or she causes.

Some commentators have argued that the affluent nations, especially colonial powers, are morally responsible to the starving because they created the conditions which make world-wide starvation possible, and perhaps inevitable (O'Neill 1993: 263–264). We find such claims plausible. But, such claims, although plausible, are contentious. Hence, for purposes of argument, we will assume that we in affluent nations are in no way causally responsible for the plight of the starving. If we can show we are (morally) responsible to the children, even if we are not (causally) responsible for their plight, then our responsibility to them will be all the stronger if, as we suspect, these causal claims are true.

Shared Responsibility

If we are the cause of harm, then we are responsible *to* the "victim" because we are responsible *for* their condition. For instance, we assume biological parents have *some* responsibility *to* children because they were responsible *for* bringing them into the world. However, being the cause of harm is not the only condition that creates a responsibility *to* someone. We are also responsible to those whom we have explicitly agreed or promised to help. For instance, by assuming a job as a lifeguard, I have agreed to care for those who swim at my beach or pool, even if they, through lack of care or foresight, put themselves into jeopardy.

More important for the current argument, responsibilities also arise from actions which, although not explicit agreements, nonetheless create reasonable expectations of care. For example, although *some* of the parents' responsibilities to their children is explained by their being the cause of the children's existence, this clearly does not explain the full *range* of parental responsibilities. For even when an agent is indisputably responsible *for* the harm to another, we would *never* think the agent is obliged to change the "victim's" soiled pants, to hold her at night when she is sick, or to listen patiently as she recounts her afternoon's activities. Yet we *do* expect this—and much more—of parents.

Our ordinary understanding of parental responsibilities makes no attempt to ground specific responsibilities *to* the child on any causal claims about the parents' responsibility *for* the child's condition. Rather, this understanding focusses on the needs of the child, and the fact that the parents are in the best position to respond to those needs. This is exactly where the focus should be.

Although for any number of reasons these responsibilities typically fall to the child's biological parents, the responsibilities are not limited to the parents. Others of us (individually or collectively) have a responsibility to care for children whose parents die or abandon them. It matters not that we neither brought these children into the world nor did we voluntarily agree to care for them. Rather, as responsible people we should care for children in need, especially since they are paradigmatically vulnerable and innocent. This is our natural sympathetic reaction. "No quality of human nature is more remarkable, both in itself and in its consequences, than the propensity we have to sympathize with others" (Hume 1978: 316).

This helps explain our shared moral responsibility to care for children who are not being cared for by their parents. Since the range of parental responsibilities cannot be explained either by the parents being the cause of the child's existence or by their explicitly agreeing to care for the child, it should not be surprising that our shared responsibility likewise does not depend on an explicit agreement or an implicit assumption of responsibility. We assume responsible people will, in fact, care for abandoned children. This shared responsibility springs from our common vulnerability, and from our ability to respond to others who are similarly situated.

Acute Need

Until now we have spoken as if all starvation and malnutrition were created equal. They are not. The hunger with which we are most familiar—the hunger whose images often appear on our television sets—is hunger caused by famine. And famines tend to be episodic; often they are unpredictable. An extended drought or a devastating flood may destroy crops in a region, so that the people of that region can no longer feed themselves. (Or, as is more often the case, these environmental catastrophes may not destroy all crops, but primarily that portion of the crop which is used to feed the local population; crops used for export may be protected in some way.) In these cases, the problem may emerge quickly and, with some assistance, may disappear quickly. Such need is acute.

The nature of our responsibility to the starving arguably depends on the nature of their need. Peter Singer offers a vivid example of acute need and claims his example shows we have a serious moral obligation to relieve world starvation.

> If I am walking past a shallow pond and see a child drowning in it, I ought to wade in and pull the child out. That will mean getting my clothes muddy, but this is insignificant when the death of the child would presumably be a very bad thing (1971: 231)

This case, Singer claims, illustrates the intuitive appeal of the following moral principle: "if it is in our power to prevent something bad from happening, without thereby sacrificing something of comparable moral importance, we ought, morally, to do it." In the case in question, this is sage moral advice. If muddying my clothes saves the life of an innocent child, then it is time for me to send the cleaners some additional business.

Singer's example vividly illustrates our fundamental moral responsibility to meet acute need, especially the acute need of children—those who are paradigmatically vulnerable and innocent. In Singer's example, the child is in immediate danger; with relatively little effort we can remove her from danger. As we argued earlier, we have a shared moral responsibility which arises from our common vulnerability. None of us has complete control over our lives. All of us are vulnerable to circumstances beyond our control: floods, hurricanes, droughts, and so forth. Through no fault of our own, our lives and welfare may be jeopardized. Admittedly, some acute need results from our ignorance or stupidity. Even so, others should assist us when feasible, at least if the cost to them is slight. After all, even the most careful person occasionally makes mistakes. When need is caused by natural disaster or personal error, we each want others to come to our aid. Indeed, we think they *should* come to our aid. If, on reflection, our desire for assistance is reasonable when *we* are in need, then, by extension, we should acknowledge that we should help others in similar need. Shared responsibility and sympathy conspire to create the sense that we should go to the aid of those who cannot alleviate their own acute needs.

Although we are here emphasizing responsibility rather than justice (narrowly defined), it is noteworthy that the conditions that generate responsibility to help others in acute need resemble the conditions Hume cites as generating our sense of justice: "... *'tis only from selfishness and confin'd generosity of man, along with the scanty provision nature has made for his wants, that justice derives its origin.*" (1978: 495; emphasis his). Our common vulnerability to circumstances and to the "scanty provision nature has made" leads us to seek ways to protect ourselves against misfortune and error. Natural disasters occur. They may occur where I live; they may not. Prudent people will recognize that we are all more secure, and thus, better off, if we recognize a shared responsibility to assist others in acute need.

As we have suggested throughout this essay, this responsibility is all the more apparent when those in need cannot care for themselves and are in no way responsible for their plight. In short, the responsibility is greatest (and less contentious) when children are the victims. In fact, when children are in acute need, especially when many are in a position to help, there is little moral difference between the responsibility of biological parents and others. If a child is drowning, then even if the parents (or some third party) tossed the child into the pond (and are thus singularly responsible for the child's plight), we should still rescue her if we can. Similarly, if a child is starving, and her need is acute, then even if the child's parents and government have acted irresponsibly, we should still feed the child if we can.

Arguably the problem is different if the acute need is so substantial and so widespread as to require us to make considerable sacrifices to help those in need. In this case our responsibilities *to* the children in acute need may resemble our responsibilities to children in chronic need.

Chronic Need

Acute need arises once (or at least relatively infrequently). It requires immediate action, which, if successful, often alleviates the need. But most hunger is not acute, it is chronic. Chronic hunger is the hunger of persistently malnourished children, where the causes of hunger are neither episodic nor easily removed. If the need can be met at all, it can be met only through more substantial, sustained effort, and often only by making numerous (and perhaps fundamental) institutional changes, both within our countries, and the other countries in need of aid.

That is why Singer's case is disanalogous with most world hunger. The drowning child is in acute need. Suppose, however, that Singer's fictional child lives on the edge of a pond where she is relatively unsupervised. We cannot protect this child by simply dirtying our clothes once. Rather, we must camp on the pond's edge, poised to rescue her whenever she falls or slips into the water. However, can we reasonably expect anyone to devote her entire life (or even the next 6 years) as this child's lifeguard? It is difficult to see how. The expectation seems even less appropriate if there are many children living beside the pond.

Likely the only sensible way to protect the child from harm is to relocate her away from the pond. Or perhaps we could teach her to swim. But are we responsible to make these efforts? Do we have the authority to forcibly relocate the child or to erect an impregnable fence around the pond? Can we *require* her to take swimming lessons? Can we *force* her government to make substantial internal economic and political changes? In short, even though we are morally responsible to assist those in acute need (and especially children), we cannot straight-forwardly infer that we must assist those (even children) in chronic need.

For instance, if we try to save a child from famine, we may have reason to think that quick action will yield substantial results. Not so with chronic hunger. Since we are less likely to see the fruits of our efforts and, we may be less motivated to assist. Moreover, some have argued that we can alleviate chronic need only if we exert enormous effort, over a long period of time. If so, expecting someone to respond to chronic need arguably burdens her unduly. Responsible people need not spend all their time and resources helping those in chronic need, especially if there is only a small chance of success. This is surely the insight in Arthur's view.

Consider the following analogy which illuminates that insight. Suppose an adult couple builds a house by the side of a river that floods every few years. After the first flood we may help them, thinking we should respond to someone who appears to be in acute need. However, after the second or third flood, we will feel it is asking too much of us to continue to help. We would probably conclude that they have intentionally chosen a risky lifestyle. They have made their own bed; now they must sleep in it.

Although this case may well be disanalagous to the plight of starving adults—since most have little control over the weather, soil erosion, or governmental policy—nonetheless, many people in affluent nations think it is analogous.

What is indisputable, however, is that the case is totally disanalogous to the plight of children. Children did not choose to live in an economically deprived country or in a country with a corrupt government. Nor can they abandon their parents and relocate in a land of plenty, or in a democratic regime. Hence, they are completely innocent—in no sense did they cause their own predicament. Moreover, they are paradigms of vulnerability.

Since they are the principal victims of chronic malnutrition, it is inappropriate to refuse to help them unless someone can show that assisting them would require an unacceptable sacrifice. That, of course, demands that we draw a line between reasonable and unreasonable sacrifice. We do not know how to draw that line. Perhaps, though, before drawing the line we should ask: If it were our child who was starving, where would we want the line to be drawn?

A Dose of Reality

Evidence suggests, however, that this whole line of inquiry is beside the point. Although it would be theoretically interesting to determine how to draw the line between reasonable and unreasonable sacrifices, this is not a determination we need make when discussing world hunger. Doomsayers like Garrett Hardin claim we have long-since crossed that line: that feeding starving children requires more than we can reasonably expect even highly responsible people to do; indeed, Hardin claims such assistance is effectively suicide (1974; reprinted here). However, the doomsayers are mistaken. Current efforts to alleviate hunger have been far short of efforts that would require a substantial sacrifice from any of us. Nonetheless, even these relatively measly efforts have made a noticeable dent in the problem of world hunger. And these successes have been achieved with smaller than anticipated growth in population. According to the FAO:

The number of chronically undernourished people in developing
countries with populations exceeding 1 million is estimated at
786 million for 1988–90, reflecting a decline from 941 million in
1969–71 and a lowering of their proportion of the population from
36 to 20 percent ..." (FAO 1992b: 1)

During the same period, the average number of calories consumed
per person per day went from 2,430 to 2,700—more than a 10 percent increase (FAO 1992b: 3).

Since the relatively meager efforts to assist the starving has
made a noticeably dent in the incidence of world hunger, then,
although enormous problems clearly remain, we have good reason to
think that heightened efforts—efforts still *far* short of those requiring substantial sacrifices from the affluent—could seriously curtail,
if not completely eliminate, world starvation. If so, we do not need to
decide where the line should be drawn. We are still some distance
from that line. Put differently, many of the world's poor are not like
the unsupervised child who lives on the side of the lake. Even though
their need may be chronic, their needs can be met short of the enormous efforts that would require us to camp next to the pond for the
remainder of our days. To that extent, our responsibility to chronically starving children is, despite first appearances, similar to our
responsibility to children in acute need.

How to Act Responsibly

Many people are already motivated to help others (and especially
children) in need. Indeed, this helps explain the influence and appeal
of Singer's essay more than two decades after its publication. Thus,
the claim that we have a shared responsibility to meet the needs of
others in acute need is psychologically plausible. Even so, it is often
difficult to motivate people to respond to others in chronic need.
Many in affluent nations feel or fear that aid just won't do anything
more than line the pockets of charitable organizations or corrupt
governments. Doubtless some money sent for aid does not reach its
intended source. But that may simply reflect our inability to determine which relief agencies are most effective. Moreover, even if some
aid does not reach those in need, it is even more obvious that most
relief aid *does* reach its desired target. That is what the statistics
cited in the last section demonstrate.

We suspect that the strongest barrier to helping those in chronic need is more psychological than philosophical: most people just
don't feel any connection with someone starving half-way around the

world (or, for that matter, in the ghetto across town). As Hume noted, most of us do tend to feel more sympathy for what we see than for what we do not see. This at least partly explains why many of us are less willing to help starving children in foreign lands—we don't see them, and thus, don't feel a tie or connection to them. As we have argued here, this is the core insight in Arthur's view: moral obligations which require us to abandon what is important to us, especially in the absence of some connection with those in need, will rarely be met by many people—and thus, will make no moral difference. Someone might argue, on more abstract philosophical grounds, that we should not need that link. Perhaps that is true. But, whether we should need to feel this connection, the fact is, most people do need it. And our concern is how to help meet the needs of the children. Thus, we want to know what will *actually* motivate people to act.

Of course, just as we should not take our initial sense of responsibility *to* children as *determining* our moral obligations, neither should we put too much weight on the unanalyzed notion of "normal ties." Doing so ignores ways in which our moral feelings can be shaped for good and for ill. Perhaps the better question is not whether we have such feelings, but whether we could cultivate them in ourselves and perhaps all humanity, and, if so, whether that would be appropriate. We suspect, though, that many of us cannot develop a sense of shared responsibility for *every* person in need. More likely we must rely on a more limited sense of shared responsibility; certainly that is not beyond the psychological reach of most of us. Indeed, it is already present in many of us. Thus, working to cultivate this sense of responsibility in ourselves and others would increase the likelihood that we could curtail starvation.

Since people have a natural sympathetic response to the cry of children, the best way to cultivate this connection is to keep people focussed on children as the real victims of starvation and malnutrition. If we keep this fact firmly in the fore of our minds, we are more likely, individually and collectively to feel and act on this sense of shared responsibility.

But even if we acknowledge this responsibility, how should we meet it? Should we provide food directly? Perhaps sometimes. But this direct approach will not solve chronic starvation. More likely we should empower the children's primary caretakers so they can feed and care for their children. To this extent our shared responsibility to hungry children is mediated by the choices and actions of others. Thus, it might be best conceptualized as akin to (although obviously not exactly like) our responsibility to provide education. Our responsibility is not to ensure that each child receives an education (although we will be bothered if a child "slips through the cracks.") Rather, our responsibility is to establish institutions which make it more likely that all will be educated. By analogy, since it is virtually impossible to feed children directly, our responsibility is not to particular children, but a responsibility to change the circumstances which make starvation likely.

Changing those circumstances might occasionally require that we be a bit heavy-handed. Perhaps such heavy-handedness is unavoidable if we wish to achieve the desired results. OXFAM, for example, provides aid to empower people in lands prone to famine and malnutrition to feed themselves and their children. If the recipients do not use the aid wisely, then OXFAM will be less likely to provide aid again. This is only a bit Draconian, but perhaps not so much as to be morally objectionable.

Conclusion

In both cases of chronic and acute need, we must remember the children who are the real victims of world hunger. The suffering child is paradigmatically vulnerable and innocent. Since we can, without serious damage to our relatively affluent lifestyles, aid these children, we should help. We share a responsibility *to* them because we are well placed to help them, and because we can do so without substantially sacrificing our own interests. This is so even if we in *no way* caused or sustained the conditions that make their hunger likely.

However, if the stronger claim that we *caused* their starvation (or created the conditions which made their starvation more likely) can be defended—as we think it probably can—this responsibility becomes a stronger imperative. Thus, if the views of Sen, Crocker, and Balakrishnan/Narayan (this volume) are correct—and we suspect they are—then most of our responsibility is to cease supporting national and international institutions which cause and sustain conditions that make hunger likely. And *this* responsibility could be explained much more simply as a responsibility to not harm others.[1]

NOTE

1. We wish to thank William Aiken, John Hardwig, and Carl Wellman for helpful comments on earlier drafts of this paper.

REFERENCES

Arthur, J. 1977. "Rights and the Duty to Bring Aid," Aiken, W. and LaFollette, H. eds. *World Hunger and Moral Obligation*. Englewood Cliffs, NJ: Prentice-Hall. Reprinted here.

Brown, L. and 1994. *The State of the World 1994: A World Watch Institute Report on Progress Toward a Sustainable Society*. New York: W.W. Norton.
———1974. *In the Human Interest*. New York: W.W. Norton.

Food and Agricultural Organization (FAO) 1992a. *World Food Supplies and Prevalence of Chronic Undernutrition in Developing Regions as Assessed in 1992*. Rome: FAO Press.
———1992b. "FAO News Release." Rome: FAO Press.
———1989. *World Hunger*. Rome: FAO Press.

Hardin, G. 1975. *Exploring a New Ethics for Survival*. New York: Penguin.
———1974. "Lifeboat Ethics: The Case Against Helping the Poor." *Psychology Today* 8:38–43, 123–126. Reprinted here.
Hart, H., and Honore, A. 1959. *Causation in the Law*. Oxford: Oxford University Press.
Hume, D. 1978. *A Treatise of Human Nature*, Selby-Bigge L.A., ed. Oxford: Oxford University Press.

Jonas, H. 1984. *The Imperative of Responsibility*. Chicago: University of Chicago Press.

Kegan, S. 1988. *The Limits of Morality*. Oxford: Oxford University Press.

LaFollette, H. 1989. "The Truth in Psychological Egoism." Feinberg J, ed. *Reason and Responsibility*. Belmont, CA: Wadsworth Publishing.

May, L. 1996. *Socially Responsible* Self, forthcoming.
———1992. *Sharing Responsibility*. Chicago: University of Chicago Press.
Mesarovic, M., and Pestel, E. 1974. *Mankind at the Turning Point*. New York: Signet Books.

O'Neill, O. 1993. "Ending World Hunger," Regan T., ed. *Matters of Life and Death*. New York: McGraw-Hill.

Parfit, D. 1984. *Reasons and Persons*. Oxford: Oxford University Press.

Singer, P. 1972. "Famine, Affluence, and Morality," *Philosophy and Public Affairs*, 1:229–243. Reprinted here.

United Nations Children's Fund (UNICEF) 1993. *The State of the World's Children 1993*. Oxford: Oxford University Press.

Wilson, J. 1993. *The Moral Sense*. New York: The Free Press.

World Health Organization (WHO) 1974. *Health Statistics Report*. Geneva: World Health Organization.

Ending World Hunger*

ONORA O'NEILL

Onora O'Neill is Principal of Newnham College, Cambridge University. She previously taught at Bernard College and at the University of Essex. She is author of Faces of Hunger and Constructions of Reason.

. . .

II. The Facts of Hunger and Famine

An enormous amount is known about the numbers of people now living and about the resources they have to live on. There are also many careful and scrupulous studies of the likely rate of growth of population and resources in various regions and countries. It may then seem easy to discover whether the world either is or will be overpopulated, whether and where there will be persisting hunger and poverty, and a continued danger of famine. It turns out that this is not easy, indeed, that the experts disagree passionately. They don't, on the whole, disagree with passion about the particular figures (which all accept as being no more than careful estimates); they often do disagree about the import of these figures.

§7 The Look of Hunger and Famine[4]

Hunger and famine are hidden killers, twin dark horses. In the Book of Revelation, other killers are symbolized by highly visible horses and horsemen: the white horse of Conquest, the red horse of War, and the pale horse of Death itself.[5] But Famine is symbolized by a black horse and horseman. And so it is in human experience. When famine strikes, relatively few people die "of hunger." They die for the most part of illnesses they would easily have survived if hunger had not weakened them. They die of flu and of intestinal troubles, and disproportionately many of those who die are very young or old. When there is famine, the survivors too are affected in hidden ways.

*ONeill, Onora, "Ending World Hunger" from Matters of Life and Death, 3/e edited by Tom Regan, 1993, McGraw-Hill, Inc. Reproduced with permission of McGraw-Hill, Inc.

Children may suffer brain damage as a result of early malnutrition; whole populations may be listless and lethargic, unable to muster the energy needed for economic advance, still living but permanently weakened. Even lesser hunger—which persists even in some very rich countries—shortens and shatters lives, stunts growth, and retards learning.

We have all seen pictures of starving, skeletal children in the appeals of famine-relief charities. But such emanciation is only the visible and publicizable fraction of the damage the black horse can do. We must remember that most of the impact of hunger is less dramatic. Whenever death rates are higher than they would be with adequate nutrition, hunger is *already* taking its toll. Perhaps there will be future famines that are far more visible than today's hunger, large-scale versions of the disastrous famines that have recently occurred in the southern Sahara, in Bangladesh, and in Ethiopia. Perhaps there will be nothing so dramatic but rather many lives of unrelenting hunger and premature death, without mass migration in search of food or any of the other horrors of extreme famine. If we remember that most of the impact of hunger is of this sort, then we can see that famine is not some unknown evil that might strike human populations in the future, but a more virulent case of evil suffered by many now living. The practical question that divides the experts is whether the endemic hunger and malnutrition that millions now live with can be ended or will persist. If it persists, famines will remain a risk; if it can be ended, so too will famines end.

Hunger does not have to produce dramatic and catastrophic episodes of famine to inflict acute suffering. Hunger destroys lives in two senses: it literally kills—destroys—the biological basis of life, and it also destroys the lives persons lead, their biographical lives, even when it leaves the biological organism functioning. The survivors suffer the biological deaths of those they love, and their own biographical lives are often shattered by hunger and the destruction of ways of life.

§8 The Extent of Hunger

To get a feel for the extent of these miseries, it helps to have a few figures. The population of the world is well over five billion—and rising very fast. If we project present rates of growth, we can imagine a world whose human population doubles and redoubles every few decades. But a *projection* of existing trends is not *prediction*. There is no point in projecting this sort of figure and arriving at the fantasy of a world without resources but weighed down by or literally covered with living humans. Long before this point is reached, the availability of resources will limit the population that can remain alive.

In the last two centuries, rapid increases in available resources have permitted a corresponding growth in human population. Two centuries ago there were only 800 million human beings alive. We do not know how many there will be in another two centuries. But however few or many there are, there will not be more alive than there are resources to sustain them. (There may be fewer, since some or all persons may live at a higher-than-subsistence standard.) Sustained overpopulation is impossible: as soon as there are more people than there are resources, some people die. When populations expand beyond resources available to them, they are pruned by poverty, hunger, and famine. But we do not have to be at their mercy. Populations can control their own rates of growth and ensure that they don't grow faster than the resources available to them. A population that succeeds in this task (and some have) need not suffer hunger or risk famine. It can be free not only of the spectacular miseries of catastrophic famines but also of the slower, hidden hunger that shows itself in premature deaths, lack of resistance to illness, and lack of energy. On these matters the experts do not disagree.

§9 Controversies about Preventing Famines and Ending Hunger

When we ask *how* famine and hunger can best be ended and whether it is at all likely that they will be ended, we find great controversy. All agree that the task of ending hunger, or even ending famine, is at best enormous and daunting. But even experts disagree about what is possible. Some awareness of these disagreements is helpful in considering moral problems raised by famine.

Some experts—often spoken of as neo-Malthusians[6]—think that the only secure way to end famine is by limiting population growth. In the long run no increase in available food could match population increase. Other experts, often called *developmentalists*, think that the first aim must be economic growth, which is a prerequisite of lowering population growth. The same division among the experts can be found in discussions of domestic poverty and hunger in rich countries, where opponents of welfare oppose action to help the poor, while advocates of welfare insist that poverty can and should be ended by public action, and that failure to do so in a rich society is moral dereliction.

Developmentalists themselves disagree whether the most important changes are economic or political. They debate whether economic policies available within current political structures, including foreign aid and international loans, investment by transnational corporations, and the public policies of developing countries, provide an adequate framework to develop the now underdeveloped world. Are there—as some political economists believe—features of the present structure of aid and trade that prevent such policies from transforming the economic prospects of underdeveloped regions but that might be changed by political transformations? Is it even possible that an obstacle to economic growth in the poorest regions lies in the present international economic order, despite its ostensible commitment to the goal of development?

These debates are ethically important because social inquiry itself is no matter of ethically neutral "facts." The debates between different experts often show that their disputes are *already* moral disagreements. There is no way in which those who want to do something about world hunger and poverty can hope that experts will present "the facts," and equally no way in which those who take action can shirk making informed judgments about what is possible.

§10 Malthusian Controversies

Neo-Malthusians take their name from Thomas Malthus (1766–1834), who noted in his *Summary View of the Principle of Population* (1830), "a tendency in mankind to increase, if unchecked, beyond the possibility of an adequate supply of food in a limited territory."[7]

Of course, Malthus knew well enough that such increase always was "checked." The check might be what he called "prudential restraint on marriage and population," or it might be high mortality. If there was much "imprudence," the ultimate check might even be the highly visible mortality of famine.

Recent neo-Malthusians hold that famine is not only the *ultimate* check on population growth but an imminent one. Some characterize population growth as a 'bomb' that economic growth cannot defuse, whose explosion threatens all. Others compare the lives of the well-off to the plight of passengers on a lifeboat, who can rescue those who drown around them only at the risk of sinking and drowning everybody. Still others allege that the only responsible approach to the distribution of resources must follow the tough-minded principle of "triage," offering help neither to the better off nor to the destitute but only to the "best risks" for whom alone (they think) help can make a difference. These violent images proclaim that population growth cannot be sustained indefinitely and that, to avoid catastrophe, we must forthwith abandon rather than rescue the neediest.[8]

Various reasons are given for these views. Some neo-Malthusians claim that the rapid growth of population of recent centuries cannot be sustained because readily exploited natural resources have already been used and further exploitation will be harder because of pollution and low yields. Hunger will blight more and more lives unless there is sustained technological advance, which we cannot guarantee. Other neo-Malthusians stress economic and political rather than natural barriers to sustained economic growth. It is apparent enough that there is nothing automatic about economic growth and that long periods of history have shown nothing more fundamental than succeeding lean and fat years. The risk of hunger and famine is greatest in just those places where economic growth will be hardest. Underdeveloped countries may lack investment capital and know-how; there may be resistance to the introduction of technology that will change existing and preferred ways of life, and an often accurate perception that not everybody will share the economic benefits that new technology is said to bring. Nor it is easy to transfer resources from areas of economic surplus to poorer regions. The rich nations are reluctant to share their surplus, and the very process of transfer can harm the economic system of undeveloped regions.

In the eyes of neo-Malthusians, these obstacles to economic growth are matched by difficulty in controlling population growth. In spite of the "contraceptive revolution," the only wholly safe and reliable modes of contraception are forms of sterilization that are not reliably reversible and are therefore unpopular. Reversible techniques (IUDs, rubber devices, chemical contraception) may be neither entirely reliable nor safe nor easy for those living in great poverty to use or to afford. They are also rejected by some on religious grounds. Abortion is even more widely rejected, and it is least available and safe where poverty is harshest.

Even if these difficulties were overcome, some neo-Malthusians argue,[9] the populations that most risk famine might not have the "prudence" to limit their increasing populations. Access to contraceptive technology does not guarantee smaller families; nor does lack of access always prevent reduction in family size. In the now developed countries of Europe and North America, a *demographic transition* has taken place, and these countries now have, despite long-lived populations and little emigration, either low or negative rates of population increase. No such demographic transition has yet taken place in many now underdeveloped countries. Death rates have fallen, but fertility levels remain high and population increase is rapid. In other Third World countries, fertility is now falling. This fall is particularly evident in some Southeast Asian countries.

An interesting and vitally important question to ask these neo-Malthusians is why they are so pessimistic about the longer-term prospects for economic development and fertility control in the Third World. Why, for example, do they not construe the economic development and controlled population growth of the now developed world as evidence that success is possible? After all, it is not so long since the whole world was underdeveloped. What is it that makes the development of the now underdeveloped world appear so hard that it demands abandoning those most at risk? Harsh measures may be necessary in certain emergencies, but it would be wrong to take or advocate emergency measures if less harsh options are available.

§11 Developmentalist Rejoinders

Developmentalist views of prospects for economic growth in the underdeveloped world and for ending the risk of famine are more optimistic. Like neo-Malthusians, these writers hold a great variety of views, and only a selection can be mentioned.[10] The optimism that developmentalist writers often show is only a *relative* optimism. Most of them do not think that economic development and ending hunger and reducing population growth can be either easy or rapid; many stress that huge political and social as well as economic changes may have to be made if the enterprise is to succeed.

The optimism is based on an awareness of the many ways in which economic advance takes place. Recent growth rates in parts of the Third World have often been high. However, the picture is one only of *qualified* optimism for several reasons. First, many of the poor do not benefit from growth; second, when population growth remains rapid, improvement in living standards must be slight even if the benefits of economic growth are evenly distributed. Few developmentalist writers today expect economic growth in poor   untries to resolve all problems of dire poverty and hunger merely by some automatic "trickle down" of benefits toward the most vulnerable. There are plenty of examples of rapid growth without eradication of dire poverty (e.g., Brazil) and others of strong action against acute poverty without much economic growth (e.g., Costa Rica).

Developmentalists do not think that population growth is an insuperable barrier to economic growth. They point out that fertility rates have generally fallen after and not before economic growth. The demographic transition of the now developed world followed rises in standards of living. They point out that, for the very poor, large families may appear an asset rather than a liability. Their children have a shorter period of economic dependence than children of richer families, and only children can provide for old age or illness or other contingencies which in richer countries may be handled by social or private insurance schemes. Developmentalists think that this can be changed: Third World populations will undergo a demographic transition *only when they begin to be less poor.* Trying to achieve economic growth by limiting population growth is going about the problem the wrong way round. "Prudence" in having children cannot be expected of those who can best secure their future by having many children.[11]

Developmentalists also view the present economic plight of poorer countries less as a natural inevitability, to which these countries must prudently adapt their expectations and their population growth, and more as the result of changeable economic and political structures. Many point out that the poverty of specific Third World countries is in part due to a history of colonialism, under which these economies stagnated because the imperial power either prevented or discouraged certain forms of trade or manufacture, or encouraged the production of goods that did not compete with the industries of the developed world (such as palm oil, coffee, rubber, and other tropical agricultural products that were often grown on the plantation system). Others point to the persistent wars in the Third World, and to the massive sale of arms by corporations in the developed world. While the *political* independence of former colonies is now virtually complete, the trade and economic policies of former imperial powers and other powerful developed nations may hinder development.

Developmentalist writers disagree not only about the detailed interpretation of the sources of economic vulnerability of Third World economies but also about the best strategy for economic progress and the part that redistribution has to play in it. Some stress the unnecessary consumption of developed countries and the grotesque size of their own armaments expenditure, and the resulting possibilities for redistribution of resources. But many are unsure how these resources can be redistributed to the benefit of the poorest.

One common view has been that policies stressing foreign aid, and in particular food aid, have a major part to play in overcoming the risk of famine. What could seem more sensible than the provision of food from the unsaleable agricultural surpluses of wealthier temperate-zone nations, particularly in North America and western Europe? But while such aid clearly benefits the farmers of the developed world, its impact on the Third World is often ambiguous. Food relieves hunger; in some emergencies, only the rapid delivery of food can prevent famine deaths. But when free or subsidized grain is standardly available, marginal farmers in poor regions may be unable to sell their crops; they may stop growing grain and even migrate to the shantytowns of Third World cities where their chance of sharing in food aid is greater but their prospects of economic progress may be slight. Over the last thirty years, many countries have become dependent on food imports and food aid, especially in

Africa.[12] The transfer of food can harm even when it is intended to benefit.

Many developmentalist writers have therefore focused less on the (far from simple) policy of transferring *food* to those who are hungry than on the (even more complex) requirements for achieving *economic development* within Third World countries. Food aid is now often said to be important only where famine prevention has failed, or would otherwise fail. The long-term aim must be to end hunger and the very risk of famine by securing and increasing the entitlement to the necessities of life of the very poorest. The underlying thought is the simple one expressed in the proverb often quoted by famine relief agencies. Give a man a fish and you feed him for a day; teach a man to fish and he will be fed for life. The proverb may have an obvious interpretation in a simple and traditional social world; but its interpretation in an interdependent world is no more obvious than the interpretation of the parable of the good Samaritan. Economic development needs capital investment, technological innovation, and trading opportunities. All three are scarce or difficult to acquire for most Third World countries. Poor countries cannot easily raise large capital sums for development projects: their problem is, after all, precisely that they still lack a developed economy in which there is accumulated capital. But they can attract international capital only if they offer comparatively favorable investment opportunities. Investment then has to reflect criteria other than those of need. For example, if irrigation or rural development projects would meet more needs but offer little return on investment, investment will not be in these areas but if selling luxury goods to the small urban elite who already have more than subsistence incomes is profitable, then such less needed development will attract investment.

Technological innovation, even if successful, may not benefit most those who need most. For example, "miracle" strains of rice or wheat may need fertilizer and irrigation that only wealthier farmers can afford. Agricultural mechanization may reduce opportunities for work and earnings for the landless poor.

Trading opportunities nowadays are internationally regulated, and the developed world can often meet its own needs more cheaply without trading with Third World countries (except for a few tropical products). Even when Third World products are cheaper, developed countries may prevent their import, since competition from "cheap labor" is not acceptable to the high-earning workers of richer countries. In other cases automated production in the industrialized world may undercut Third World production costs, despite their low wages.

In spite of these difficulties, developmentalist writers argue that there is no more fundamental reason why the Third World should remain poverty-stricken forever than there was in the case of the developed world. Development was and is *always* difficult. It is true that Third World countries lack both colonies, whose imports they can keep cheap or whose markets they can preserve for their own industry, and a frontier or colonies for their own expanding population, and they do not control the international economic order. However, they have some advantages. Many forms of technology, including contraceptive technology, are already developed; there are interests and groups within the developed world that seek global development and are prepared to argue and agitate for aid, trade, and other policies that may help Third World countries develop. Above all, it is now well established that economic development and a better-than-subsistence standard of life can be reached by whole populations. We can no longer take it as inevitable that "the poor are always with us."

§12 Social and Moral Inquiry

This brief account of issues that distinguish Malthusian and developmentalist perspectives on famine and world hunger may suggest that problems of famine aren't primarily *moral* problems at all. The controversies just mentioned arise within various lines of social inquiry; they are controversies between economists, demographers, political analysts, and others. However, this does not show that we can do without moral inquiry into problems of famine. At most we might conclude that serious moral inquiry must take account of the divisions between different approaches to social and political inquiry and that it may not reach conclusions about some matters until these economic and social issues are better understood. We cannot, however, conclude that poverty and world hunger are "purely" economic or demographic or social problems, to which moral inquiry is irrelevant. Even if we had complete social knowledge, for example, we would still need to work out what to do about hunger and the risk of famine. We shall now consider whether either Kantian or utilitarian ethical reasoning can help us do so.

. . .

IV. Kantian Approaches to Some Famine Problems

The second moral theory whose scope and determinacy in dealing with famine problems I shall consider was developed by the German philosopher Immanuel Kant (1724-1804). I shall offer a simplified version of Kantian ethics[25] in §18 through §22. In §23 through §25

I shall set out some of its implilcations for action toward those who are hungry and at risk of famine, and from §26 onward I shall summarize some differences between utilitarian and Kantian ethics

§18 A Simplified Account of Kant's Ethics

Kant's theory is frequently and misleadingly assimilated to theories of human rights. It is, in fact, a theory of human obligations; therefore it is wider in scope than a theory of human rights. (Not all obligations have corresponding rights.) Kant does not, however, try to generate a set of precise rules defining human obligations in all possible circumstances; instead, he attempts to provide a set of *principles of obligation* that can be used as the starting points for moral reasoning in actual contexts of action. The primary focus of Kantian ethics is, then, on *action* rather than either *results*, as in utilitarian thinking, or *entitlements*, as in theories that make human rights their fundamental category. Morality requires action of certain sorts. But to know *what* sort of action is required (or forbidden) in which circumstances, we should not look just at the expected results of action or at others' supposed entitlements but, in the first instance, at the nature of the proposed actions themselves.

When we engage in moral reasoning, we often need go no further than to refer to some quite specific principle or tradition. We may say to one another, or to ourselves, things like "It would be hypocritical to pretend that our good fortune is achieved without harm to the Third World" or "Redistributive taxation shouldn't cross national boundaries." But when these specific claims are challenged, we may find ourselves pushed to justify or reject or modify them. Such moral debate, on Kant's account, rests on appeals to what he calls the *Supreme Principle of Morality*, which can (he thinks) be used to work out more specific principles of obligation. This principle, the famous Categorical Imperative, plays the same role in Kantian thinking that the Greatest Happiness Principle plays in utilitarian thought.

A second reason why Kant's moral thought often appears difficult is that he offers a number of different versions of this principle, which he claims are equivalent but which look very different. A straightforward way in which to simplify Kantian moral thought is to concentrate on just one of these formulations of the Categorical Imperative. For present purposes I shall choose the version to which he gives the sonorous name, *The Formula of the End in Itself.*

§19 The Formula of the End in Itself

The Formula of the End in Itself runs as follows:

> Act in such a way that you always treat humanity, whether in your own person or in the person of any other, never simply as a means but always at the same time as an end.[26]

To understand this principle we need in the first place to understand what Kant means by the term "maxim." The maxim of an act or policy or activity is the *underlying principle* of the act, policy, or activity, by which other, more superficial aspects of action are guided. Very often interpretations of Kant have supposed that maxims can only be the (underlying) intentions of individual human agents. If that were the case it would limit the usefulness of Kantian modes of moral thought in dealing with world hunger and famine problems. For it is clear enough that individual action (while often important) cannot deal with all the problems of Third World poverty. A moral theory that addresses *only* individual actors does not have adequate scope for discussing famine problems. As we have seen, one of the main attractions of utilitarianism as an approach to Third World poverty is that its scope is so broad: it can be applied with equal appropriateness to the practical deliberations of individuals, of institutions and groups, and even of nation states and international agencies. Kantian ethical thinking can be interpreted (though it usually isn't) to have equally broad scope.

Since maxims are *underlying* principles of action, they may not always be obvious either to the individuals or institutions whose maxims they are, or to others. We can determine what the underlying principles of some activity or institution are only by seeing the patterns made by various more superficial aspects of acts, policies, and activities. Only those principles that would generate that pattern of activity are maxims of action. Sometimes more than one principle might lie behind a given pattern of activity, and we may be unsure what the maxim of the act was. For example, we might wonder (as Kant does) how to tell whether somebody gives change accurately only out of concern to have an honest reputation or whether he or she would do so anyhow. In such cases we can sometimes set up an "isolation test"—for example, a situation in which it would be open to somebody to be dishonest without any chance of a damaged reputation. But quite often we cannot set up any such situation and may be to some extent unsure which maxim lies behind a given act. Usually we have to rely on whatever individual actors tell us about their maxims of action and on what policymakers or social scientists may tell us about the underlying principles of institutional or group action. What they tell us may well be mistaken. While mistakes can be reduced by care and thoughtfulness, there is no guarantee that we can always work out which maxim of action should be scrutinized for purposes of judging what others do. On the other hand, there is no problem when we are trying to guide our own action: if we can find out what duty demands, we can try to meet those demands.

It is helpful to think of some examples of maxims that might be used to guide action in contexts where poverty and the risk of famine are issues. Somebody who contributes to famine-relief work or advocates development might have an underlying principle such as, "Try to help reduce the risk or severity of world hunger." This commitment might be reflected in varied surface action in varied situations. In one context a gift of money might be relevant; in another some political activity such as lobbying for or against certain types of aid and trade might express the same underlying commitment. Sometimes superficial aspects of action may seem at variance with the underlying maxim they in fact express. For example, if there is reason to think that indiscriminate food aid damages the agricultural economy of the area to which food is given, then the maxim of seeking to relieve hunger might be expressed in action aimed at *limiting* the extent of food aid. More lavish use of food aid might *seem* to treat the needy more generously, but if in fact it will damage their medium- or long-term economic prospects, then it is not (contrary to superficial appearances) aimed at improving and securing their access to subsistence. On a Kantian theory, the basis for judging action should be its *fundamental* principle or policy, and superficially similar acts may be judged morally very different. Regulating food aid in order to drive up prices and profit from them is one matter; regulating food aid in order to enable local farmers to sell their crops and to stay in the business of growing food is quite another.

When we want to work out whether a proposed act or policy is morally required we should not, on Kant's view, try to find out whether it would produce more happiness than other available acts. Rather we should see whether the act or policy is required if we are to avoid acting on maxims that use others as mere means and act on maxims that treat others as ends in themselves. These two aspects of Kantian duty can each be spelled out and shown to have determinate implications for acts and policies that may affect the persistence of hunger and the risk and course of famines.

§20 Using Others as Mere Means

We use others as *mere means* if what we do reflects some maxim *to which they could not in principle consent*. Kant does not suggest that there is anything wrong about using someone as a means. Evidently every cooperative scheme of action does this. A government that agrees to provide free or subsidized food to famine-relief agencies both uses and is used by the agencies; a peasant who sells food in a local market both uses and is used by those who buy the food. In such examples each party to the transaction can and does consent to take part in that transaction. Kant would say that the parties to such transactions use one another but do not use one another as *mere means*. Each party assumes that the other has its own maxims of action and is not just a thing or prop to be used or manipulated.

But there are other cases where one party to an arrangement or transaction not only uses the other but does so in ways that could only be done on the basis of a fundamental principle or maxim to which the other could not in principle consent. If, for example, a false promise is given, the party that accepts the promise is not just used but used as a mere means, because it is *impossible* for consent to be given to the fundamental principle or project of deception that must guide every false promise, whatever its surface character. Those who accept false promises *must* be kept ignorant of the underlying principle or maxim on which the "undertaking" is based. If this isn't kept concealed, the attempted promise will either be rejected or will not be a *false* promise at all. In false promising, the deceived party becomes, as it were, a prop or tool—a *mere means*—in the false promisor's scheme. Action based on any such maxim of deception would be wrong in Kantian terms, whether it is a matter of a breach of treaty obligations, of contractual undertakings, or of accepted and relied upon modes of interaction. Maxims of deception *standardly* use others as mere means, and acts that could only be based on such maxims are unjust.

Other standard ways of using others as mere means is by violence or coercion. Here too victims have no possibility of refusing what is done to them. If a rich or powerful landowner or nation destroys a poorer or more vulnerable person, group, or nation or threatens some intolerable difficulty unless a concession is made, the more vulnerable party is denied a genuine choice between consent and dissent. While the boundary that divides violence and coercion from mere bargaining and negotiation varies and is therefore often hard to discern, we have no doubt about the clearer cases. Maxims of violence destroy or damage agents or their capabilities.

Maxims of coercion may threaten physical force, seizure of possessions, destruction of opportunities, or any other harm that the
coerced party is thought to be unable to absorb without grave injury
or danger. For example, a grain dealer in a Third World village who
threatens not to make or renew an indispensable loan without which
survival until the next harvest would be impossible, unless he is sold
the current crop at pitifully low prices, uses the peasant as mere
means. The peasant does not have the possibility of genuinely con-
senting to the "offer he can't refuse." In this way the outward form of
some coercive transactions may *look* like ordinary commercial dealings: but we know very well that some action that is superficially of
this sort is based on maxims of coercion. To avoid coercion, action
must be governed by maxims that the other party can choose to
refuse and is not forced to accept. The more vulnerable the other
party in any transaction or negotiation, the less that party's scope
for refusal, and the more demanding it is likely to be to ensure that
action is noncoercive.

In Kant's view, acts done on maxims that endanger, coerce, or
deceive others, and thus cannot in principle have the consent of
those others, are wrong. When individuals, institutions, or nation
states act in ways that can only be based on such maxims, they fail
in their duty. They treat the parties who are either deceived or
coerced unjustly. To avoid unjust action it is not enough to observe
the outward forms of free agreement, cooperation, and market disciplines; it is also essential to see that the weaker party to any
arrangement has a genuine option to refuse the fundamental character of the proposal.

§21 Treating Others as Ends in Themselves

For Kant, as for utilitarians, justice is only one part of duty. We may
fail in our duty, even when we don't use anyone as mere means, if
we fail to treat others as "ends in themselves." To treat others as
ends in themselves we must not only avoid using them as mere
means but also treat them as rational and autonomous beings with
their own maxims. In doing so we must also remember that (as Kant
repeatedly stressed, but later Kantians have often forgotten) human
beings are *finite* rational beings in several ways. First, human beings
are not ideal rational calculators. We *standardly* have neither a complete list of the actions possible in a given situation nor more than a
partial view of their likely consequences. In addition, abilities to
assess and to use available information are usually quite limited.
Second, these cognitive limitations are *standardly* complemented by
limited autonomy. Human action is limited not only by various sorts

of physical barrier and inability but by further sorts of (mutual or asymmetrical) *dependence*. To treat one another as ends in themselves such beings have to base their action on principles that do not undermine but rather sustain and extend one another's capacities for autonomous action. A central requirement for doing so is to share and support one another's ends and activities to some extent. Since finite rational beings cannot generally achieve their aims without some help and support from others, a general refusal of help and support amounts to failure to treat others as rational and autonomous beings, that is, as ends in themselves. Hence Kantian principles require us not only to act justly, that is, in accordance with maxims that don't injure, coerce, or deceive others, but also to avoid manipulation and to lend some support to others' plans and activities. Since hunger, great poverty, and powerlessness all undercut the possibility of autonomous action, and the requirement of treating others as ends in themselves demands that Kantians standardly act to support the possibility of autonomous action where it is most vulnerable, Kantians are required to do what they can to avert, reduce, and remedy hunger. They cannot of course do everything to avert hunger: but they may not do nothing.

§22 Justice and Beneficence in Kant's Thought

Kant is often thought to hold that justice is morally required, but beneficence is morally less important. He does indeed, like Mill, speak of justice as a *perfect duty* and of beneficence as an *imperfect duty*. But he does not mean by this that beneficence is any less a duty; rather, he holds that it has (unlike justice) to be selective. We cannot share or even support *all* others' maxims *all* of the time. Hence support for others' autonomy is always selective. By contrast we can make all action and institutions conform fundamentally to standards of nondeception and noncoercion. Kant's understanding of the distinction between perfect and imperfect duties differs from Mill's. In a Kantian perspective, justice is more than the core of beneficence, as in Mill's theory, and beneficence isn't just an attractive but optional moral embellishment of just arrangements (as tends to be assumed in most theories that take human rights as fundamental).

§23 Justice to the Vulnerable in Kantian Thinking

For Kantians, justice requires action that conforms (at least outwardly) to what could be done in a given situation while acting on maxims that use nobody. Since anyone hungry or destitute is more than usually vulnerable to deception, violence, and coercion, the possibilities and temptations to injustice are then especially strong. They are often strongest for those who are nearest to acute poverty and hunger, so could (if they chose) exploit others' need.

Examples are easily suggested, I shall begin with some situations that might arise for somebody who happened to be part of a famine-stricken population. Where shortage of food is being dealt with by a reasonably fair rationing scheme, any mode of cheating to get more than one's allocated share involves using some others and is unjust. Equally, taking advantage of others' desperation to profiteer—for example, selling food at colossal prices or making loans on the security of others' future livelihood, when these are "offers they can't refuse"—constitutes coercion, uses others as mere means, and so is unjust. Transactions that have the outward form of normal commercial dealings may be coercive when one party is desperate. Equally, forms of corruption that work by deception—such as bribing officials to gain special benefits from development schemes, or deceiving others about these entitlements—use others unjustly. Such requirements are far from trivial and are frequently violated in hard times; acting justly in such conditions may involve risking one's own life and livelihood and may require the greatest courage.

It is not so immediately obvious what justice, Kantianly conceived, requires of agents and agencies who are remote from destitution. Might it not be sufficient to argue that those of us fortunate enough to live in the developed world are far from famine and destitution, so if we do nothing but go about our usual business will successfully avoid injustice to the destitute? This conclusion has often been reached by those who take an abstract view of rationality and forget the limits of human rationality and autonomy. To such people it seems that there is nothing more to just action than noninterference with others. But once we remember the limitations of human rationality and autonomy, and the particular ways in which they are limited for those living close to the margins of subsistence, we can see that mere "noninterfering" conformity to ordinary standards of commercial honesty and political bargaining is not enough for justice toward the destitute. If the demands of the powerful constitute "offers that cannot be refused" by the government or by the citizens of a poor country, or if the concessions required for investment by a transnational corporation or a development project reflect the desperation of recipients rather than an appropriate contribution to the project, then (however benevolent the motives of some parties) the weaker party to such agreements is used by the stronger.

In the earlier days of European colonial penetration of the now underdeveloped world it was evident enough that some of the ways in which "agreements" were made with native peoples were in fact violent, deceptive, or coercive—or all three. "Sales" of land by those who had no grasp of market practices and "cession of sovereignty" by those whose forms of life were prepolitical constitute only spurious consent to the agreements struck. But it is not only in these original forms of bargaining between powerful and powerless that injustice is frequent. There are many contemporary examples. For example, if capital investment in a poorer country requires the receiving country or some of its institutions or citizens to contribute disproportionately to the maintenance of a developed, urban "enclave" economy that offers little local employment but lavish standards of life for a small number of (possibly expatriate) "experts," while guaranteeing long-term exemption from local taxation for the investors, then we may doubt that the agreement could have been struck without the element of coercion provided by the desperation of the weaker party. Often enough the coercers in such cases are members of the local as well as the international elite. Or if a trade agreement extracts political advantages (such as military bases) that are incompatible with the fundamental political interests of the country concerned, we may judge that at least some leaders of that country have been "bought" in a sense that is not consonant with ordinary commercial practice.

Even when the actions of those who are party to an agreement don't reflect a fundamental principle of violence, coercion, or deception, the agreement may alter the life circumstances and prospects of third parties in ways to which they patently could not have not consented. For example, a system of food aid and imports agreed on by the government of a Third World country and certain developed states or international agencies may give the elite of that Third World country access to subsidized grain. If that grain is then used to control the urban population and also produces destitution among peasants (who used to grow food for that urban population), then those who are newly destitute probably have not been offered any opening or possibility of refusing their new and worsened conditions of life. If a policy is imposed, those affected *cannot* have been given a chance to refuse it: had the chance been there, they would either have assented (and so the policy would not have been *imposed*) or refused (and so proceeding with the policy would have been evidently coercive), or they would have been able to renegotiate the terms of trade.

§24 Beneficence to the Vulnerable in Kantian Thinking

In Kantian moral reasoning, the basis for beneficent action is that without it we fail to treat others of limited rationality and autonomy as ends in themselves. This is not to say that Kantian beneficence won't make others happier, for it will do so whenever they would be happier if (more) capable of autonomous action, but that happiness secured by purely paternalistic means, or at the cost (for example) of manipulating others' desires, will not count as beneficent in the Kantian picture. Clearly the vulnerable position of those who lack the very means of life, and their severely curtailed possibilities for autonomous action, offer many different ways in which it might be possible for others to act beneficently. Where the means of life are meager, almost any material or organizational advance may help extend possibilities for autonomy. Individual or institutional action that aims to advance economic or social development can proceed on many routes. The provision of clean water, of improved agricultural techniques, of better grain storage systems, or of adequate means of local transport may all help transform material prospects. Equally, help in the development of new forms of social organization— whether peasant self-help groups, urban cooperatives, medical and contraceptive services, or improvements in education or in the position of women—may help to extend possibilities for autonomous action. While the central core of such development projects will be requirements of justice, their full development will also demand concern to treat others as ends in themselves, by paying attention to their particular needs and desires. Kantian thinking does not provide a means by which all possible ways of treating others as ends in themselves could be listed and ranked. But where some activity helps secure possibilities for autonomous action for more people, or is likely to achieve a permanent improvement in the position of the most vulnerable, or is one that can be done with more reliable success, this provides reason for furthering that way of treating others as ends.

Clearly the alleviation of need must rank far ahead of the furthering of happiness in other ways in the Kantian picture. I might make my friends very happy by throwing extravagant parties: but this would probably not increase anybody's possibility for autonomous action to any great extent. But the sorts of development-oriented changes that have just been mentioned may *transform* the possibilities for action of some. Since hunger and the risk of famine are always and evidently highly damaging to human autonomy, any action that helps avoid or reduce famine must have a strong claim on any Kantian who is thinking through what beneficence requires. Depending on circumstances, such action may have to take the form of individual contribution to famine relief and development organizations, of individual or collective effort to influence the trade and aid policies of developed countries, or of attempts to influence the activities of those Third World elites for whom development does not seem to be an urgent priority. Some approaches can best be undertaken by private citizens of developed countries by way of lobbying, publicity, and education; others are best approached by those who work for governments, international agencies, or transnational corporations, who can "work from within" to influence the decisions and policies of these institutions. Perhaps the most dramatic possibilities to act for a just or an unjust, a beneficent or selfish future belongs to those who hold positions of power or influence within the Third World. But wherever we find ourselves, our duties are not, on the Kantian picture, limited to those close at hand. Duties of justice arise whenever there is some involvement between parties—and in the modern world this is never wholly lacking. Duties of beneficence arise whenever destitution puts the possibility of autonomous action in question for the more vulnerable. When famines were not only far away, but nothing could be done to relieve them, beneficence or charity legitimately began—and stayed—near home. In an interconnected world, the moral significance of distance has shrunk, and we may be able to affect the capacities for autonomous action of those who are far away.

§25 The Scope of Kantian Deliberations about Hunger and Famine

In many ways Kantian moral reasoning is less ambitious than utilitarian moral reasoning. It does not propose a process of moral reasoning that can (in principle) rank *all* possible actions or all possible institutional arrangements from the happiness-maximizing "right" action or institution downward. It aims rather to offer a pattern of reasoning by which we can identify whether *proposed action or institutional arrangements* would be just or unjust, beneficent or lacking in beneficence. While *some* knowledge of causal connections is needed for Kantian reasoning, it is far less sensitive than is utilitarian reasoning to gaps in our causal knowledge. It may therefore help us reach conclusions that are broadly accurate even if they are imprecise. The conclusions reached about particular proposals for action or about institutional arrangements will not hold for all time, but be relevant for the contexts for which action is proposed. For example, if it is judged that some institution—say, the World Bank—provides, under present circumstances, a just approach to certain development problems, it will not follow that under all other circumstances such an institution would be part of a just approach. There may be other institutional arrangements that are also just; and there may be other circumstances under which the institutional structure of the World Bank would be shown to be in some ways unjust.

These points show us that Kantian deliberations about hunger can lead only to conclusions that are useful in determinate contexts. This, however, is standardly what we need to know for action, whether individual or institutional. We do not need to be able to generate a complete list of available actions in order to determine whether proposed lines of action are not unjust and whether any are beneficent. Kantian patterns of moral reasoning cannot be guaranteed to identify the optimal course of action in a situation. They provide methods neither for listing nor for ranking all possible proposals for action. But any line of action that is considered can be checked to see whether it is part of what justice and beneficence require—or of what they forbid.

The reason this pattern of reasoning will not show any action or arrangement of the most beneficent one available is that the Kantian picture of beneficence is less mathematically structured than the utilitarian one. It judges beneficence by its overall contribution to the prospects for human autonomy and not by the quantity of happiness expected to result. To the extent that the autonomous pursuit of goals is what Mill called "one of the principal ingredients of human happiness" (but only to that extent),[27] the requirements of Kantian and of utilitarian beneficence will coincide. But whenever expected happiness is not a function of the scope for autonomous action, the two accounts of beneficent action diverge. For utilitarians, paternalistic imposition of, for example, certain forms of aid and development assistance need not be wrong and may even be required. But for Kantians, who think that beneficence should secure others' possibilities for autonomous action, the case for paternalistic imposition of aid or development projects without the recipients' involvement must always be questionable.

In terms of some categories in which development projects are discussed, utilitarian reasoning may well endorse "top-down" aid and development projects that override whatever capacities for autonomous choice and action the poor of a certain area now have in the hopes of securing a happier future. If the calculations work out in a certain way, utilitarians may even think a "generation of sacrifice"—or of forced labor or of imposed population-control policies—not only permissible but mandated. In their darkest Malthusian moments some utilitarians have thought that average happiness might best be maximized not by improving the lot of the poor but by minimizing their numbers, and so have advocated policies of harsh neglect of the poorest and most desperate. Kantian patterns of reasoning are likely to endorse less global and less autonomy-overriding aid and development projects; they are not likely to endorse neglect or abandoning of those who are most vulnerable and lacking in autonomy. If the aim of beneficence is to keep or put others in a position to act for themselves, then emphasis must be placed on "bottom-up" projects, which from the start draw on, foster, and establish indigenous capacities and practices for self-help and local action.

. . .

§27 Respect for Life in Kantian Reasoning

I shall consider only some implications of human capacities for (partially) autonomous action in Kantian thinking on respect for human life in contexts of acute vulnerability, such as destitution and (threatened) hunger.

The fundamental idea behind the Categorical Imperative is that the actions of a plurality of rational beings can be mutually consistent. A minimal condition for their mutual consistency is that each, in acting autonomously, not preclude others' autonomous action. This requirement can be spelled out, as in the formula of the end in itself, by insisting that each avoid action that the other could not freely join in (hence avoid violence, deception, and coercion) and that each seek to foster and secure others' capacities for autonomous action. What this actually takes will, as we have seen, vary with circumstances. But it is clear enough that the partial autonomy of human beings is undermined by life-threatening and destroying circumstances, such as hunger and destitution. Hence a fundamental Kantian commitment must be to preserve life in two senses. First, others must not be deprived of life. The dead (as well as the moribund, the gravely ill, and the famine-stricken) cannot act. Second, others' lives must be preserved in forms that offer them sufficient physical energy, psychological space, and social security for action. Partial autonomy is vulnerable autonomy, and in human life psychological and social as well as material needs must be met if any but the most meager possibility of autonomous action is to be preserved. Kantians are therefore committed to the preservation not only of biological but of biographical life. To act in the typical ways humans are capable of, we must not only be alive, but have a life to lead.

On a Kantian view, we may justifiably—even nobly—risk or sacrifice our lives for others. When we do so, we act autonomously, and nobody uses us as a mere means. But we cannot justly use others (nor they us) as mere means in a scheme that could only be based on violence, deception, or coercion. Nor may we always refuse others the help they need to sustain the very possibility of autonomous action. Of course, no amount of beneficence could put anyone in the position to do all possible actions: that is not what we need to be concerned about. What we do need to be concerned about is failure to secure for others a possibility of some range of autonomous action.

Where others' possibilities for autonomous action are eroded by poverty and malnutrition, the necessary action must clearly include moves to change the picture. But these moves will not meet Kantian requirements if they provide merely calories and basic medicine; they must also seek to enable those who began to be adequately fed to act autonomously. They must foster the capabilities that human beings need to function effectively. They must therefore aim at least at minimal security and subsistence. Hence, the changes that Kantians argue or work for must always be oriented to development plans that create enough economic self-sufficiency and social security for independence in action to be feasible and sustainable. There is no royal road to this result and no set of actions that is likely to be either universally or totally effective. Too many changes are needed, and we have too little understanding of the precise causal connections that limit some possibilities and guarantee others. But some broadly accurate, if imprecise indication of ranges of required action, or ranges of action from which at least some are required, is possible.

VI. Nearby Hunger and Poverty

§28 Hunger and Welfare in Rich Countries

So far we have been considering how we might think about and respond to the poverty, hunger, and famine that are characteristic of parts of the developing world. However, both poverty and hunger can be found nearer home. Poverty in the developed world is nowhere so widespread or acute as to risk famine; but it is well documented.[28] Hunger in the developed world is doubly hidden. As always, it shows more in the blighting of lives and health than in literal deaths. However, in contrast to Third World poverty, poverty in rich countries is a minority problem that affects parts of the population whom not everybody meets. Perhaps the most visible aspect of this poverty-amid-wealth in the 1990s is the number of homeless people now to be found on the streets of great and once-great cities in some of the richest societies of the world. In the warmer climates of the Third World, the need for warm and decent housing is also often unmet—but homelessness is nowhere a worse experience than in the colder parts of the developed world. Although the homeless of the rich world may be able to command money that would constitute wealth in a very poor country, its purchasing power where they are is not enough for minimal housing, decent hygiene, and clothing and may not be enough for adequate food. Apart from the highly visible homeless there are many others in the richer countries who for one reason or another go hungry.

The utilitarian and Kantian ways of thinking considered in this chapter have clear implications for responses to nearby hunger. For utilitarians there will be no doubt that this hunger too produces misery, and should be ended by whatever means will add to the total of human happiness. Many of the strategies that have been used successfully to eradicate hunger in some developed countries have been strongly influenced by this utilitarian thinking. For example, in many western European states social welfare systems guarantee basic welfare, including health care for all, and minimal income. The public policies of these welfare states are funded by taxation, and there would be wide public agreement that these policies produce a greater total happiness than would *laissez-faire* policies, which would leave the poor without a publicly funded "safety net." Opposition to welfare state policies, which can reliably reduce poverty and end hunger, is not likely to come from utilitarians. On the contrary, utilitarian activism has been one of the major forces behind the emergence of welfare states.[29]

Opposition to a welfare state has, however, been vocal among some sorts of human rights thinkers. They articulate the worry that a welfare state, like foreign aid or food aid, is unjust to those who are taxed to provide the funds, and damaging to those who become dependent on what they often disparagingly call welfare handouts.

The objection to redistributive taxation has been part of a long-standing polemic between advocates of "equality" and of "liberty" during the period of the Cold War. Some of the advocates of liberty (often called *libertarians*) have adopted an extreme view of the demands of liberty, and argue that unrestricted rights to property-without-taxation are a human right. They conclude that the welfare state is an attack on human liberty. Equally, some advocates of equality have argued for a very strong imposition of material equality, which would indeed make heavy inroads into individual liberty. The underlying arguments for both extreme positions, and for their favored interpretations of human rights, are quite unconvincing. In practice, societies have to strike some balance between liberty and equality. Good social welfare policies are an attractive way of accommodating liberty and equality because they ensure that nobody is so vulnerable that their liberty is wholly eroded, but they do so without a heavy reduction of liberty of those who pay the necessary taxes. The even-handed collection of just taxes leaves richer citizens very great liberty to lead their lives as they will, and enables poorer citizens to reach a minimally decent standard of living that secures their capabilities for leading their lives with dignity. The real issues for social policymakers in the area of taxation have to do with questions about the containment of costs, the fairness of taxation, and the efficiency of its collection rather than with illusory attempts to create societies that embody liberty without equality, or equality without liberty.

The second of these worries, that welfare creates dependence, is a rather implausible objection to policies that end hunger: nothing damages autonomy and creates vulnerability and dependence as much as debilitating hunger and demeaning homelessness. A lack of welfare systems perhaps guarantees that the poor do not depend on the state, but it increases rather than ends their dependence. Worries about dependence have a limited appropriate role in considering *what sort* of welfare policies to pursue. Should welfare payments be in cash or in kind? How far is means testing needed? Should support go to families or to individuals? Do some welfare systems damage the incentive to work? These detailed questions, rather than ideological defense either of unrestricted liberty or of unrestricted equality, are the real issues for social policymakers today.

The Kantian position presented here stresses the importance of not using others as mere means and of treating them as ends in themselves. This position demands commitment to institutions that enable people to become and remain autonomous agents. Hence Kantians would be particularly concerned to prevent the extremes of poverty that lead to hunger and homelessness. The hungry and homeless are particularly vulnerable to every sort of injustice, and above all to violence, coercion, and deception, all of which use people as mere means. On the other hand, this same commitment to autonomy would lead Kantians to demand that welfare policies leave welfare recipients as much in charge of their lives as possible. They would argue that welfare policies (e.g., minimum wage, health care, unemployment pay, child benefit, and many others) can all be structured to enhance rather than restrict the autonomy of those who receive benefits or payments. Good welfare policies manifest rather than damage respect for persons. Kantians do not, of course, advocate justice alone, but also insist that beneficence is important and should be manifested in support and concern for particular others and for their projects. This commitment would also be relevant to actions to relieve poverty, hunger, and homelessness. A society that manages not to use any of its members as mere means, and funds adequate levels of welfare payment, can either succeed in treating its more vulnerable members as ends in themselves, whose particular lives and plans must be respected, or fail to do so by leaving them to the undermining and humiliating procedures of an ill-trained welfare bureaucracy. Because Kantians are concerned for justice and beneficence, they would never see beneficence alone as an adequate response to poverty, homelessness, and hunger at home or abroad. Mere charity is too capricious to secure for the poor capabilities to lead their own lives. Equally, unlike persons with rights-based sorts of ethical thinking, they would never see justice alone as a morally adequate response to human vulnerability.

Whether poverty and hunger are in the next street or far away, whether we articulate the task in utilitarian, in Kantian, or in other terms, the claims of justice and of beneficence for the two cases are similar. What may differ in the two cases are our opportunities for action. Sometimes we have far greater possibilities to affect what goes on in the next street than we do to affect what goes on on distant continents. Since nobody can do everything, we not only *may* but *must* put our efforts where they will bear fruit. This, however, provides no license for injustice to distant others. Nearby neighbors need justice, but they are not entitled to justice at the expense of those who are far away. Hence, legitimate concern for justice and welfare for those who are nearby fellow-citizens has always to work with and not against the vast efforts of countless agents and institutions across the world and across the generations of mankind to put an end to world hunger. In a world in which action affects distant others, justice cannot be stopped at local or national boundaries: there is no such thing as social justice in one country. It is only our activism, and not our thinking or concern, that can legitimately be local. If we act by the ecologist's slogan "Think globally, act locally" not only in protecting vulnerable environments but in protecting vulnerable humans, we may, however, become part of the solution rather than part of the problem of world hunger.

· · ·

NOTES

· · ·

4. For the background to this summary of famine and hunger issues, see the works listed under "For Further Reading," §7, below.

5. Revelations 6:5.

6. For a short list of Malthusian works and discussions of these views, see the suggested readings for §9, below..

7. Thomas Malthus, *Summary View of the Principle of Population*, reprinted in *On Population: Three Essays*, Notestein, F. ed. New York: Mentor, 1960, p. 55.

8. Again, see the list under §9 below.

9. This line of argument has been pressed by Garrett Hardin: see references in Note 17 and in §9 below.

10. Again, see the list §7 below.

11. See, for example, Ester Boserup, *Population and Technology*. Oxford, England: Blackwell, 1981, especially Chapter 14.

12. See in particular Tony Jackson, *Against the Grain: The Dilemma of Project Food Aid*. Oxford: England: Oxfam, 1982. See also works by Cassen and Griffin, listed under "For Further Reading."

· · ·

25. The main Kantian text in which these points are articulated is the supposedly introductory, but actually rather difficult, *Groundwork of the Metaphysic of Morals*, translated by H. J. Paton as *The Moral Law*. London: Hutcheson, 1953. Many contemporary discussions of Kantian ethics take rights as basic. Kant takes duties as basic. For a succinct account of the differences between Kant's ethics and recent Kantian ethics see Onora O'Neill, "Kantian Ethics," in Peter Singer, ed. *Companion to Ethics*. Oxford: Blackwell, 1991. For a more detailed account of Kant's ethics see R. Sullivan, *Kant's Moral Theory*. Cambridge: Cambridge University Press, 1988. For a different view of it see Onora O'Neill, *Constructions of Reason: Explorations of Kant's Practical Philosophy*. Cambridge: Cambridge University Press, 1989.

26. Kant, op. cit., p. 430 (Prussian Academy pagination).

27. John Stuart Mill, *On Liberty*. In Warnock, op. cit., p. 185.

28. For the United States see Harvard School of Public Health, *Hunger in America: The Growing Epidemic*. Cambridge, MA: Harvard University Press, 1985; and *Hunger Reaches Blue Collar America*. Same publisher, 1987.

29. Robert Goodin, *Protecting the Vulnerable: A Reanalysis of Our Social Responsibilities*. Chicago: University of Chicago Press, 1985.

· · ·

FOR FURTHER READING

The literature on world hunger, famine, and development problems is so large that any selection is in various ways arbitrary. The books mentioned here are generally accessible and recent apart from some of the neo-Malthusian references. This is not to say that Malthusian perspectives have been wholly discredited or abandoned, but only that current debates are less centered on them.

For §7 and Later Discussions of Development

Drèze, Jean, and Sen, Amartya, 1989. *Hunger and Public Action.* Oxford: Clarendon Press. This book is enormously informative and comprehensive about the analysis of hunger problems and about the policies that have turned out best at reducing hunger in different parts of the world. It has a long and very useful bibliography. If you read one book on poverty and hunger, read this one.

Drèze and Sen have also edited three volumes under the general title *The Political Economy of Hunger* (Oxford: Clarendon, 1991), which deal respectively with entitlement and well-being (Vol. 1), famine prevention (Vol. 2), and endemic hunger (Vol. 3).

World Bank, 1988. *The Challenge of Hunger: A Call to Action.* Washington, DC: World Bank. Other World Bank publications are also highly informative.

Arnold, D. 1988. *Famine: Social Crisis and Historical Change.* Oxford: Blackwell.

Bennett, Jon, with Susan George, 1987. *The Hunger Machine.* Oxford: Blackwell. Accessible and vivid.

Cassen, R. et al., 1986. *Does Aid Work?* Oxford: Clarendon Press.

George, Susan, 1977. *How the Other Half Dies: The Real Reasons for World Hunger.* Montclair, NJ: Allanheld.
———1988. *A Fate Worse than Debt.* Harmondsworth, UK: Penguin.
Griffin, K., 1987. *World Hunger and the World Economy.* London: Macmillan.

Harrisson, G.A., ed. 1988. *Famine.* Oxford: Oxford University Press, 1988.

Lappé, Frances Moore, 1988. *World Hunger: Twelve Myths.* London: Earthscan Publications.

O'Neill, Onora, 1986. *Faces of Hunger: An Essay on Poverty, Development and Justice.* London: George Allen and Unwin.
———1991. "Transnational Justice," David Held, ed. *Political Theory Today.* Stanford, CA: Stanford University Press, pp. 276–304. Surveys theoretical work on global distributive justice.

Timberlake, Lloyd, 1988. *Africa in Crisis.* London: Earthscan Publications.

For §9 and Later Discussions of Malthusian Positions

Malthus, Thomas, 1798. *Essay on the Principle of Population as It Affects the Future Improvement of Society.* London: 1798, and see Note 4.

Lucas, George R., and Ogletree, Thomas W., eds. 1976. *Lifeboat Ethics: The Moral Dilemmas of World Hunger.* New York: Harper & Row. The bibliography in this book is a useful source of references.

Hardin, Garrett, 1972. *Exploring the New Ethics for Survival.* New York: Viking: and the bibliography in Lucas and Ogletree, op. cit.

Ehrlich, Paul, 1971. *The Population Bomb.* New York: Ballantine.

Paddock, Paul, and Paddock, William, 1967. *Famine—1975.* Boston: Little, Brown.

For more recent work, journals are particularly useful: you might browse through *People Population Studies, Population and Development Review,* or *Population and Environment.*

For §28 and Other Points on Poverty and Hunger in Developed Countries:

Harvard School of Public Health, *Hunger in America: The Growing Epidemic.* Cambridge, Mass.: Harvard University Press, 1985.

Harvard School of Public Health, *Hunger Reaches Blue Collar America.* Cambridge, Mass.: Harvard University Press, 1987.

Robert Goodin, *Protecting the Vulnerable: A Reanalysis of Our Social Responsibilities.* Chicago: University of Chicago Press, 1985.

Norman Daniels, *Just Health Care.* Cambridge: Cambridge University Press, 1985.

III. RIGHTS AND JUSTICE

Solidarity among Strangers and the Right to Food

HENRY SHUE

Henry Shue is the Wyn and William Y. Hutchinson Professor of Ethics & Public Life at Cornell University. He is the author of *Basic Rights: Subsistence, Affluence, and U.S. Foreign Policy* (Princeton, 1980), which is soon to appear in a Second Edition. His current research primarily concerns issues of international justice that arise from attempts to prevent global climate change. Shue was a founding member of the Institute for Philosophy and Public Policy at the University of Maryland.

It is this solidarity among strangers, this transformation through the division of labor of needs into rights and rights into care that gives us whatever fragile basis we have for saying that we live in a moral community.[1]

Rights are for the bad days. It is difficult for those of us who are among the best-off members of the best-off societies in human history to appreciate fully that, for a billion or so of our contemporaries, every day is a bad day, although some days are still worse than others and, for many young people, the days are few.[2]

People decide which rights to grant to each other. A human does not come into life accompanied by a printed list of his or her rights, like a new toaster with its limited warranty, set of instructions ("Do not submerge in water"), and list of addresses of authorized repair stations. But decisions about which rights are to be granted need not be made arbitrarily and cannot be made individualistically. Judgments about rights are made for reasons, which embody our best understanding of the realities of human life. Sifting through the various considerations advanced as reasons for acknowledging or not acknowledging specific rights is a deeply social, and gradually evolving, process. Or so I will now argue.

Justifying Rights and Duties

Much paper has been consumed by debates about whether rights are natural. The answer is: yes and no. If "natural" means given— "just there" to be seen by any clear-eyed observer—then rights are not natural. For individual persons, there are no instructions from the manufacturer (and no manufacturer). Not much is natural in the sense of given independent of human judgment, of course, since social choices about the boundaries of any concept contribute to the determination of what does and does not fall within the concept. If, on the other hand, "natural" means based on what individual humans and human societies are actually like—what persons need and what enables them to thrive as humans—then rights are natur- al. The concept of human thriving or flourishing—like all concepts— becomes highly debatable on its outer edges, with increasing scope for judgment and ultimately perhaps for bare preference, but the concept's core of needs is as firm and well established as any.

Vital   We have a reason to make something the content of a funda- mental right only if it is vital to human life, but different things are vitally important in radically different, almost opposite ways. Some liberties, on the one hand, are vital because they are preconditions for the crowning glories of human life: the creativity and refinement that seem to be possible only for humans, among this planet's species. Food, clean water, and clean air (and some other liberties), on the other hand, are vital because they are preconditions for the bare maintenance of human life. Ingesting basic nutrition and exer- cising artistic freedom are about as different as activities can be, but each is essential to a flourishing human life. The first step in show- ing that something ought to be the content of a right is showing that it is vital—either literally necessary to, or highly valuable to, living as a human.

Vulnerable   The second step in justifying a right is showing that, besides being vital, the thing in question is generally vulnerable: subject to widespread threats that individuals on their own often could not ward off. Besides taking in nutrition regularly, we also need, for example, for our hearts to beat regularly. But we face no general threat to regular heartbeat that is analogous to the general threat to regular nutrition constituted by fragile food-systems. If we were born with hearts that depended on rechargeable batteries—everyone in effect had an inborn pacemaker from the start—and there were millions of people who could not reach recharging equipment, just as there now are (hundreds of) millions who cannot grow or otherwise obtain adequate food under our current arrangements, it might make sense to propose "access to recharging equipment" as a human right. Although in the end many of us will die of failing hearts, ordinarily a person can lead a long and vigorous life without needing to rely on special social arrangements to keep her heart beating. Normally, heartbeat itself is not subject to chronic direct threats that individuals cannot handle on their own, so it needs no special protection. It is vital but not generally vulnerable. Food is vital, and food supplies are highly vulnerable.

I noted already that "we have a reason to make something the content of a right only if it is vital to human life, but different things are vitally important in radically different, almost opposite ways." Jeremy Waldron sums up Joseph Raz's widely accepted definition of a right as follows: "to have a right is for it to be the case that one's interest justifies holding someone else to have a duty."[3] One's interest must, in my terms, be "vitally important" in order for it to deserve to be the subject of a right—so important that, as Raz emphasizes, other people (who may not even know me, or may know me but not like me) can justifiably be expected to conduct their lives so that this interest of mine is protected or promoted.

There is a reason why starving children are usually dressed in rags, and wandering far from home. The reason is that the distributions of different material commodities like food, clothing, and shelter are not so discrete, or distinct from each other, that a person is likely to be missing out on just one commodity while being well supplied with the others.[4] The fact that things tend to come in bundles is one reason why rights should come in bundles as well. Nevertheless, since this book is about hunger and food, I will focus on reasons for the right to food, but with frequent comparisons with other equally fundamental rights.[5]

People often say something like the following: "A right to food? Sure. Without food you die; and if you are dead, you can't exercise any rights. If there were no right to food, no other right would mean much." Unfortunately—since I welcome its conclusion that there is a right to food—this is not a convincing argument. This argument is too quick and too simple, but we can note some important features of better arguments by seeing why. The observation that "without food you die" functions as an appeal to some such tacit premise as: a person has a right to whatever she needs in order to stay alive.[6]

But this premise is much too strong. Few of us believe that a person has a right to whatever she needs in order to stay alive, and we could not afford to act on this premise for long if we did believe it. The premise would commit us, for example, to the judgment that if a 75-year-old person would die without a mechanical heart, she has a right to a mechanical heart.[7]

The most important reason why we do not make this judgment is the extraordinary nature of the medical care currently constituted by implantation of a mechanical heart and its resultant extraordinary expense. This, of course, could change. Surgery, antibiotics, and all kinds of care now taken for granted (in rich societies) were extraordinary even during the lifetimes of current 75-year olds. Maybe someday mechanical hearts will be mass produced and as readily provided as, say, contact lenses are now; if so, they will have then become routine and be part of ordinary care at that time. In those circumstances it might well be plausible to argue that everyone who needs one has a right to be provided one if he or she cannot afford it on one's own, just as one can argue now that every child has a right to, say, polio vaccine as part of any elementary package of preventive medicine in spite of the fact that polio vaccine did not even exist in 1950. How can it be that there was no right to polio vaccine in 1950, but there is in 1995?

The short answer is that there is an enduring general right to protection against common, easily and cheaply preventable threats to life and that a cheap protection against a severe threat to life became available between 1950 and now. The basic right to life always entailed a package of protections; it became affordable to add an item—polio vaccine—to the package. Today it is outrageous to deny a child a dose of polio vaccine because he or she cannot pay for it, because we are refusing to implement one's right to life for the sake of a trivial amount of money. If a dose of polio vaccine still cost as much as a mechanical heart now does, we would have to refuse to guarantee it to all children. As with police protection and all other protections for our lives entailed by rights, the measures we judge appropriate do depend partly on cost. Costs of technologies often decline as they are mass produced, the extraordinary becomes the ordinary, and it becomes reasonable to insist that everyone have it. This is one way that rights change. How much it would take to keep someone going—hundreds of thousands of dollars of hightech medical care or a few dollars a day of ordinary food—cannot be ignored. Expense is an issue, as we will see more fully, because it affects the reasonableness of the duties that the recognition of the right would impose on the duty-bearers.

So what can we see generally about what it takes for an interest to justify holding someone else to have a duty? As indicated in the beginning, there is no one feature of an interest that qualifies it to be the content of a right. This can now be seen to be true for two different reasons. On the one hand, the interest must be important or vital, but "important" and "vital" are general categories and can be specified in multiple ways. On the other hand, importance to potential right-bearers—however exactly it is spelled out—is not definitive by itself. A mechanical heart may be supremely important to an aged person with a failing heart, but that by itself is not a sufficient ground for concluding that (all or some of) the rest of us have a duty to provide it. We must in addition consider which measures are normal and which are extraordinary, because we must consider cost. It is possible for what can satisfy a vital need inexpensively to be the content of a right, while what could satisfy another equally vital need, but only at great expense, not to be.

What it is reasonable to demand of others depends partly on what it would cost them to fulfill the demand. What I have so far called "vital" is what the content of a right means to the bearer of the right. But one must also inquire what fulfillment of a possible right would mean to those who would fulfill it, the duty-bearers. If fulfillment of a duty integral to a right would cost the duty-bearer something vital, that is a weighty reason against imposing the duty.[8]

Solidarity with Strangers

Rights are profoundly social.[9] The social solidarity involved in rights may be less readily apparent than their individualistic aspects, but it comes through when, and if, consideration of possible rights turns to their costs to duty-bearers, as I have just been advocating. Some proponents of rights appear to find such consideration of costs at best undignified, even ignoble, or mean-spirited.[10] Rights seem to them to be too elevated a matter for discussions of expenses to be dragged in. I am suggesting, on the contrary, that the refusal to enter into serious examination of the duties entailed by any proposed right not only is intellectually irresponsible, leaving the right largely unspecified and blowing in the wind, but fails to appreciate the full social basis of the right, which rests on the responses of other people. To ignore the point of view of duty-bearers, while considering only the point of view of right-bearers, is to construct an extremely truncated picture of how rights actually work.

It is not enough simply to declare that everyone has a right to, say, security and privacy in his or her own home, even if one adds: "So the rest of us must not interfere—we must leave them alone." Of course this right involves such a negative duty not to invade the security and privacy of others.[11] The significance of our interest in security and privacy justifies the imposition of a duty on everyone else not to interfere with us. While this duty is at the heart of rights to security and privacy, it is far from the whole story because in fact many people will choose to violate their negative duty to leave others alone and will, for example, break into houses in order to steal money or easily saleable electronic equipment in order, for instance, to maintain their drug habits. It is utterly fatuous to say: "Oh, now you are bringing up the problem of drugs—I was talking about human rights." Talk about rights to privacy and security in the home is at least half empty if one does not ask at least the questions: "What are the most serious threats to this right, and what would it cost to protect the enjoyment of the right against those main threats?"

Every night in this country homes are broken into, and pedestrians are mugged, by people who are addicted to hard drugs and consequently desperately want money. Drug addiction is one of the most serious threats to genuine enjoyment of security in one's home. Everyone, including people with addictions, certainly has a negative duty not to mug or burglarize. To think, however, that one was doing something significant to implement the right to security if one simply reminded or admonished the people with the addictions not to violate their duties would be a joke. In order to protect security we need to do something about the political conditions that allow drug dealing to thrive. That would be dangerous and expensive. Consequently, any analysis of the duties correlative to this right has to ask, who will bear the danger and who will bear the expense, that is, how are the positive duties to be allocated?

Ignoring the positive duties correlative to a right, and their costs, is like saying: "we believe people have a 'right not to be flooded,' but we don't want to talk about dams, which are expensive economic projects"—what would a "right not to be flooded" mean if nothing were done to block the flow of water? The positive protections for a right are the dams against the threats to the right. Environmentally well-informed people know, of course, that dams are often not the best, and sometimes are not even a good, measure for preventing flooding. One often must, for example, also prevent deforestation in the watershed of the stream in question or dams will merely redistribute the flooding to different locations. A serious flood prevention program is not merely a dam-building program. This too has its analogue in the case of the right to security in the home. An approach to implementation that is not politically cynical must involve measures that go deeper than more police and more jails and must move aggressively to stop drug-dealing from consistently having one of the highest profit margins of any business in the world.

Two different points are intertwined here. One is that serious-ness about rights leads to seriousness about duties. It is irresponsi-bly dreamy simply to muse wishfully about rights that it might be nice for people to have without moving to the next step of consider-ing what arrangements, formal or informal, local or global, govern-mental or nongovernmental, are necessary for the rights imagined to be implemented. The other point is that seriousness about duties opens up the underlying social character of rights, the respects in which, while the rights belong to individuals, their protection is an expression of solidarity across a community. In order for that soli-darity to be forthcoming, in many cases, and certainly in order for the cooperation required by the implementation of rights to be fair to all concerned, consideration must be given not only to the impor-tance of the interests at stake for potential right-bearers in whether a particular right is recognized but also to the importance of the interests at stake for potential duty-bearers. For just as certain interests will be made secure if a particular right is recognized and implemented, that very implementation will involve costs and/or burdens to be borne by those who are assigned the correlative duties. The reasonableness of those duties is part of the reasonable-ness of the rights they implement. If it would not be reasonable to expect those who would bear the necessary duties to perform them, it cannot be reasonable to acknowledge the right.[12]

One common response to questions about the allocation of the burdens of implementing rights is to point out that right-bearers and duty-bearers are not two separate classes such that some people are exclusively right-bearers and receive only the benefits of whatever rights there are, while other people are exclusively duty-bearers and simply carry burdens. If a right is a universal human right, it belongs to everyone, and anyone can invoke its protections when the interest that it protects is threatened. So the very right whose imple-mentation may sometimes impose burdens of duty on me may also protect the same interest in my own case on the day that my own cri-sis comes.

Now this is correct, and it is important, but its practical signif-icance can easily be misconstrued. I am certainly not immune to dis-aster, and I might very well someday find myself hungry and home-less, especially in a country like the United States where even the basic entitlements in the social safety net are under sustained assault by political reactionaries. So institutional arrangements to implement a right to food will not necessarily always find even peo-ple as well-off as I am now on the giving, rather than the receiving, end. Nevertheless, in practice the probability of my actually needing to invoke the right to food is orders of magnitude smaller than the probability that, say, many children in Burundi or Harlem will need to invoke it. Hunger is the least of my current worries about myself. Odds definitely are that, with regard to the right to food, I will always find myself in the status of a duty-bearer and never function actively as a right-bearer, a fact that of course it is only sane to welcome, not to regret. (Should I instead hope to have the problems of Burundian children so that I can receive "my share" of the material benefits from the social acknowledgment of the right to food?) The point is only that it would be implausible to maintain that the right to food is going to be equally advantageous materially to everyone just because it does indeed belong to everyone.[13] Anatole France's famous observation, "The law in its majestic equality forbids the rich as well as the poor to sleep under the bridges," poignantly captures the importance of differences in circumstances.[14] The same prohibition, or the same right, will have very different material benefits for people in different situations.

This discussion of benefits from rights is so far extremely simplistic, especially in two respects. First, one must distinguish what might be called insurance benefits from direct material benefits. Rights are in important respects like insurance policies, providing protection against eventualities that one hopes will not occur, like early death. Suppose there are two young couples, the Roses and the Thorns, each with a young child. Each couple decides to buy life insurance for the breadwinner(s) of the family in order that their child will have enough money to pay for college even if the breadwinner(s) should die young. The breadwinner for the Rose family does in fact meet an early death, and the survivor and their child collect the insurance. The Thorns on the other hand, enjoy a long and happy life, living to see their grandchildren while still paying annual premiums on the life insurance policies, until finally they just cancel the life insurance policies, until finally they just cancel the life insurance policies without ever collecting any 'death benefits.' Do we judge, then, that while the Roses benefitted from one of their life insurance policies, because one of them died young and the spouse and child collected money that they needed, the Thorns failed to benefit? No. None of the Thorns benefitted materially by receiving a check for a death benefit from the insurance company, but they did benefit from the security provided for their child's education. The insurance policy guaranteed the Thorns that, whether they lived or died, their child would have its education paid for. That security is itself a benefit–and an objective one. That is, it is not merely that they felt secure subjectively about their child's education–that could have resulted from their mistakenly believing they were covered by a policy that did not in fact cover them. Their child's education was objectively secure: it was in reality going to be paid for, one way or another. Their life insurance did them a lot of good. It provided them what I am calling insurance benefits.

Rights also provide insurance benefits, as well as material benefits. I do not benefit from a right to food only when I am too weak to secure my own meals. I benefit from the fact–or would benefit if in this country it were the fact–that arrangements are in place for the day, should it come, when I become so weak. Since this is not one of the problems I worry about, I would not benefit subjectively–not be relieved of any anxiety on this score. Nevertheless, I would be objectively better-off, specifically more secure, than I am without institutions guaranteeing food to those unable to get it for themselves.

The second respect in which the initial discussion above of rights and benefits is simplistic is in attempting to look at only one right at a time. Specific rights protect against specific threats to specific interests. At any one time some people will be subject to any given threat, other people will definitely not be the subject, and others still will be more or less likely to be subject to it. Every right does have insurance benefits even if it protects against threats that are, at any given time, distant or irrelevant, as we noticed just above. It is also important, however, that any one right normally comes in a system of rights. For any given person, while certain rights protect against threats that are not immediate, other rights protect against other threats that are. A particular person is likely to be receiving material benefits from a few rights and insurance benefits from many others, if she is lucky, or, if she is not as lucky, material benefits from many rights. The more threats from which one would actually suffer but for one's rights, the more material benefits one receives from the system of rights.

Often a kind of mirror effect occurs between different rights. I am not worried about running out of food because I have more than enough wealth to buy food for myself. That, in turn, may mean that what I have to worry about protecting is my wealth. If I have enough wealth not to need to invoke any arrangements for implementing the right to food, I may well benefit instead from the arrangements for the right to physical security that protect me against any assault that would be involved in taking some of my wealth from me by force. This is a certain sort of reciprocity among rights.

Reciprocity among Right-bearers

A far more important reciprocity holds among persons, if they are the bearers of rights. This reciprocity is the specific form that systems of rights give to solidarity with strangers. I might, for instance, resonably expect a hungry child–let us call her Wanda[15]–not to attack me physically in order to take some of my money for food, just as she might reasonably expect that I will not merely turn away clutching my money and let her starve. The interest protected in the case of each of us would be physical survival. A well–designed system of rights could protect the vital interest of us both equally well, if we each performed our duties.

Her duty may be far more onerous than mine in spite of the fact that, in the encounter I have just sketched, mine is positive and hers is negative. My duty might be, say, to provide her with enough money for food for a month while she looks for a job. If I were her last hope–as I might or might not be–my failure to do my duty in implementing her right to food would have as its effect her death within the next month from starvation. The cost to me of fulfilling my duty to her might be, assuming she lives in a poor Third World country and could eat for a little more than $1 a day, say $50. My duty is positive, but in this one case taken by itself, trivial in amount for a member of the U.S. middle-class; I might just get inside the door of a Broadway show for this amount (leaving aside what it would cost me to get to New York City and to have a comfortable bed for the night).[16]

Her duty in implementing my right to physical security, on the other hand, is the purely negative one of not attacking and attempting to rob me, irrespective of whether I turn and start walking away from her. The effect on me of her failure to do her duty toward me might be, assuming that she is weak from malnutrition and not armed, that I fight her off with only cuts and bruises or that I buy her off at the last minute, under direct threat of attack, with the contents of my wallet, which–let us assume for the sake of neatness–is $50. The effect upon her of her doing her purely negative duty of leaving me alone, if I am in fact walking away from her, is death within the next month from starvation, assuming that I am the only rich-country tourist passing through the village and there is no one else available over the short-term either to help her voluntarily, to employ her, or to be robbed by her. In short, my performance of my positive duty would cost me $50; her performance of her negative duty would cost her her life. Contrary to common assumption, the fulfillment of a positive duty need not be more costly or more difficult than the fulfillment of a negative duty. No such generalizations are available at the high level of abstraction represented by the concepts of positive and negative duties; one must look at specific duties and at features other than whether they are positive or negative, which is a feature of little real significance in spite of its popularity in abstract theories.[17]

On the other hand, while avoiding for a month the death of one malnourished youth in the Third World may cost only a trivial amount like $50 (less than the cost of most new books), tens of millions of other young people fit Wanda's general description. Reiterating fulfillment of the same modest duty endlessly could exhaust any one person's resources. If that were the implication of acknowledging a right for Wanda, the apparent unreasonableness of the implication might be taken to show the unreasonableness of the premise from which it follows. A supposed right that implied such unreasonable duties would be an unreasonable right. However, it is usually thought that, if Wanda has a general right to help from someone, it can only be from someone who has not yet done his or her share to fulfill such general rights.[18] Do we each have a share, the performance of which is the limit on our general duties?

Now it is obvious that a person's general duties—that is, duties in response to general rights (rights belonging to everyone)—either are limited or are not limited. If they are not limited, then one is never finished with one's general duties; however much one has done or given, more—endlessly more—remains. This is not an obviously incoherent view. It is only an overwhelming view. If it is correct, one's duty is simply never done until one's last breath is gone, precisely as many martyrs, saints, and other passionate servants of humanity have believed. In this age, this view would be a hard sell, but that may tell us more about the age than about the view.

If, on the other hand, a person's general duties are limited, there is such a thing as having done all that one has any duty to do. One can be finished doing everything that one ought to do for the sake of human rights. Since the planet contains at least a billion people whose rights are not being protected or respected, one is very likely—more likely in some places than others—to encounter people who are desperate because interests important enough to deserve the protection of rights are, in their cases, going unprotected and unfulfilled. Still, if the notion of a limit to duty is to mean anything at all, one must be entitled at some point to walk by on the other side of the road. One is entitled to look the Wandas of the world in the eye, sadly but not guiltily, and walk calmly away.

Or maybe not so calmly. It may be—unless I am an insensitive brute, it will be—uncomfortable for me to walk away from Wanda's desperate need. I will be greatly tempted to deceive myself into believing that she will, if I leave her, somehow be taken care of, even if I have absolutely no good reason for this optimism. I am free of course to be generous in excess of my fair share of general duty—nothing prohibits me from helping people I am under no duty to help. If, however, my "generosity" is a salve for feelings of guilt at the thought of walking away, my guilt is irrational if my limited duty had already been done. It is, in a way, just bad luck for me that I have encountered Wanda—and of course bad luck for her that it was me, not someone with unfulfilled general duties, that encountered her. If

I were in my home, not hers, I wouldn't see her; and I would not have to avoid her plaintive eyes as I turn to leave her.

If I were at home, she would of course still be where she is, just as desperate. But I know that wherever I happen to be, there or at home, hundreds of thousands of other desperately hungry youths stand on hundreds of thousands of other dirty street corners. They cannot all be my responsibility—that would make my duty absurdly great and thereby demonstrate the supposed right to be unreasonable. The others do not threaten to haunt me the way that Wanda does, but that is only because I can see her face—must see her face. That I see her face is perhaps merely an arbitrary contingency, an unfortunate coincidence, like seeing a terrible accident on the highway that occurs just before one happens to pass. If her face is otherwise going to haunt me, perhaps I should give her the $50 to buy myself the peace of mind (and stay out of the Third World in the future). But if I do give it to her, I should admit to myself that this is irrational guilt-money, more weakness than generosity.

And yet I believe that it is right that we should hesitate to become the kind of people who are really good at walking away. The reluctance that decent people feel seems to me to be healthfully human and even morally admirable. That the reluctance is felt shows that the sense of solidarity undergirding systems of rights is in fact deeply felt. The implication cannot, however, simply be not to walk away. That would be to deny, after all, that duty has a limit. And that would just be to go around the circle one more time: either a person's general duties are limited or they are not.... At this level the logic is inescapable. We need a fresh perspective.

Individual Rights and Social Forces

The greatest failing of rights theories, I believe, has been their tendency to rest content with an asocial individualistic level of descriptive analysis.[19] The right to food is an individual right, that is, a right of each individual person. It thus has, if you like, an individualistic grounding: it is the importance to each individual of her interest in adequate food that makes food an appropriate subject for recognition as a right. The right to food has, then, its individualistic aspect. But this is no excuse for settling for simplistic pictures of social reality that implicitly portray human societies as if they were piles of undifferentiated grains of sand. Normative individualism does not entail or presuppose descriptive individualism. And descriptive individualism is clearly inadequate.

Currently in the neighborhood of a billion people on this planet are malnourished, and hundreds are starving to death at any given moment. It would be deeply silly to think that an adequate analysis of what to do about a problem this engrained and persistent could possibly take the form of random individuals relating directly to other random individuals, for example, my giving or not giving $50 to Wanda. This would be analogous to thinking about how, in the early 1940s, to recapture the European continent from the Nazis by saying: "Well, you could get a rowboat and cross the English Channel; and I'll get another rowboat, and we'll rendezvous at Normandy—be sure to bring a rifle and plenty of ammunition." Or thinking that, since putting a man on the moon was about an individual, the first question should be: which man? Ultimately in all these cases—invading Normandy, putting a man on the moon, and eliminating widespread human hunger—duties for individuals must be specified, and individuals must then act as they ought. But only hopeless ignorance of the functioning of social institutions could allow us to think that the form of analysis by means of which we should arrive at the responsibilities of individuals is to imagine isolated human atoms each trying to do her duty: "I will give $50 to Wanda and five relevantly similar individuals, and you provide seeds and a plow to Abdul and five relevantly similar individuals." This is as fatuous as thinking that a plan for the Normandy invasion would have the form: "You shoot every Nazi you see, and meanwhile I will fix us some lunch." In order to arrive at a sane allocation of responsibilities to individuals, one needs an adequate analysis of the critical social forces and institutions: a reasonably accurate account of the political economy of why so many people on a planet this wealthy lack adequate food and how that can be changed.

That I can say that what we need is an adequate analysis of the social dynamics and how to change them does not, unfortunately, mean that I myself have the analysis ready to give.[20] But it is possible to indicate directions for reorientation of our thinking. Negatively, but importantly, it is no good just anguishing about terrible choices for individuals acting in isolation, like whether I should hand $50 to Wanda or let her starve during the subsequent few weeks. Hard choices will doubtless always be with us no matter how creative we are about our institutional innovation, but to think that they are the heart of the matter would be to accept a hopelessly atomistic, individualistic picture of the problem: the world's population consists of individuals with unfulfilled rights, like Wanda, wandering around their villages and of other individuals, like me, who blunder in with $50 in their pocket and wonder what to do with it.

It is no surprise that it seems impossible to decide what an individual should do, since such uncoordinated individual actions are virtually certain not to solve the underlying problems. Actions must be coordinated, and effective institutions must be built just as they are in any other serious undertaking.

Also negatively but importantly, we can begin by admitting that so far things have not gone well. What our normative individualism—that is, our commitment to arranging to protect the interests vital to individual persons—tells us is that the world is extremely badly run when in some parts of it children die like flies while in other parts of it resources abound. It may seem perverse to insist on such a negative judgment, but in the wake of the end of the Cold War we in this part of the world are suffering an orgy of self-congratulation about the splendors of our political economy. Ours is certainly superior to the former Soviet one, but that is not saying much. And everything is going beautifully for us only if "us" excludes the billion or so human beings mired in desperate poverty. Being more constructive is difficult. But the need to be constructive—and imaginative and innovative—can be clear only if we are not smothered in smugness about how well the economy of the "Free World" already works.

The one thing that can be said in favor of examples like "Wanda" is that they try to put names and faces on human beings. That is important. It helps to keep the normative individualism, the sense that no individual person is expendable, alive. But it is not enough— we must also harness whatever real understanding we can put together from political science, economics, anthropology, and the other social sciences, granted that much of them too, like much of ethics, is devoted to simplistic and useless abstractions.

More positively, we can be sure that we must think in terms of divisions of moral labor, because the duties involved in implementing the right to food must be assigned in a manner that satisfies at least two criteria: (1) the interest of right-bearers in a secure food supply is actually guaranteed as well as is humanly possible and (2) at the same time the same and other vital interests of duty-bearers are similarly guaranteed. In short, the right to food cannot be guaranteed by an assignment of duties that ignores equally vital interests on the part of duty-bearers.[21]

One of the misleading clichés within what is supposed to be commonsense about rights is: if a right is universal, the correlative duties must be universal too. This is false, however often it is repeated, as I hope I have shown. It is not the case that everyone's duties are the same, even if everyone's rights are the same. The cliché arises from ignoring all the duties necessary to the implementation of a

right except the purely negative ones, which indeed must be universal. For example, if everyone has a right to physical security, everyone else—literally, everyone—has toward everyone else—literally,
everyone else—a duty not to torture, a duty not to execute arbitrarily, a duty not to rape, a duty not to assault, and so on. It is impossible for anyone to be exempt from these negative duties toward anyone else because a person who was exempt even with regard to a few
other people—call him Mr. Special—would be free to, say, assault
those people as he wished. In the *ante bellum* South, for example, a
slave-owner was Mr. Special. A slave had the duty not to assault
toward everyone else, slave and free: he or she was not to assault
anyone, although the punishment was certainly incomparably more
severe if the person assaulted was free, that is, "white." Mr. Special
probably was understood to have the duty not to assault generally
toward other adult free people—there, of course, was some "disci-
plining" of wives as well as of slaves—but was certainly understood
not to have any such duty toward slaves. Slaves could be struck,
beaten, whipped, and raped. It was not in one's interest to damage
one's property, so there were in fact fewer severe beatings than there
could have been, but not out of any sense of a duty owed to the slave.
This is a system in which negative duties are not universal, and it is
repulsive.

Another crucial element in the implementation of any right, as
we saw earlier, is fulfillment of the duty to protect right-bearers
against the people who do not honor, or mistakenly think they do not
have, negative duties. If the only actions taken to fulfill rights were
efforts to convince people of their negative duties, many rights would
be violated. Even if we do not fully understand the sources of human
violence against humans, we know perfectly well that preventing it
involves more than promulgating negative duties and attempting to
persuade people that they all have them all. In order for people to be
reasonably physically secure they must be protected against those
who violate their negative duties. To some extent people need to be
guarded by, for example, police on the beat.

What I am calling "the duty to protect" is whatever set of institutional arrangements would most effectively provide for persons'
physical security, while also respecting their other crucial interests.
It is possible to debate whether these arrangements should include
an Uzzi in every home and dozens of new prisons, or what I would
take to be saner programs. What is abundantly clear either way is
that positive duties will have to be performed. Police will have to be
on the streets, judges will have to be in the criminal courts, at least
guards—possibly teachers and counselors—will have to be in the
prisons, and so on. On the other hand, not everyone needs to join

the police force, the criminal justice system, or the prison system. There is a division of labor in the fulfillment of the duty to protect physical security.

Now it would be difficult to say whether the causes of violence or the causes of hunger are less well understood.[22] Concerning hunger too, we have serious disputes. Is the World Bank part of the solution, or part of the problem? Will U.S.A.I.D. ever stop spending huge portions of its budget on U.S. academics (as consultants)? Can weak national governments in poor countries, desperate for foreign exchange to service crushing debts, ever protect their agricultural sectors against distortions by multinational agribusinesses with no interest in local diets but interest only in exports to rich countries? And so on. What we do know, however, is that agricultural systems do need protection from all sorts of market-driven predators, including wolves in sheep's clothing, since feeding poor people is rarely the most profitable use of valuable resources. If there were lots of profit to be made in solving the world's hunger problem, market forces would presumably have sent people rushing in to solve it long ago.

Individual donations by individual donors—I give $50 to Wanda, who is already malnourished—are at best too little, too late, too uncoordinated. They may also be myopically off-target by focusing too directly on food itself; for many Third World countries, more or less food assistance, or even agricultural development aid, is far less important than some solution to their staggering burdens of debt to foreign, rich-country banks, which is one of the main forces driving the diversion of land and other resources out of the production of food. The philosophical point is that the duties necessary to implement the right to food depend on the design of effective institutions for food security. The design of effective institutions for food security depends on sources other than philosophy, namely our best understanding of political economy and of social dynamics generally.

Serious efforts at social analysis provide more assistance with the question of what kind of action to take than with the question of how much sacrifice of one's own material interests to make in taking the action. I understand one's duty is to play a role in operating an existing, effective institution, or in creating an effective institution where none exists. Different persons will play different roles. Most roles will probably require intelligence, imagination, and other human virtues, besides a willingness to share the resources that one commands, because whatever resources one sacrifices should be invested in changing fundamental dynamics, not merely consumed in smoothing over some bad effects of existing dynamics. Blocking further deprivations of food by others who are ignoring their own duties and creating mechanisms that will multiply the effectiveness of attempts to help the deprived is much more valuable than merely patching up bad effects while leaving their causes to continue doing harm.[23]

The question, how much one should sacrifice in these efforts? remains, however. The superficial answer is that one's duty is at least to do one's fair share in the overall task of guaranteeing this, and other equally basic, rights. The specification of a fair share raises further questions that I cannot take up here. First, if the right to food is one of a bundle of equally basic rights, as I believe, it may be a discretionary matter whether one does more to guarantee this right and less to guarantee others, or vice versa. Especially if a right cannot be guaranteed in isolation from other equally basic rights, arranging for the whole bundle of rights is the only available option in any case. Consequently, it may be a good thing if different people work on different rights.

Second, and much more troubling, is the question whether one's fair share is to be calculated on the ideal assumption that everyone else will do his or her fair share, which it is perfectly obvious is not in fact happening, or is to be calculated on the realistic basis of the way things actually are, namely that many people are by no stretch of the imagination doing their share of the positive duties and quite a few are in addition violating their negative duties. If one's share is calculated on the realistic basis, one's share will be considerably greater than otherwise, and one will in fact be picking up balls dropped by others; on the other hand, the job of guaranteeing the right for everyone may be accomplished. If one's share is calculated on the ideal assumption that everyone who should carry out duties will do so, one's share will be much less; on the other hand, the job of guaranteeing the right for everyone will surely not be accomplished. While we think about whether we are bound to do our share according to the more demanding calculation, we might get started doing our share on the less demanding one.

NOTES

1. Michael Ignatieff, *The Needs of Strangers*. London: Chatto and Windus, 1984, pp. 9–10. Quoted in Jeremy Waldron, *Liberal Rights: Collected Papers, 1981–1991*. New York: Cambridge University Press, 1993, p. 382.

2. One good source of general information is: *Causes of Hunger. Hunger 1995*, Fifth Annual Report on the State of World Hunger.

Silver Spring, MD: Bread for the World Institute, 1994.

3. Jeremy Waldron, *Liberal Rights: Collected Papers, 1981–1991*. New York: Cambridge University Press, 1993, p. 353. For Raz's own account, see Joseph Raz, "Right-based Moralities," *Theories of Rights*, Waldron, Jeremy, ed. Oxford: Oxford University Press, 1984, p. 183.

4. That was much more likely before the commodification of almost everything. When people made their own clothes and grew their own food, rather than purchasing them from others, it was quite possible to have enough food but no coat because the sheep had died, leaving no wool for a coat, and no one made coats in order to sell them. Now, if you have the money, you can buy anything; and if you don't, you are likely not to have it unless you are entitled to it by right. I am not suggesting that we should, or even could, "go back," but it is important to understand that not every feature of the modern is good—see Karl Polanyi, *The Great Transformation: The Political and Economic Origins of Our Time*. Boston: Beacon Press, 1957.

5. I mean a moral right to food, even if the moral right is not embodied in legal rights. Legal rights to food have, however, come to be fairly well entrenched—see Philip Alston, "International Law and the Human Right to Food," *The Right to Food*, Alston, P., and Tomasevski, K. eds. Dordrecht: Martinus Nijhoff for the Netherlands Institute for Human Rights, 1984, pp. 9–68.

6. The argument, then, is something like this: a person has a meaningful right only if she will be alive to exercise it; she will be alive to exercise it only if she has whatever she needs to stay alive; she needs food; so if a person is to have any meaningful right, she needs food. If we want people to have meaningful rights, then we must, as a means to that end, guarantee them food.

7. On this kind of case more generally, see Daniel Callahan, *The Troubled Dream of Life: Living with Mortality*. New York: Simon & Schuster, 1993.

8. Not necessarily a decisive reason: most people seem to think that a young person can have a duty to sacrifice his or her life, if need be, in defense of a state or nation (leaving aside here exactly what we refer to by "state" and "nation") in spite of the fact that fulfillment of that duty may cost something utterly vital.

9. The significance of this has been missed by some contemporary critics of rights like Mary Ann Glendon in *Rights Talk: The Impoverishment of Political Discourse*. New York: Free Press, 1991.

10. James W. Nickel deserves credit for having persisted in working out this unpopular side of the theory of rights. See, for example, James W. Nickel, *Making Sense of Human Rights: Philosophical Reflections on the Universal Declaration of Human Rights*. Berkeley: University of California Press, 1987, Chapter 7, "Resources and Rights."

11. A negative duty is a duty to refrain from acting; a positive duty is a duty to act. In the course of this essay I will note various respects in which this simple negative/positive distinction, which is often invoked in the literature about rights as if it is momentous, is largely inconsequential even where it is worth noticing for a little additional clarity.

12. The issue consequently is not only whether the duties are reasonable in themselves (whatever exactly that would mean) but whether they are reasonable demands specifically upon the [kinds of] people upon whom they would fall.

13. Nor is there, of course, any reason why arrangements about rights need to be mutually advantageous for all participants in order for the arrangements to be justified. The justification of morality does not depend upon mutual advantage.

14. Anatole France, *Le Lys Rouge*, rev. ed. Paris: 1923, pp. 117–118; quoted and translated in Waldron, *Liberal Rights*, p. 460.

15. Yes, if you like, you may call her Rwanda.

16. I realize that there may be other cases—I am coming to that. This problem of numbers has been emphasized by James S. Fishkin, *The Limits of Obligation*. New Haven, CT: Yale University Press, 1982. Compare Henry Shue, *"Fishkin, The Limits of Obligation,"* *Political Theory*, vol. 11 (1983), pp. 269–272.

17. This is argued more fully in Shue, *Basic Rights*, Chapter 2, "Correlative Duties."

18. General rights are rights that belong to every person and are not contingent on any special relationships between right-bearer and duty-bearer or any particular histories involving them with each other.

19. I will not take up here the vexed question of whether, in addition to rights of individuals, there are also rights of groups of some kind. Valuable discussions include Philip Alston, "Making Space for New Human Rights: The Case of the Right to Development," *Human Rights Yearbook*, vol. 1 (1988), pp. 3–40; and Waldron, *Liberal Rights*, Chapter 14, "Can Communal Goods be Human Rights?"

20. An excellent example of the kind of analysis I mean is: Jean Drèze and Amartya Sen, *Hunger and Public Action*, WIDER Studies in Development Economics. Oxford: Clarendon Press, 1989.

21. It may be that the assignment of duties must respect as well *some* less important, but nevertheless genuinely important, interests on the part of duty-bearers. This is a complex but critical issue, at least partly about the interpretation of human equality, at which I took a fairly simple crack in Shue, *Basic Rights*, Chapter 5, "Affluence and Responsibility" (summarized in the table on p. 115). For a different view, see Samuel Scheffler, *Human Morality*. New York: Oxford

University Press, 1992.

22. My bet, for what it is worth, is that we understand the dynamics of hunger better. I am not sure that the eradication of violence is possible, but I do not see why widespread malnutrition could not be eliminated.

23. See the chapter by James W. Nickel.

Global Justice

JAMES P. STERBA

James P. Sterba is Professor of Philosophy at the University of
Notre Dame, and has published 14 books—most recently
Contemporary Social and Political Philosophy (1994) and *Earth
Ethics* (1994)—and over 130 articles. He is also president of the
North American Society for Social Philosophy and past president
of Concerned Philosophers for Peace.

At the present moment, over one billion people, one out of every five,
live in conditions of "absolute poverty," defined as "a condition of life
so limited by malnutrition, illiteracy, disease, squalid surroundings,
high infant mortality, and low life expectancy as to be beneath any
reasonable definition of human decency."[1] Recent trends are also
ominous. From 1984 to 1993, grain output per capita fell 11 percent.[2] From 1989 to 1993, the world seafood supplies per capita fell
9 percent.[3] From 1978 to 1993, per capita irrigated land, which
plays a disproportionate role in meeting the world's food needs, fell
6 percent.[4] If current trends continue, by 2010 per capita availability of rangeland, will drop by 22 percent, seafood supplies by 10 percent, irrigated land by 12 percent, cropland by 21 percent and
forestland by 30 percent.[5] If current trends continue, by 2030, per
capital grain availability levels will decline to those of 1950, before
the introduction of the Green Revolution.[6]

Yet even in the face of such evidence, there is reason for hope.
Presently, there is still enough resources worldwide to put an end to
absolute poverty. The problem is still one of distribution. In 1989
(the latest year for which this figure is available) the richest 20 percent of the world's people received 83 percent of global income and
the poorest 20 percent only 1.4 percent.[7] By transferring income
from the rich to the poor and by radically reducing population
growth worldwide, we could both put an end to absolute poverty and
halt the downward trend in per capita food-related resources. So let
us suppose that the poor were willing to bring their population
growth under control provided that they could acquire sufficient
income and resources to meet their basic needs. Would the poor then
be justified in appropriating income and resources from the rich in

order to meet their basic needs?[8] What are the requirements of justice here?

While it is generally agreed that justice is giving people what they deserve, there is considerable disagreement over what it is that people deserve. For libertarian justice, what people deserve is determined by an ideal of liberty. For welfare liberal justice, it is determined by an ideal of fairness. For socialist justice, it is determined by ideal of equality. For communitarian justice, it is determined by ideal of the common good. And for feminist justice, it is determined ideal of a gender-free society. Now I have argued elsewhere that when these five conceptions of justice are correctly interpreted, they all can be seen to support the same basic practical requirements.[9] Since I cannot in this paper lay out my entire practical reconciliation argument, what I propose to do is to focus on the most contentious part of that argument in which I attempt to show that libertarians should endorse a right to a basic needs minimum that extends to both distant peoples and future generations. In setting out the argument, I will try to make it more perspicuous than I have in the past and relate it to recent work done by libertarians, especially by libertarians who have objected to the argument.

Liberty and Welfare

Let us begin by interpreting the ideal of liberty as a negative ideal in the manner favored by libertarians.[10] So understood, liberty is the absence of interference by other people from doing what one wants or is able to do. Interpreting their ideal in this way, libertarians claim to derive a number of more specific requirements, in particular, a right to life, a right to freedom of speech, press and assembly, and a right to property. Here it is important to observe that the libertarian's right to life is not a right to receive from others the goods and resources necessary for preserving one's life; it is simply a right not to be killed unjustly. Correspondingly, the libertarian's right to property is not a right to receive from others the goods and resources necessary for one's welfare, but rather a right to acquire goods and resources either by initial acquisition or by voluntary agreement.

Of course, libertarians would allow that it would be nice of the rich to share their surplus resources with the poor. Nevertheless, according to libertarians, such acts of charity should not be coercively required. For this reason, libertarians are opposed to coercively supported welfare programs.

Now when the conflict between the rich and the poor is viewed as a conflict of liberties, either we can say that the rich should have the liberty not to be interfered with in using their surplus resources for luxury purposes, or we can say that the poor should have the liberty not to be interfered with in taking from the rich what they require to meet their basic needs. If we choose one liberty, we must reject the other. What needs to be determined, therefore, is which liberty is morally preferable: the liberty of the rich or the liberty of the poor.

Two Principles

In order to see that the liberty of the poor not to be interfered with in taking from the surplus resources of the rich what is required to meet their basic needs is morally preferable to the liberty of the rich not to be interfered with in using their surplus resources for luxury purposes, we need appeal to one of the most fundamental principles of morality, one that is common to all political perspectives. This is: The "Ought" Implies "Can" Principle

> People are not morally required to do what they lack the power to do or what would involve so great a sacrifice that it would be unreasonable to ask them to perform such an action, and/or in the case of severe conflicts of interest, unreasonable to require them to perform such an action.[11]

For example, suppose I promised to attend a departmental meeting on Friday, but on Thursday I am involved in a serious car accident that leaves me in a coma. Surely it is no longer the case that I ought to attend the meeting, now that I lack the power to do so. Or suppose instead that on Thursday I develop a severe case of pneumonia for which I am hospitalized. Surely I could legitimately claim that I cannot attend the meeting, on the grounds that the risk to my health involved in attending is a sacrifice that it would be unreasonable to ask me to bear. Or suppose the risk to my health from having pneumonia is not so serious that it would be unreasonable to ask me to attend the meeting (a supererogatory request), it might still be serious enough to be unreasonable to require my attendance at the meeting (a demand that is backed up by blame or coercion).

What is distinctive about this formulation of the "ought" implies "can" principle is that it claims that the requirements of morality cannot, all things considered, be unreasonable to ask, and/or in cases of severe conflict of interest, unreasonable to require people to abide by. The principle claims that reason and morality must be linked in an appropriate way, especially if we are going to be able to justifiably use blame or coercion to get people to abide by the requirements of morality. It should be noted, however, that although major figures in the history of philosophy, and most philosophers today, including virtually all libertarian philosophers, accept this linkage between reason and morality, this linkage is not usually conceived to be part of the "ought" implies "can" principle.[12] Nevertheless, I claim that there are good reasons for associating this linkage with the principle, namely, our use of the word "can" as in the example just given, and the natural progression from logical, physical, and psychological possibility found in the traditional "ought" implies "can" principle to the notion of moral possibility found in this formulation of the principle. In any case, the acceptability of this formulation of the "ought" implies "can" principle is determined by the virtually universal acceptance of its components and not by the manner in which I have proposed to join those components together.[13]

Now applying the "ought" implies "can" principle to the case at hand, it seems clear that the poor have it within their power to willingly relinquish such an important liberty as the liberty not to be interfered with in taking from the rich what they require to meet their basic needs. Nevertheless, it would be unreasonable to ask or require them to make so great a sacrifice. In the extreme case, it would involve asking or requiring the poor to sit back and starve to death. Of course, the poor may have no real alternative to relinquishing this liberty. To do anything else may involve worse consequences for themselves and their loved ones and may invite a painful death. Accordingly, we may expect that the poor would acquiesce, albeit unwillingly, to a political system that denies them the right to welfare supported by such a liberty, at the same time that we recognize that such a system imposes an unreasonable sacrifice on the poor—a sacrifice that we can not morally blame the poor for trying to evade.[14] Analogously, we might expect that a woman whose life was threatened would submit to a rapist's demands, at the same time that we recognize the utter unreasonableness of those demands.

By contrast, it would not be unreasonable to ask and require the rich to sacrifice the liberty to meet some of their luxury needs so that the poor can have the liberty to meet their basic needs.[15] Naturally, we might expect that the rich, for reasons of self-interest and past contribution, might be disinclined to make such a sacrifice. We might even suppose that the past contribution of the rich provides a good reason for not sacrificing their liberty to use their surplus for luxury purposes. Yet, unlike the poor, the rich could not claim that relinquishing such a liberty would involve so great a sacrifice that it would be unreasonable to ask and require them to make it; unlike the poor, the rich could be morally blameworthy for failing to make such a sacrifice.

Notice that by virtue of the "ought" implies "can" principle, this argument establishes the following:

1. (a) Since it would be unreasonable to ask or require the poor to sacrifice the liberty not to be interfered with when taking from the surplus resources of the rich what is necessary to meet their basic needs, (b) it is not the case that the poor are morally required to make such a sacrifice.
2. (a) Since it would not be unreasonable to ask and require the rich to sacrifice the liberty not to be interfered when using their surplus resources for luxury purposes, (b) it may be the case that the rich are morally required to make such a sacrifice.

What the argument does not establish is that it is the case that the rich are *morally required* to sacrifice (some of) their surplus so that the basic needs of the poor can be met. To clearly establish that conclusion, we need to appeal to a principle, which is, in fact, simply the contrapositive of the "ought" implies "can" principle. It is the conflict resolution principle.

The Conflict Resolution Principle

> What people are morally required to do is what is either reasonable to ask everyone affected to accept, or in the case of severe conflicts of interest, reasonable to require everyone affected to accept.

While the "ought" implies "can" principle claims that if any action is *not reasonable to ask or require* a person to do, all things considered, that action is *not morally required* for that person, all things considered, the conflict resolution principle claims that if any action is *morally required* for a person to do, all things considered, that action is *reasonable to ask or require* that person to do, all things considered.

This conflict resolution principle accords with the generally accepted view of morality as a system of reasons for resolving interpersonal conflicts of interest. Of course, morality is not limited to such a system of reasons. Most surely it also includes reasons of self-development. All that is being claimed by the principle is that moral resolutions of interpersonal conflicts of interest cannot be contrary to reason to ask everyone affected to accept or, in the case of severe interpersonal conflicts of interest, unreasonable to require everyone affected to accept. The reason for the distinction between the two kinds of cases is that when interpersonal conflicts of interest are not severe, moral resolutions must still be reasonable to ask everyone affected to accept but they need not be reasonable to *require* everyone affected to accept. This is because not all moral resolutions can be justifiably enforced; only moral resolutions of severe interpersonal conflicts of interest can and *should* be justifiably enforced. Furthermore, the reason why moral resolutions of severe interpersonal conflicts of interest should be enforced is that if the parties are simply asked but not required to abide by a moral resolution in such cases of conflict, then it will be morally permissible, and even likely, that the stronger party will violate the resolution and that would be unreasonable to ask or require the weaker party to accept.

When we apply the conflict resolution principle to our example of severe conflict between the rich and the poor, there are three possible moral resolutions:

I. A moral resolution that would require the rich to sacrifice the liberty not to be interfered with when using their surplus resources for luxury purposes so that the poor can have the liberty not to be interfered with when taking from the surplus resources of the rich what is necessary to meet their basic needs.

II. A moral resolution that would require the poor to sacrifice the liberty not to be interfered with when taking from the surplus resources of the rich what is necessary to meet their basic needs so that the rich can have the liberty not to be interfered with when using their surplus resources for luxury purposes.

III. A moral resolution that would require the rich and the poor to accept the results of a power struggle in which both the rich and the poor are at liberty to appropriate and use the surplus resources of the rich.

Applying our previous discussion of the "ought" implies "can" principle to these three possible moral resolutions, it is clear that 1a (it would be unreasonable to ask or require the poor....) rules out II, but 2a (it would not be unreasonable to ask and require the rich ...) does not rule out I. But what about III? Some libertarians have contended that III is the proper resolution of severe conflicts of interest between the rich and the poor.[16] But a resolution, such as III that sanctions the results of a power struggle between the rich and the poor, is a resolution that, by and large, favors the rich over the poor. All things considered, it would be no more reasonable to require the poor to accept III than it would be to require them to accept II. This means that only I satisfies the conflict resolution principle by being a resolution that is reasonable to require everyone affected to accept. Consequently, if we assume that, however else we specify the requirements of morality, they cannot violate the "ought" implies "can" principle or the conflict resolution principle, it follows that, despite what libertarians claim, the basic right to liberty endorsed by them, as determined by a weighing of the relevant competing liberties according to these two principles, actually favors the liberty of the poor over the liberty of the rich.[17]

Yet couldn't libertarians object to this conclusion, claiming that it would be unreasonable to require the rich to sacrifice the liberty to meet some of their luxury needs so that the poor could have the liberty to meet their basic needs? As has been pointed out, libertarians don't usually see the situation as a conflict of liberties, but suppose they did. How plausible would such an objection be? Not very plausible at all.

Consider the following: What are libertarians going to say about the poor? Isn't it clearly unreasonable to require the poor to sacrifice the liberty to meet their basic needs so that the rich can have the liberty to meet their luxury needs? Isn't it clearly unreasonable to require the poor to sit back and starve to death? If it is, then there is no resolution of this conflict that would be reasonable to require both the rich and the poor to accept. But that would mean that libertarians could not be putting forth a moral resolution, because according to the conflict resolution principle, in cases of severe conflict of interest, a moral resolution resolves conflicts of interest in ways that it would be reasonable to require everyone affected to accept. Therefore, as long as libertarians think of themselves as putting forth a moral resolution for cases of severe conflict of interest, they cannot allow that it would be unreasonable *both* to require the rich to sacrifice the liberty to meet some of their luxury needs in order to benefit the poor and to require the poor to sacrifice the liberty to meet their basic needs in order to benefit the rich. I submit that if one of these requirements is to be judged reasonable, then, by any neutral assessment, it must be the requirement that the rich sacrifice the liberty to meet some of their luxury needs so that the poor can have the liberty to meet their basic needs. There is no other plausible resolution if libertarians intend to be putting forth a moral resolution.

It should also be noted that this case for restricting the liberty of the rich depends on the willingness of the poor to take advantage of whatever opportunities are available to them to engage in mutually beneficial work, so that failure of the poor to take advantage of such opportunities would normally cancel or at least significantly reduce the obligation of the rich to restrict their own liberty for the benefit of the poor.[18] In addition, the poor would be required to return the equivalent of any surplus possessions they have taken from the rich once they are able to do so and still satisfy their basic needs. Nor would the poor be required to keep the liberty to which they are entitled. They could give up part of it, or all of it, or risk losing it on the chance of gaining a greater share of liberties or other social goods.[19] Consequently, the case for restricting the liberty of the rich for the benefit of the poor is neither unconditional nor inalienable.

Of course, there will be cases in which the poor fail to satisfy their basic needs, not because of any direct restriction of liberty on the part of the rich but because the poor are in such dire need that they are unable even to attempt to take from the rich, what they require to meet their basic needs. In such cases, the rich would not be performing any act of commission that would prevent the poor from taking what they require. Yet, even in such cases, the rich would normally be performing acts of commission that would prevent other persons from taking part of the rich's own surplus possessions and using it to aid the poor. When assessed from a moral point of view, restricting the liberty of these allies or agents of the poor would not be morally justified for the very same reason that restricting the liberty of the poor to meet their own basic needs would not be morally justified: it would not be reasonable to require all of those affected to accept such a restriction of liberty.

In brief, I have argued that a libertarian ideal of liberty can be seen to support a right to welfare through an application of the "ought" implies "can" principle to conflicts between the rich and the poor. In the interpretation I have used, the principle supports such rights by favoring the liberty of the poor over the liberty of the rich. In another interpretation (developed elsewhere), the principle supports such rights by favoring a conditional right to property over an unconditional right to property.[20] In either interpretation, what is crucial to the derivation of these rights is the claim that it would be unreasonable to require the poor to deny their basic needs and accept anything less than these rights as the condition for their willing cooperation.

In his book, *Individuals and Their Rights*, Tibor Machan criticizes my argument that a libertarian ideal of liberty leads to welfare rights, accepting its theoretical thrust but denying its practical significance.[21] He appreciates the force of the argument enough to grant that if the type of conflict cases I describe between the rich and the poor actually obtained, the poor would have welfare rights. But he denies that such cases—in which the poor have done all that they legitimately can to satisfy their basic needs in a libertarian society— actually obtain. "Normally," he writes, "persons do not lack the opportunities and resources to satisfy their basic needs."[22]

But this response virtually concedes everything that defenders of welfare rights had hoped to established. For the poor's right to welfare is not unconditional. It is conditional principally on the poor doing all that they legitimately can to meet their own basic needs. Therefore, it is only when the poor lack sufficient opportunity to satisfy their own basic needs that a right to welfare has moral force. Accordingly, on libertarian grounds, Machan has conceded the legitimacy of just the kind of right to welfare that defenders of welfare had hoped to establish.

The only difference that remains is a practical one. Machan thinks that virtually all of the poor have sufficient opportunities and resources to satisfy their basic needs and that, therefore, a right to welfare has no practical moral force. In contrast, I would think that many of the poor do not have sufficient opportunities and resources to satisfy their basic needs and that, therefore, a right to welfare has considerable practical moral force.

But isn't this practical disagreement resolvable? Who could deny that most of the more than one billion people who are currently living in conditions of absolute poverty "lack the opportunities and resources to satisfy their basic needs?"[23] And even within our own country, it is estimated that some 36 million Americans live below the official poverty index, and that one fifth of American children are growing up in poverty.[24] It is impossible to deny that many of these Americans also "lack the opportunities and resources to satisfy their basic needs." Given the impossibility of reasonably denying these factual claims, Machan would have to concede that the right to welfare, which he grants can be theoretically established on libertarian premises, also has practical moral force.

Recently, John Hospers has objected to my argument by questioning whether the poor would be better off demanding welfare even if they have a right to it.[25] Hospers cites the example of Ernst Mahler, an entrepreneurial genius who employed more than 100,000 and produced newsprint and tissue products that are now used by more than two billion people. Hospers suggests that once rich people, like Mahler, realize that the poor should have the liberty not to be interfered with when taking from the surplus possessions of the rich what they require to satisfy their basic needs, they should stop producing any surplus whatsoever. Yet clearly it would be in the interest of the rich to stop producing a surplus only if (a) they did not enjoy producing a surplus, (b) their recognition of the rightful claims of the poor would exhaust their surplus, and (c) the poor would never be in a position to be obligated to repay what they appropriated from them. Fortunately for the poor, not all of these conditions are likely to obtain.[26] But suppose they all did. Wouldn't the poor be justified in appropriating, or threatening to appropriate, even the nonsurplus possessions of those who can produce more in order to get them to do so? Surely this would not seem to be an unreasonable imposition on those who can produce more, because it would not seem to be unreasonable to require them to be more productive when the alternative is that the poor would, through no fault of their own, fail to meet their basic needs. It would be unreasonable to require the poor to do anything less when their basic needs are at stake.

This is an important conclusion in our assessment of the libertarian ideal, because it shows that ultimately the right of the poor to appropriate what they require to meet their basic needs does not depend, as many have thought, on the talented having sufficient self-interested incentives to produce a surplus. All that is necessary is that the talented can produce a surplus and that the poor cannot meet their basic needs in any other way.

Distant Peoples and Future Generations

Now it is possible that libertarians convinced to some extent by this argument might want to accept a right to a basic needs minimum for members of one's own society but then deny that this right extends to distant peoples and future generations. Since it is only recently that philosophers have begun to discuss the question of what rights distant peoples and future generations might legitimately claim against us, a generally acceptable way of discussing the question has yet to be developed. Some philosophers have even attempted to "answer" the question, or at least part of it, by arguing that talk about "the rights of future generations" is conceptually incoherent and thus analogous to talk about "square circles." Thus Richard DeGeorge writes:

> The argument in favor of the principle that only existing entities have rights is straightforward and simple: Nonexistent entities by definition do not exist. What does not exist cannot be subject or bearer of anything. Hence, it cannot be the subject or bearer of rights.[27]

Accordingly, the key question that must be answered first is this: Can we meaningfully speak of distant peoples and future generations as having rights against us or of our having corresponding obligations to them?

Answering this question with respect to distant peoples is much easier than answering it with respect to future generations. Few philosophers have thought that the mere fact that people are at a distance from us precludes our having any obligations to them or their having any rights against us. Some philosophers, however, have argued that our ignorance of the specific membership of the class of distant peoples does rule out these moral relationships. Yet this cannot be right, given that in other contexts we recognize obligations to indeterminate classes of people, such as a police officer's obligation to help people in distress or the obligation of food producers not to harm those who consume their products.

Yet others have argued that while there may be valid moral claims respecting the welfare of distant peoples, such claims cannot be rights because they fail to hold against determinate individuals and groups.[28] But in what sense do such claims fail to hold against determinate individuals and groups? Surely all would agreee that existing laws rarely specify the determinate individuals and groups against whom such claims hold. But morality is frequently determinate where existing laws are not. There seems to be no conceptual impossibility to claiming that distant peoples have rights against us and that we have corresponding obligations to them.

Of course, before distant peoples can be said to have rights against us, we must be capable of acting across the distance that separates us. As long as this condition is met—as it typically is for people living in most technologically advanced societies—it would certainly seem possible for distant peoples to have rights against us and we corresponding obligations to them.

By contrast, answering the question with respect to future generations is much more difficult and has been the subject of considerable debate among contemporary philosophers.

One issue concerns the referent of the term *future generations*. Most philosophers seem to agree that the class of future generations is not "the class of all persons who simply *could* come into existence." But there is some disagreement concerning whether we should refer to the class of future generations as "the class of persons who will definitely come into existence, assuming that there are such" or as "the class of persons we can reasonably expect to come into existence." The first approach is more "existential," specifying the class of future generations in terms of what will exist; the second approach is more "epistemological," specifying the class of future generations in terms of our knowledge. Fortunately, there does not appear to be any practical moral significance to the choice of either approach.

Another issue relevant to whether we can meaningfully speak of future generations as having rights against us or our having obligations to them concerns whether it is logically coherent to speak of future generations as having rights now. Of course, no one who finds talk about rights to be generally meaningful should question whether we can coherently claim that future generations *will* have rights at some point in the future (specifically, when they come into existence and are no longer *future* generations). But what is questioned, since it is of considerable practical significance, is whether we can coherently claim that future generations have rights *now* when they don't yet exist.

Let us suppose, for example that we continue to use up the earth's resources at present or even greater rates, and, as a result, it turns out that the most pessimistic forecasts for the twenty-second century are realized.[29] This means that future generations will face widespread famine, depleted resources, insufficient new technology to handle the crisis, and a drastic decline in the quality of life for nearly everyone. If this were to happen, could persons living in the twenty-second century legitimately claim that we in the twentieth century violated their rights by not restraining our consumption of the world's resources? Surely it would be odd to say that we violated their rights over one hundred years before they existed. But what exactly is the oddness?

Is it that future generations generally have no way of claiming their rights against existing generations? While this does make the recognition and enforcement of rights much more difficult (future generations would need strong advocates in the existing generations), it does not make it impossible for there to be such rights. After all, it is quite obvious that the recognition and enforcement of the rights of distant peoples is a difficult task as well.

Or is it that we don't believe that rights can legitimately exercise their influence over long durations of time? But if we can foresee and control at least some of the effects our actions will have on the ability of future generations to satisfy their basic needs, why should we not be responsible for those same effects? And if we are responsible for them, why should not future generations have a right that we take them into account?

Perhaps what troubles us is that future generations don't exist when their rights are said to demand action. But how else could persons have a right to benefit from the effects our actions will have in the distant future if they did not exist just when those effects would be felt? Our contemporaries cannot legitimately make the same demand, for they will not be around to experience those effects. Only future generations could have a right that the effects our actions will have in the distant future contribute to their well-being. Nor need we assume that in order for persons to have rights, they must exist when their rights demand action. Thus, to say that future generations have rights against existing generations we can simply mean that there are enforceable requirements on existing generations that would benefit or prevent harm to future generations. Most likely what really bothers us is that we cannot know for sure what effects our actions will have on future generations. For example, we may at some cost to ourselves conserve resources that will be valueless to future generations who may develop different technologies. Or, because we regard them as useless, we may destroy or deplete resources that future generations will find to be essential to their well-being. Nevertheless, we should not allow such possibilities to blind us to the necessity for a social policy in this regard. After all, whatever we do will have its effect on future generations. The best approach, therefore, is to use the knowledge that we presently have and assume that future generations will also require those basic resources we now find to be valuable. If it turns out that future generations will require different resources to meet their basic needs, at least we will not be blamable for acting on the basis of the knowledge we have.[30]

Notice too that present existence could not be a logical requirement for having rights now for the simple reason that past people don't presently exist in our society, yet we continue to respect their rights, for example, through the enforcement of the terms of their wills. If past people, who do not presently exist, can have rights against us, it should be possible for future people, who don't presently exist but who will exist in the future, to presently have rights against us. Hence, there is nothing logically incoherent in the possibility of future generations presently having rights against us.

Once it is recognized that we can meaningfully speak of distant peoples and future generations as having rights against us and we corresponding obligations to them, there is no reason not to extend the argument for a basic needs minimum grounded on libertarian premises that I have developed here to distant peoples and future generations as well as to the members of one's own society. This is because the argument is perfectly general and applies whenever serious conflicts of liberty arise between those who can have rights against us and we corresponding obligations to them.

It might be objected that the welfare rights that this argument establishes from libertarian premises are not the same as the welfare rights endorsed by welfare liberals and socialists. This is correct. We could mark this difference by referring to the rights that this argument establishes as "negative welfare rights" and by referring to the rights endorsed by welfare liberals and socialists as "positive welfare rights." The significance of this difference is that a person's negative welfare rights can be violated only when other people through acts of commission interfere with their exercise, whereas a person's positive welfare rights can be violated not only by such acts of commission but by acts of omission as well. Nonetheless, this difference will have little practical import. In recognizing the legitimacy of negative welfare rights, libertarians will come to see that virtually any use of their surplus possessions is likely to violate the negative welfare rights of the poor by preventing the poor from appropriating (some part of) their surplus resources. In order to insure that they will not be engaging in such wrongful actions, it will be incumbent on them to institute adequate positive welfare rights for the poor. Only then will they be able to legitimately use any remaining surplus possessions to meet their own nonbasic needs. Furthermore, in the absence of adequate positive welfare rights, the poor, either acting by themselves or through their allies or agents, would have some discretion in determining when and how to exercise their negative welfare rights.[31] In order not to be subject to that discretion, libertarians will tend to favor the only morally legitimate way of preventing the exercise of such rights: they will institute adequate positive welfare rights that will then take precedence over the exercise of negative welfare rights. For these reasons, recognizing the negative welfare rights of the poor will ultimately lead libertarians to endorse the same sort of welfare institutions favored by welfare liberals and socialists.

Now it is important to see how moral and pragmatic considerations are combined in this argument from negative welfare rights to positive welfare rights. What needs to be seen is that the moral consideration is primary and the pragmatic consideration secondary. The moral consideration is that until positive welfare rights for the poor are guaranteed, any use by the rich of their surplus possessions to meet their nonbasic needs is likely to violate the negative welfare rights of the poor by preventing the poor from appropriating (some part of) their surplus resources. The pragmatic consideration is that, in the absence of positive welfare rights, the rich would have to put up with the discretion of the poor, either acting by themselves or through their allies or agents, in choosing when and how to exercise their negative welfare rights. Obviously, distant peoples who are separated from the rich by significant distances will be able to exercise their negative welfare rights only by either negotiating the distances involved or by having allies or agents in the right place, willing to act on their behalf. With respect to future generations, their rights can be exercised only if they too have allies and agents in the right place and time, willing to act on their behalf. Unless distant peoples are good at negotiating distances or unless distant peoples and future generations have ample allies and agents in the right place and time, the pragmatic consideration leading the rich to endorse positive welfare rights will diminish in importance in their regard. Fortunately, the moral consideration alone is sufficient to carry the argument here and elsewhere: libertarians should endorse positive welfare rights because it is the only way that they can be assured of not violating the negative welfare rights of the poor by preventing the poor from appropriating their surplus resources.

Specifically, what are the practical implications of recognizing a right to a basic needs minimum that extends to distant peoples and future generations? Consider that at present there is a sufficient worldwide supply of goods and resources to meet the normal costs of satisfying the basic nutritional needs of all existing persons, according to former U.S. Secretary of Agriculture, Bob Bergland.

For the past 20 years, if the available world food supply had been evenly divided and distributed, each person would have received more than the minimum number of calories.[32] Other authorities have made similar assessments of the available world food supply.[33]

Needless to say, the adoption of a policy of supporting a right to welfare for all existing persons would necessitate significant changes, especially in developed countries. For example, the large percentage of the U.S. population whose food consumption clearly exceeds even an adequately adjusted poverty index would have to substantially alter their eating habits. In particular, they would have to reduce their consumption of beef and pork so as to make more grain available for direct human consumption. (Presently, the amount of grain fed American livestock is as much as all the people of China and India eat in a year.) Thus, at least the satisfaction of some of the nonbasic needs of the more advantaged in developed countries would have to be forgone if the basic nutritional needs of all existing persons in developing and underdeveloped countries are to be met. Furthermore, to raise the standard of living in developing and underdeveloped countries will require substantial increases in the consumption of energy and other resources. But such an increase would have to be matched by a substantial decrease in the consumption of these goods in developed countries, otherwise global ecological disaster would result from increased global warming, ozone depletion, and acid rain, lowering virtually everyone's standard of living.[34]

In addition, once the basic nutritional needs of future generations are also taken into account, the satisfaction of the nonbasic needs of the more advantaged in developed countries would have to be further restricted in order to preserve the fertility of cropland and other food-related natural resources for the use of future generations. Obviously, the only assured way to guarantee the energy and resources necessary for the satisfaction of the basic needs of future generations is by setting aside resources that would otherwise be used to satisfy the nonbasic needs of existing generations. Once basic needs other than nutritional needs are taken into account as well, still further restrictions would be required. For example, it has been estimated that presently a North American uses fifty times more resources than an Indian. This means that in terms of resource consumption the North American continent's population is the equivalent of 12.5 billion Indians. Obviously, this would have to be radically altered if the basic needs of distant peoples and future generations are to be met.[35] Thus, eventually the practice of utilizing more and more efficient means of satisifying people's basic needs in developed societies would appear to have the effect of equalizing the normal costs of meeting people's basic needs across societies.

The welfare rights of future generations are also closely connected with the population policy of existing generations. For example, under a population policy that places restrictions on the size of families and requires genetic screening, some persons will not be brought into existence who otherwise would have come into existence. Thus, the membership of future generations will surely be affected by whatever population policy existing generations adopt. Given that the size and genetic health of future generations will obviously affect their ability to provide for their basic needs, the welfare rights of future generations would require existing generations to adopt a population policy that takes these factors into account.

Fortunately, a policy with the desired restrictions can be grounded on the welfare rights of existing and future generations. As we have seen, the welfare rights of future generations require existing generations to make provision for the basic needs of future generations. As a result, existing generations would have to evaluate their ability to provide both for their own basic needs and for the basic needs of future generations. Since existing generations by bringing persons into existence would be determining the membership of future generations, they would have to evaluate whether they are able to provide for that membership. Existing generations should not have to sacrifice the satisfaction of their basic needs for the sake of future generations, although they would be required to sacrifice some of their nonbasic needs on this account. Thus, if existing generations believe that were population to increase beyond a certain point, they would lack sufficient resources to make the necessary provision for each person's basic needs, it would be incumbent on them to restrict the membership of future generations so as not to exceed their ability to provide for each person's basic needs. If the rights of existing and future generations are respected, the membership of future generations would never increase beyond the ability of existing generations to make the necessary provision for the basic needs of future generations.

While the particular requirements that the welfare rights of distant peoples and future generations would place on those in developed affluent societies are obviously quite severe, they are not unconditional. Those in developing and underdeveloped societies are under a corresponding obligation to do what they can to meet their own basic nutritional needs, for example, by bringing all arable land under optimal cultivation and by controlling population growth. We should not be unreasonable in judging what particular developing and underdeveloped societies have managed to accomplish in this regard. In the final analysis, such societies should be judged on the basis of what they have managed to accomplish, *given the options available to them.* For example, developing and underdeveloped societies today lack many of the options, such as exporting their excess population to sparsely populated and resource rich continents, that Western European societies utilized during the course of their economic development. In this and other respects, developing and underdeveloped societies today lack many of the options Western European societies were able to utilize in the course of their economic and social development. Consequently, in judging what developing and underdeveloped societies have managed to accomplish, we must take into account the options that they actually have available to them in their particular circumstances. Nevertheless, in the near future, it should be reasonable to expect that all existing persons accept the population policy just proposed, according to which the membership of future generations would never be allowed to increase beyond the ability of existing generations to make the necessary provision for the basic needs of future generations.

In sum, I have argued that even a libertarian ideal of liberty, which initially seems opposed to welfare rights, can be seen to require a right to a basic needs minimum that extends to distant peoples and future generations and is conditional on the poor doing whatever they reasonably can to meet their own basic needs, including bringing their population growth under control. Given that, as I have argued elsewhere, welfare liberal, socialist, communitarian, and feminist political ideals can be easily seen to support this same right to a basic needs minimum, showing how a libertarian ideal of liberty supports the right should go a long way toward solving the problem of what all people, whether near or distant, present or future, deserve, which is the problem of global justice.

NOTES

1. Ruth Leger Sivard, *World Military and Social Expenditures*. Washington DC: World Priorities, 1993, p. 24. This particular definition of absolute poverty comes from Robert McNamara.

2. Lester R. Brown, "Facing Food Insecurity," Lester R. Brown, et al. eds. *State of the World 1994*. New York: Norton, 1994, p. 177.

3. Lester Brown, Hal Kane, David Malin Roodman, *Vital Signs 1994*. New York: Norton, 1994, p. 19.

4. Sandra Postel, "Carrying Capacity: Earth's Bottom Line," Lester R. Brown, et al. eds. *State of the World 1994*, p. 12.

5. Sandra Postel, "Carrying Capacity: Earth's Bottom Line," p. 4.

6. Brown, "Facing Food Insecurity," p. 186.

7. Sandra Postel, "Carrying Capacity: Earth's Bottom Line," p. 5 In 1960, the richest 20 percent of the world's people received 70 percent of the global income, the poorest 20 percent only 2.3 percent.

8. Basic needs, if not satisfied, lead to significant lacks or deficiencies with respect to a standard of mental and physical well-being. Thus, a person's needs for food, shelter, medical care, protection, companionship, and self-development are, at least in part, needs of this sort. For a discussion of basic needs, see my *How To Make People Just*, Totowa: Rowman and Littlefield, 1988, pp. 45–48.

9. See *How To Make People Just* Totowa: Rowman and Littlefield, 1988, and also "From Liberty to Welfare," *Ethics* (1994).

10. See John Hospers, *Libertarianism*. Los Angeles: Nash Press, 1971.

11. I first appealed to this interpretation of the "ought" implies "can" principle to bring libertarians around to the practical requirements of welfare liberalism in an expanded version of an article entitled "Neo-Libertarianism," which appeared in the fall of 1979. In 1982, T. M. Scanlon in "Contractualism and Utilitarianism," Amartya Sen and Bernard Williams, eds. *Utilitarianism and Beyond*. Cambridge: Cambridge University Press, 1982, pp. 103–128 appealed to much the same standard to arbitrate the debate between contractarians and utilitarians. In my judgment, however, this standard embedded in the "ought" implies "can" principle can be more effectively used in the debate with libertarians than in the debate with utilitarians, because sacrifices libertarians standardly seek to impose on the less advantaged are more outrageous and, hence, more easily shown to be contrary to reason.

12. This linkage between morality and reason is expressed by the belief that (true) morality and (right) reason cannot conflict. Some supporters of this linkage have developed separate theories of rationality and reasonableness, contending, for example, that, while egoists are rational, those who are committed to morality are both rational and reasonable. On this interpretation, morality is rationally permissible but not rationally required since egoism is also rationally permissible. Other supporters of the linkage between reason and morality reject the idea of separate theories of rationality and reasonableness, contending that morality is not just rationally permissible but also rationally required and that egoism is rationally impermissible. But despite their disagreement over whether there is a separate theory of rationality distinct from a theory of reasonableness, both groups link morality with a notion of reasonableness that incorporates a certain degree of altruism. For further discussion of these issues, see *How To Make People Just*, Chapter 11.

13. I am indebted to Alasdair MacIntyre for helping me make this point clearer.

14. See James P. Sterba, "Is There a Rationale for Punishment?" *American Journal of Jurisprudence* 29 (1984): 29–43.

15. By the liberty of the rich to meet their luxury needs I continue to mean the liberty of the rich not to be interfered with when using their surplus possessions for luxury purposes. Similarly, by the liberty of the poor to meet their basic needs I continue to mean the liberty of the poor not to be interfered with when taking what they require to meet their basic needs from the surplus possessions of the rich.

16. See, for example, Eric Mack, "Individualism, Rights and the Open Society," edited by Tibor Machan, ed. *The Libertarian Alternative*. Chicago: Nelson-Hall, 1974.

17. Since the conflict resolution principle is the contrapositive of the "ought" implies "can" principle, whatever logically follows from the one principle logically follows from the other, nevertheless, by first appealing to the one principle and then the other, as I have here, I maintain that the conclusions that I derive can be seen to follow more clearly.

18. The employment opportunities offered to the poor must be honorable and supportive of self-respect. To do otherwise would be to offer the poor the opportunity to meet some of their basic needs at the cost of denying some of their other basic needs.

19. The poor cannot, however, give up the liberty to which their children are entitled.

20. For this other interpretation, see my *How To Make People Just*, Chapter 5.

21. Tibor Machan, *Individuals and Their Rights*. La Salle: Open Court, 1989, pp. 100–111.

22. Ibid., p. 107.

23. Ruth Leger Sivard, *World Military and Social Expenditures*, p. 24.

24. Ibid. pp. 38–39 and Alan Durning, "Life on the Brink," *World Watch* 3(2) 1990:29.

25. John Hospers, "Some Unquestioned Assumptions," *Journal of Social Philosophy* (1991).

26. Although given what I have said about the welfare rights of distant peoples and future generations, it would seem that (b) and (c) are unlikely to obtain.

27. Richard DeGeorge, "Do We Owe the Future Anything?" in *Law and the Ecological Challenge* (1978) pp. 180–190.

28. Rex Martin, *Rawls and Rights*. Lawrence: University of Kansas, 1984, Chapter 2.

29. Anita Gordon and David Suzuki, *It's a Matter of Survival*. Cambridge, Harvard University Press, 1990. See also Donella H. Meadows, Dennis L. Meadows, Jorgen Randers, and William W. Behrens III, *The Limits to Growth*, 2nd ed. New York: New American Library, 1974, Chapters 3 and 4.

30. For a somewhat opposing view, see M. P. Golding, "Obligations to Future Generations," *The Monist*, 56 (1972):85–99.

31. When the poor are acting collectively in conjunction with their agents and allies to exercise their negative welfare rights, they will want, in turn, to institute adequate positive welfare rights to secure a proper distribution of the goods and resources they are acquiring.

32. Bob Bergland, "Attacking the Problem of World Hunger," *The National Forum* 69(2) 1979:4.

33. Ruth Leger Sivard, *World Military and Social Expenditures*, p. 28.

34. For a discussion of these causal connections, see Cheryl Silver, *One Earth One Future*. Washington DC: National Academy Press, 1990; Bill McKibben, *The End of Nature*. New York: Anchor Books, 1989; Jeremy Leggett, ed., *Global Warming*. New York: Oxford University Press, 1990; Lester Brown, ed., *The World Watch Reader*. New York: Nelson, 1991.

35. Successes in meeting the most basic needs of the poor in particular regions of developing countries (e.g., the Indian state of Kerala) should not blind us to the growing numbers of people living in conditions of absolute poverty and how difficult it will be to meet the basic needs of all these people in a sustainable way that will allow future generations to have their basic needs met as well, especially when we reflect on the fact that the way we in the developed world are living is not sustainable at all!

Making Sense of the Right to Food [1]

XIAORONG LI

Xiaorong Li is a research scholar at the Institute for Philosophy and Public Policy, University of Maryland, College Park.

Everyone has the right to a standard of living adequate for the health and well-being of himself and his family, including adequate food, clothing and housing, and to the continuous improvement of living conditions.

Universal Declaration of Human Rights, Article 11

Between 1988 and 1990, 786 million people in the world's developing regions were undernourished.[2] Assuming that these people did not choose to deprive themselves, it is safe to say that their right to food "adequate for [their] health and well-being" was not satisfied.

The purpose of this essay is to facilitate debate on what makes the claim to food a right; how the right to food for all can be respected, at least partially; and who should take responsibility for its implementation. I will defend the following claims. The right to food should be understood as a need-based right. The right to food is a right to access to the means to procure adequate food. The right to food must be supported by social practices conducive to a stable social and economic order. Such an order is necessary to prevent deprivation and to insure that each person has the opportunity to secure adequate access to food. Governments are primarily responsible for instituting and maintaining this order and thus for protecting the right to food.

Subsistence Rights as Need-Based Claims

I postulate that a claim to subsistence (or services) is a human right if it is a claim to the satisfaction of a basic human need. Satisfaction of basic needs is essential because it enables persons to develop and function in such a way that they can pursue their well-being. Basic human needs differ from other, nonbasic needs. The term "basic" refers not to all the things that we claim we need, but to those needs that T. M. Scanlon would call *objective*.[3] According to Scanlon, an *objective* criterion for assessing the importance of competing claims of needs should be independent of individuals' own assessment or preference. Individuals' own judgment of what they need would be a *subjective* criterion when used to determine the importance of their claims. In contrast, assessing a person's need for food with reference to the nutritional requirement for normal human functioning uses an objective criterion. In Norman Daniels' view, certain human needs (such as the need for health care) are "objectively ascribable" to a person independently of one's preferences and "objectively important" because they are all-purpose means to the achievement of whatever specific plans we choose. Such "course-of-life" needs (as opposed to contingent needs) have to do with developing and maintaining "normal (human) species functioning."[4]

Basic subsistence rights express the moral concern that each person's basic human needs should be met. Doubts regarding what count as basic human needs may remain, but few people would challenge the claim that human needs for food are objectively attributable and important, noncontingent needs for normal human functioning. The right to food, in the need-based account of rights, is thus a basic right. This need-based notion can be justified on the basis of Scanlon's scheme for the justification of rights: "the case for rights derives in large part from the goal of promoting an acceptable distribution of control over important factors in our lives."[5] The need-based notion regards the conditions for satisfying basic human needs as "important factors in our lives."

To conceive of the right to food as need-based resolves the problem perceived by some that such a right may dictate egalitarian distribution. Since each person's need for food (depending on his or her age and health condition at the moment) is different (children and pregnant women, for example, may have special nutritional needs), this need-based account would prescribe allocation according to specific needs in order to alleviate the plight of food deficiency and malnutrition effectively.

The claim of food (subsistence) rights as need-based is committed to the following views:

1. The right to food, as a need-based human right, carries high priority because of its tie to human dignity and its essential effect on human well-being. The human need for food is closely tied to the dignity that distinguishes human beings from animals. The sense of indignity and humili-

ation human beings often experience when they are forced to accept degrading conditions (slave labor, prostitution, stealing, or begging) in exchange for food is uniquely theirs. It is this sense of human dignity, as an essential part of human well-being, that makes the human need for food a right-claim. In describing legal rights, Joel Feinberg has stated this point eloquently:

> Rights are not mere gifts or favors, motivated by love or pity, for which gratitude is the sole fitting response. A right is something that can be demanded or insisted upon without embarrassment or shame. When that to which one has a right is not forthcoming, the appropriate reaction is indignation; when it is duly given there is no reason for gratitude, since it is simply one's own or one's due that one received. A world with claim-rights is one in which all persons, as actual or potential claimants, are dignified objects of respect, both in their own eyes and in [the] view of others. No amount of love and compassion, or obedience to higher authority, or noblesse oblige, can substitute for those values.[6]

Feinberg goes on to differentiate legal rights from "moral rights." The latter term characterizes those human rights that have not become legally established in certain societies. His view of human dignity as intrinsic to legal rights may thus not extend to these human rights. However, human rights understood as need-based, whether legal or moral, perform the same function for maintaining human dignity. Basic human needs enable people to demand and insist on their moral human rights without shame and embarrassment, even when these rights have not become legal rights.

This link between human dignity and rights leads us to another interesting perspective on the right to food. We all know of loving and compassionate individuals—some of them are rulers of societies—who generously give to the poor or to their subjects. Such benevolent actions should not be considered as acts of rights protection. In political rhetoric, generous "giving" by rulers is often applauded as an improvement of rights conditions. Authoritarian regimes may decide (most likely as a means of consolidating power) to offer the powerless an opportunity to "get rich," or to improve their abysmal standard of living. Suppose that food is thus made more accessible. Should such a policy count for implementing protection of the right to food? Not if we consider human dignity an indispensable ingredient of the right-claim. The reason is simple: those who have no access to political power cannot participate in economic policy-making. Thus, they have no way of securing the gains they make under the new policy. Access to food is given to them and can be taken away without their consent. They are in no position (because of their lack of political freedom) to claim what they have a right to.

2. The right to food is universal, applicable to societies where human rights protection is neither legally established nor even officially recognized. Such rights are not contingent on a particular view of, for example, social justice. Charles Beitz has argued otherwise; in his view, human rights are defined "by the principles of justice appropriate to the social group at issue," and "the human rights of any particular person depend upon the principles appropriate to his or her social group."[7] Here Beitz is proceeding from the Rawlsian insight that principles of justice are worked out according to the level of civilization and political-economic conditions of particular societies.[8] But this view is difficult to reconcile with the concept of universal human rights. For example, when the U.N. calls for human rights protection, is it simply asking each society to work out its own principles of justice and, in accordance with these principles, its own list of rights and their relative importance? If so, then why does the U.N. declare human rights *universal*?

There are also a number of other practical difficulties, which Beitz admits as drawbacks of his model. For example, it is impossible to know which rights persons in unjust societies could legitimately claim. How can we even tell whether a society is just or unjust if each has its own principles? Different nationals may have different rights, differently ranked; persons who are members of more than one society may have to make different claims depending on where they live at the moment.[9]

To avoid these difficulties, we may maintain that social justice, no matter how different the principles of justice may be from one society to the next, must respect basic human rights as claims, which are universal to all human beings, to basic need satisfaction. Moreover, the ranking of rights should not be left entirely to nations or states, though their level of economic development and civilization may justify putting off the full protection of certain rights. Instead, the international community should adopt general principles or guidelines for rights protection. For instance, among all the United Nations-declared rights, some should be declared "basic." Whether a specific right is "basic" will depend on whether it is a claim to the satisfaction of basic human needs.

3. The need-based right to food should be understood as a right to the opportunity to "earn" food as well as a right to welfare for those who are unable to work. Understood as a right to the opportunity to work when one is healthy and skilled enough to work, the right to food depends for its protection on society's respect for the rights to fair payment and to education or professional training that prepares one to become eligible and suitable for work. For those who are unable to work (due to sickness or physical handicap, maternity, learning disability, senility, etc.), or those whose job opportunities have disappeared for the time being (due to disasters, war, or market-induced unemployment, for example), the right to food justifies their right to welfare provisions by the state. In implementing the right to food, therefore, responsible agencies must create conditions for the implementation of a range of other rights, which have also been recognized in the U.N. Covenant on Economic, Social and Cultural Rights: the right to work and opportunity for training (Article 6), the right to fair wages and equal renumeration for work of equal value (Article 7), and the right to education (Article 13). As I shall argue, it is also necessary to protect a range of civil-political rights, such as the right to free expression and the right to free association and participation in independent unions. The right to unionize helps protect workers' rights to employment security, fair pay and benefits, and safe working conditions. Labor rights have recently emerged as one basic requirement for the protection of the right to food for millions disadvantaged by the marketization underway in developing countries.

4. Finally, the concept of need-based subsistence rights is both "positive" and "negative." The conventional positive/negative divide suggests that some rights can be protected if others simply refrain from violating them, while other rights can only be protected if others provide the substance that these rights make claims to. However, as Henry Shue has argued, the effort to characterize different rights as negative or positive, depending on whether they require refraining or providing, does not do justice to the various functions of rights.[10]

When hunger becomes a threat to well-being, one or both of the following courses of events has led to the problem: either the hungry people's access to food is blocked, or there is simply not enough food to go around. In order for one to be free from hunger (understood here as *involuntary undernourishment*, to be differentiated from voluntary underconsumption of food), two conditions must hold: (1) one must not be deprived of access to food, if there is any; and (2) food, the substance of this right, must be available. When only one of these conditions holds for someone, one's right to food cannot be respected.

Respecting the right to food, therefore, is not simply a matter of providing, nor simply a matter of refraining (by the government, police, legal instruments, and so on). For vulnerable rightholders (infants, seniors, or the poor), the right to food cannot be respected if they are simply left on their own. The right to food requires positive actions to provide food for the vulnerable. It is in this sense that this right has often been characterized as a positive right, the implementation of which requires society to do something actively and even aggressively. Such implementation involves creating or maintaining conditions under which all persons have access to food. It involves others' or society's taking action in "providing" (producing, allocating, and shipping) the food and insuring that food is affordable to all.

However, the right to food is not merely positive. It also has features of a negative right, a notion evolved from Locke's idea of "natural rights." A "negative right" is a right the implementation of which requires governments and other individuals to refrain from certain actions. The right to food is negative since it requires governments not to take away, nor to block access to, available food. Embezzlement of food reserves, governmental suspension of food delivery to rebel-occupied areas, and official rejection of foreign aid for political considerations, are familiar cases of negative violations. Less obviously, negative violations occur when governments adopt new economic plans in which local food production is abruptly interrupted and vulnerable families' conventional food sources are terminated without proper compensation. Interruption of food sources occurs when governments nationalize private farmland or privatize national plantations, or when peasants are uprooted and their land is used for industrial or transportational purposes. Thus, there are many actions that governments must *refrain from taking*, unless they can provide adequate and timely compensation, in order to protect the right to food.

For all these reasons, the right to food (and subsistence rights in general, to which I cannot extend a full discussion here) does not lend itself to either the "positive" or the "negative" label. It cuts across the positive/negative dichotomy. A parallel with the right to fair trial may help clarify some of the related issues. The right to fair trial might be very expensive to implement in poor countries. To guarantee fair trials, a society has to be able to afford a sophisticated legal profession, to pay for the training of legal workers, judges and police, and to finance educational programs informing the public of the law and involving them in public reasoning about the fairness of legal procedures. When a society cannot afford these institutional expenditures, however, it does not follow that the right to a fair trial should simply not be respected. Currently, the U.N. Working Group on Arbitrary Detention and Human Rights Watch hold governments of poor countries responsible if they fail to do what they can to insure fair trials for suspects. Although the failure to provide a fair trial may result in part from a lack of institutional tools, a government may immediately refrain from certain actions—trying defendants in closed courts, for example—that violate the right to a fair trial. Similarly, the failure to respect the right to basic sustenance may result from a lack of food that the government can do nothing about. But such failures are often the result of deliberate acts—including the active deprivation or depletion of food resources—for which the state must be held responsible.

Let me briefly mention that the implementation of the right to food requires the implementation of some commonly recognized negative rights, such as the right to free expression and free press. Information circulation and the freedom to expose policy failures can be crucial in averting famine. Information about incipient shortages, available supplies, and delivery failures plays an important role. When politicians block vital information or encourage the spread of false information, inflated reports can lead to overconsumption of dwindling supplies. Severe hunger and starvation may then follow.[11]

In contrast, deaths related to famine can be reduced if local authorities monitor early signs of food shortage. The free flow of information helps authorities to identify potential trouble spots and locate resources for aid. If governments fail to acknowledge a problem, aggressive press coverage can generate a public outcry, which will push an accountable government to respond.[12]

The breakdown of the positive/negative divide reveals a wide range of possible actions between full protection and complete disregard of the right to food. One can speak of minimum protection (by refraining from deprivation) and maximum protection (by providing access to food). Even when maximum protection cannot be achieved, the right to food as a constraint on governments forbids the state from depriving persons of access to food (if such an access is already available), even when such deprivation is intended to promote general socioeconomic development or make possible maximum protection for all in the future. Minimum protection can be significant. If Chinese peasants could have prevented their land from being collectivized, if they could have been left alone to tend the land instead of being drawn into the Great Leap Forward and other political campaigns that disrupted food production, then, other things being equal, the starvation of possibly thirty million Chinese in the early 1960s could have been avoided.

What Claim Does the Right to Food Make?

What exactly does the right to food require others or society to do for rightholders? This question cannot be addressed before we identify what the right to food is a claim to. What should people be provided with, and not deprived of, in order to guarantee their right to food? To identify the object of the right to food, we may begin by excluding inappropriate candidates.

The requirement for fulfilling this right should not be the actual use or consumption of foodstuffs necessary for the health and well-being of a particular person (female, middle-aged, and pregnant, for example). Such a requirement comes too close to the implausible claim that one's right to food is not fulfilled until one actually consumes the prescribed amount of food. Persons should be able to consume less than the amount required for their health if they choose to. They should be free to go on a diet, or on a hunger strike. If the object of the right to food were the actual consumption of food, it would prevent us from saying that those who have access to adequate food but choose to forgo food for whatever reasons have their right to food respected.[13]

"Actual enjoyment" can of course be interpreted as the actual possession of food supplies or the ready availability of food to the person who is said to have the right. A particular person's having the right refers to one's enjoying or having the opportunity to access to food if one wants it. The point here is not to argue over language but to reject one possible reading of "actual enjoyment": actually consuming a certain amount of food. Such a reading may make the right to food appear too imposing—it may seem to claim that the right to food is not respected until rightholders eat the food necessary for their health.

Nor should the right to food be understood as the rightholder's claim to an adequate amount of food no matter how little one tries to secure it, especially if he or she is healthy, capable, and has sufficient means to acquire access to food. If everyone is unconditionally entitled to food without the responsibility to work (even if he or she *can* work), then the motive to work or produce is likely to subside and productivity is likely to fall below sustainability. In the end, the effort to provide for everyone's access to adequate food will fail. The unconditionality interpretation of the right to food is virtually self-defeating: while promising food provision, the unconditional claim may contribute to a productivity decline. The communist collective farms, which promised to provide subsistence "to each according to his need," only managed (apart from exceptions in more resource-rich East European countries) to worsen rural poverty and malnutrition in spite of state subsidies.[14]

That the right to food is not a right to "free" or unconditional food,[15] proves reasonable if we consider the circumstances in which there is a reason for implementing the right to food. Suppose it became possible to guarantee the satisfaction of everyone's need for food without requiring anyone to work because there was no need to continue food production or to replace the amount of food consumed. In such a hypothetical situation, there would be no use for the right to food—food would be overly abundant and easily accessible to anyone, just like sunlight or air. ("The right to fresh air" receives attention now only because fresh air is becoming a rare good.) It would then make only trivial sense to claim that our entitlement to food should be respected and that food should be provided. The right to food makes more sense in circumstances of limited food supplies or moderate scarcity. Food is under moderate scarcity if there is not enough for unlimited taking, and yet enough for distribution in such a way as to enable all persons' basic needs to be met. Current world food supplies can be reasonably assessed to be in a state of "moderate scarcity," which necessitates a protection of the rights to food.[16]

Under such conditions, real obstacles to protection of the right to food are found in current political and economic (distributive) systems, rather than in problems of absolute scarcity.[17] Implementing the right to food thus depends on rearranging relevant institutions, a topic to be addressed in the last section of this chapter. Such rearrangements *can* be done if there exists a political will to reorganize governments and multinational institutions and to reform distributive systems.[18] We must be careful, however, not to equate what is possible for world food productivity and ideal distributive arrangements to accomplish, on the one hand, with what one person can accomplish, on the other. It is irrational to require any single person to assume an obligation to implement the right to food. But this does not mean that it is nobody's obligation. In the next section, I will argue that, for this obligation to be fulfilled, the participation of many (if not all) individuals in institutional efforts is required.

From time to time, partial or isolated situations of absolute or severe scarcity exist, where there is not enough food to go around and not all people can be fed. Because of the impossibility of feeding all persons under such situations, insisting on guaranteeing the right to food for all is similar to insisting on guaranteeing a cure for all terminal illnesses. If the terminally ill cannot be cured, it would be pointless to insist that everybody's freedom from terminal illness should be guaranteed. Society cannot be required to do what is not in its power to do. "Ought," as philosophers often remind us, implies "can." Nevertheless, a right continues to exist under such circumstances. It exists only as a goal, an ideal, which society should aim at promoting. Even if there simply is not enough food in a given situation to guarantee each person an adequate supply, the limited food may be sufficient for a distribution that ensures fair and equal access by all to a minimum amount of food. The fact that persons have a right (even just as an ideal) dictates *how* limited foods *should* be distributed. However, in our increasingly interconnected world, such severe scarcity does not have to be dealt with in isolation for a significantly long period. International assistance can be quickly arranged and food can be delivered from other places. But why should there be international assistance?

Whose Responsibility Is It to Do What?

In the remaining space, I can only argue, first, that the right to food must be seen as a social issue and thus it is society, not individuals, who is primarily responsible for protecting it. The right, to be effective, must be supported by just institutions conducive to a stable political and economic order. Such an order is necessary for preventing deprivation and insuring each person's opportunity for adequate access to food. Next, I argue that it is governments which, though often the cause of problems in this area, must ultimately be the means to respect this right in its full social complexity. I will also address the issue of foreign governments and their role in protecting the right to food. Finally, I examine the limited nature and potency of individual responsibility and its link to institutional justice.

A society is a complex of actors, including individuals, government agencies, and other cultural, political and economic entities. How should responsibility for human rights protection be apportioned among them? Are all agencies equally responsible, or should some assume major responsibility? The U.N. Covenant on Economic, Social and Cultural Rights has assigned obligations primarily to states for protecting the rights of their citizens. This Covenant states:

> Each State Party to the present Covenant undertakes to take steps, individually and through international assistance and co-operation,.... to the maximum of its available resources, with a view to achieving progressively the full realization of the rights recognized in the present Covenant by all appropriate means, including particularly the adoption of legislative measures.

The mention of "international assistance and co-operation" also indicates an international responsibility on the part of foreign governments and multinational institutions.

But why should the state be primarily responsible? Obviously, when the state fails to regulate food prices, when government officials (police officers or the military) arbitrarily take away a family's sources of income, when secret police have income-earning adults fired from work for union or opposition activities, or when the government fails to provide those who are unable to work with any access to food, so that they and their children suffer from hunger—in all these cases, we tend to hold the government responsible, not so much the employers or the parents, for violating or failing to protect the victims' right to food. If, however, female children are not given as nutritious a diet as their brothers because the parents allocate household food more favorably to their sons, the implicated parties (the parents) violate their female children's right to food. But they should be prosecuted for neglecting or abusing children under the criminal law, not by an international human rights court unless the state criminal courts have delined to prosecute them.

There is a normative reason for this difference in attribution. Governments have the power to command the police and the army, to make policies, to execute the law, and to fulfill the commitments that they have made to the people. Governments are entrusted with powers of this magnitude in order to maintain order, protect legal and constitutional rights, and make sure that citizens fulfill their various duties under the law. The political power entrusted to the government in normal situations (in the absence of war and paralyzing corruption, for example) is much more effective than any other nonofficial (individual or nongovernmental) power, precisely because of its magnitude. When private citizens violate the law, or when individual officials fail to act in accordance with the law, the government, via its legal instruments, can punish violations or extract compensation. But when the government systematically violates citizens' rights and uses its legal and military apparatus to back up its actions, citizens can become vulnerable, helpless, or desperate. When their grievances are ignored or not redressed by state institutions, they can be severely hurt and disadvantaged. They have no other higher authorities to appeal to except, if possible, international institutions such as the United Nations or the European Court. Precisely, because government violations of citizens' rights can put them in such a helplessly disadvantageous position, government responsibility to protect their rights is accordingly indispensable and vital.

Now, what about governments that override rights in the process of achieving future justice? Before rights protection can be fully actualized, are governments justified in violating rights if such violations are deemed beneficial for future protection? If we answer this question in the affirmative, then we are not taking seriously the role of human rights as a constraint on violations *here and now*. A future justice should undoubtedly provide better rights protection, and efforts toward achieving future justice should constitute an important part of the campaign for human rights. But effective human rights work, as demonstrated in the achievements of mainly

nongovernmental agencies worldwide, has focused largely on applying human rights as curbs that require immediate compliance and
on holding governments of all kinds (democratic or authoritarian)
accountable for their violations. A satisfactory theory of international human rights is thus expected to account for the role of rights as
"side constraints," a Lockean notion that captures the sense that a
right should not be overridden even if the reward is a possibly better
protection (when justice obtains) for (presumably) a larger number of
persons. To endorse a trade-off of current protection for future justice is to relinquish certain real opportunities for stopping violations
in the present.

I now turn to the issue of whether multinational agencies, such
as the United Nations (not including nongovernment organizations
[NGOs]), capable of taking responsibility, should step into "domestic"
rights disputes between individuals and their government. When
governments cease to function, have collapsed, or act in violation of
citizens' rights, should international institutions or other governments assume the responsibility for implementing rights? Suppose
that citizens of a certain state suffer from involuntary starvation—
either because authorities deprived them of food supplies or failed to
take timely measures to prevent severe food shortages caused by
famine, war, or other disasters, or because the system has failed to
distribute food in such a way that each person has access to it. The
relevant state agencies equipped with the power to protect rights
must have become incapable of or opposed to respecting the right to
food. In situations like this, should foreign governments and multinational institutions, who are in a position to save lives or to ease
suffering from hunger, assume the responsibility for rights implementation? They may have not been directly involved in depriving
these people, nor has it been their official duty to prevent disasters
or to secure food supplies for them. In what sense, then, might they
have a responsibility now to implement these people's right to food?

I have previously referred to the desirability of individual citizens' being able to appeal to international protection when they have
exhausted all possibilities of national protection. This desirability
provides an intuitive account of why there should be international
human rights bodies and why these institutions' decisions should be
legally enforced. Let us develop this argument for international protection, starting with the question of what responsibilities are generated by the right to food. As we have seen, to recognize this right is
to recognize the *universal* need for food as vital for human beings to
achieve well-being, including normal health (or healthy growth) and
a sense of dignity. Human beings have this need regardless of their
nationality or membership in certain cultural, religious, or political

communities. Thus, if states and international agencies recognize the right to food, they should also recognize the universal human need for food. In so doing, they express the moral concern that all human beings should be able to meet their basic need for food. They also acknowledge that society should be organized in such a way that citizens' right to food can be satisfied.

From these premises, however, it does not follow that members of the international community, P, have a responsibility to (re)organize the government of society X or to take charge of ensuring food access for all members of X if its current government does not respect its citizens' rights. P's recognition that some ideal state of affairs ought to be brought about does not imply that it is P's responsibility to bring about that state. But there are reasons for arguing that if P recognizes the right to food and its universal applicability to all persons alike, P has a duty to take two courses of action, depending on how severe the situation is. (1) When the government of X is not working properly to guarantee its citizens' right and some people have no access to adequate food, P should try to push for and assist institution-building so that reforms will take place toward greater rights protection. (2) When severe hunger or starvation have already occurred, P should do its best to save lives. What (2) requires is actually a humanitarian duty in life-threatening situations. It is not exactly a duty generated by a commitment to the right to food. It is, rather, a duty generated by the right to life. Failures to act are failures to respect the victims' right to life.

The states themselves, not the international community, are of course mainly responsible for ensuring their citizens' access to food; but when the states fail to do so, those institutions that recognize the universal right to food have a duty to help reform state institutions and, when starvation approaches, a humanitarian duty to save lives.

Here, the act of recognizing the right to food is crucial. The duty comes in the same package with this right: to recognize the latter is also to recognize the former. If various agents have not ratified this right, according to this account, it is difficult to pinpoint them as having the above duty. But why *should* these agents recognize the right to food? The reason, as discussed earlier, goes to the moral concern about meeting basic human needs.

Though various political agents play a key role in implementing rights, the right to food, like other human rights, cannot be truly respected unless individuals become actively and conscientiously involved. Governmental obligations are inconceivable without individuals performing their own duties and supporting an accountable government. As the U.N. Covenant on Economic, Social and Cultural

Rights also states, "the individual, having duties to other individuals and to the community to which he belongs, is under a responsibility to strive for the promotion and observance" of the right to food (The Preamble). This responsibility often requires that individuals contribute mainly in the form of taxes to enable their government to reform, to assist reforms abroad, and to aid starving people.

Admittedly, individuals' responsibility differs from that of governmental (or multinational) agencies. This difference has been compared to the difference between the duty of a passerby and that of a lifeguard in saving a drowning child. The lifeguard has accepted the duty to save anyone who is drowning in a certain area. When he or she fails to save a drowning child, he or she should be held responsible. In contrast, a passerby does not have such a responsibility. However, as a community member active in protecting the welfare of children, the passerby has a responsibility to urge community officials to make sure that children swim only when lifeguards are on duty, to insist that lifeguards be held accountable for negligence, and so on. But when a child is drowning, with or without the lifeguard on duty, the passerby has a humanitarian duty to save lives.[19]

By pledging to be bound by a constitution that protects the right to food, or by becoming a party to international human rights conventions, governments can be said to have accepted the responsibility of protecting the right to food. Individual citizens do not have the same responsibility. If they have any responsibility at all, it is a responsibility to establish, sustain, and restore just institutions[20] (that is, institutions devoted to the protection of human rights) and a moral duty to provide humanitarian aid to those whose lives are in danger.

On this account, the right to food does not generate an obligation for every individual to provide direct food assistance to those who would otherwise be hungry. Individual donations to food kitchens or food banks out of a humanitarian or charitable duty alleviate hunger, but they will not suffice to solve the problem. As long as our institutional defects remain intact, no matter how much or how often individuals are willing to contribute for hunger relief, the institutional mechanisms will continue to produce hunger. Failures to respect the right to food are rooted in social and political institutions that shape and affect the lives of individuals. The cure, therefore, is to be found in reforming or reorganizing such institutions.

NOTES

1. Valuable comments on various versions of this chapter were generously offered by Thomas Pogge and colleagues at the Institute for Philosophy and Public Policy, University of Maryland. Eric Goldstein

read earlier drafts and made helpful suggestions. I also wish to thank Arthur Evenchik and the editors of this volume for their editorial suggestions. I gratefully acknowledge support for this research from the National Endowment for the Humanities Grant #RO-22709-94.

2. Food and Agriculture Organization of the United Nations (FAO), *The State of Food and Agriculture.* Rome: FAO, 1992. See also World Resources Institute, *World Resources: A Guide to the Global Environment, 1994–1995.* New York: Oxford University Press, 1994, p. 108.

3. Thomas Scanlon (1975), p. 655–660.

4. Norman Daniels (1981), p. 152–154.

5. Thomas Scanlon (1978), p. 105.

6. Joel Feinberg (1973), pp. 58–59.

7. Charles Beitz (1979), p. 60.

8. John Rawls (1971), pp. 7–9, 152.

9. Beitz (1979), p. 60.

10. For an illuminating discussion of the problems related to the sharp distinction between "positive" and "negative" rights, see Shue (1980), pp. 35–40; and "Rights in the Light of Duties," in Brown and MacLean (1979), esp. pp. 66–71. Beitz has also discussed these problems in relation to the division between what he calls "personal rights" (which fall under "negative" rights) and political-economic rights, a division that puts political rights (which are supposedly "negative") on the other side of the divide (Beitz 1979, pp. 4–53).

11. See Ashton et al., 1984; Peng, 1987; Millman and colleagues 1990, for an analysis of similar causes of China's 1958–1960 famine.

12. Reduced famine in India in recent decades illustrates the vital role of information flow. See the study by Millman & colleagues, 1990.

13. Shue writes, "I take subsistence rights to be rights to the actual use or consumption of unpolluted air, unpolluted water, adequate food, adequate clothing" (1980, p. 70). See also Shue in Brown and MacLean (1979, pp. 13, 15).

14. A simplified description of how food production, distribution, and availability respond to income through the market may show the importance of jobs. If persons vulnerable to hunger can have jobs, they will be able to purchase some foods even when prices rise; their purchasing power, though very weak, continues to attract supplies from areas where food can be produced and dispatched. Income lures food commodities through the market into famine-stricken regions from more prosperous lands (Sen, 1990). As trade between regions increases, this chain reaction further stimulates production and creates more jobs. Food becomes more accessible to low-income families. In comparison, providing access to "free" food—the form that hunger relief has taken in African famines—saves lives but can be ineffective in easing hunger and malnutrition in the long run. Handouts of food do not give the local poor an ability to command food. They become dependent on aid, the source of which they have no control over.

15. A right to unconditional food is not the same as an unconditional right to food. A right might be unconditional, but the substance that this right is a right to can at the same time be conditional. A person's having a certain right may not be conditioned on who he or she is; but the substance that one's right is supposed to bring about can be conditioned on one having done certain things.

16. Contrary to predictions that population increase would lead to mass starvation, there has been sufficient food to sustain the expanded global population. No doubt the growth in production has been offset by the increase of consumers. But advances in technology, trade, and the specialization of agricultural production have brought about increases in the quantity and quality of food. Because of the "green revolution" between 1950 and 1991, world grain production rose by 169 percent. In developing countries, production increased by 117 percent between 1965 and 1990 (Postel 1994, Bongaarts 1994). Between 1961–1963 and 1983–1985, per capita food available for human consumption increased in developing countries (from 2,320 to 2,660 calories per day) and developed countries (from 3,160 to 3,410 calories) (Millman and colleagues, 1990, p. 311).

17. That is why many major famines in recent years (for example, in Bengal in 1943, in Ethiopia between 1973 and 1982, and in Bangladesh in 1974) took place without any decline in national food output per head (Sen, 1990).

18. For example, governments can stimulate food production and facilitate trade to exchange nonagricultural products for food. Distributive justice does not exclude productive justice.

19. This comparison and the argument are stated in John Arthur's article in Aiken and LaFollette (1977), p. 45.

20. Thomas Pogge argues that individuals "share a collective responsibility for the justice of any social order in which they participate—they must not simply cooperate in imposing an unjust social order without attempting to reform it toward greater justice" (forthcoming, p. 13).

REFERENCES

Aiken, William, and LaFollete, Hugh, ed. 1977. *World Hunger and Moral Obligation.* Englewood Cliffs, NJ: Prentice-Hall.

Ashton, B., et al. (1984) "Famine in China, 1958–1961." *Population and Development Review* 10:613–645.

Beitz, Charles, 1979. "Human Rights and Social Justice," Brown, P., and MacLean, D., eds. *Human Rights and U.S. Foreign Policy.* Lexington, MA: Lexington Books, pp. 45–63.

Bongaarts, John, 1994. "Can the Growing Human Population Feed Itself?" *Scientific American*, March 1994.

Brown, P., and MacLean, D., eds. 1979. *Human Rights and U.S. Foreign Policy.* Lexington, MA: Lexington Books.

Daniels, Norman, 1981. "Health Care and Distributive Justice," *Philosophy and Public Affairs.* Spring 10(2):146–178.

Feinberg, Joel, 1973. *Social Philosophy.* Englewood Cliffs, NJ: Prentice-Hall.

Hardin, Garrett, 1977. "Lifeboat Ethics: The Case Against Helping the Poor," Aiken, W., and LaFollette, H., eds. *World Hunger and Moral Obligation.* Englewood Cliffs, NJ: Prentice-Hall, pp. 12–21.

Lichtenberg, Judith, 1982. "The Moral Equivalence of Action and Omission," *Canadian Journal of Philosophy*, Supplementary Volume VIII.

Millman, S., et al., 1990. "Organization, Information, and Entitlement in the Emerging Global Food System," Newman, Lucile et al., eds. *Hunger in History.* Cambridge, MA: Basil Blackwell, pp. 307–330.

Nagel, Thomas, 1981. "Poverty and Food: Why Charity Is Not Enough," Brown, Peter, and Shue, Henry, eds. *Food Policy: The Responsibility of the United States in the Life and Death Choices.* New York: The Free Press, pp. 54–62.

Nozick, Robert, 1974. *Anarchy, State, and Utopia.* New York: Basic Books.

Nussbaum, Martha, 1992. "Human Functioning and Social Justice: In Defense of Aristotelian Essentialism," *Political Theory* 20 (2).

O'Neill, Onora, 1977. "Lifeboat Earth," Aiken, W., and LaFollette, H., eds. *World Hunger and Moral Obligation.* Englewood Cliffs, NJ: Prentice-Hall, pp. 148–164.

Peng, Xizhe, 1987. "Demographic Consequences of the Great Leap Forward," *Population and Development Review* 13:639–670.

Pogge, Thomas. "How Should Human Rights be Conceived?" *Annual Review of Law and Ethics*, vol. 3, (forthcoming).

Postel, Sandra, 1994. "Carrying Capacity: The Earth's Bottom Line," *State of the World 1994.* New York: W.W. Norton, 1994.

Rawls, John, 1971. *A Theory of Justice.* Cambridge, MA: Harvard University Press.

Scanlon, T. M., 1975. "Preference and Urgency," *Journal of Philosophy* 77(19) (November 1975): 655–669.

————, 1978. "Rights, Goals and Fairness," Stuart Hampshire, ed. *Public and Private Morality.* Cambridge: Cambridge University Press.

Sen, Amartya, 1981. *Poverty and Famines: An Essay on Entitlement and Deprivation.* Oxford: Clarendon Press, and New York: Oxford University Press.

————, 1990. "Food Entitlement and Economic Chains," Newman, L., et al., eds. *Hunger in History.* Cambridge, MA: Basil Blackwell, pp. 374–386.

Shue, Henry, 1979. "Rights in the Light of Duties," Brown P., and MacLeen, D., eds. *Human Rights and U.S. Foreign Policy.* Lexington, MA: Lexington Books.

Shue, Henry, 1980. *Basic Rights: Subsistence, Affluence, and U. S. Foreign Policy.* Princeton, NJ: Princeton University Press.

Singer, Peter, 1977. "Famine, Affluence, and Morality," Aiken, W., and LaFollette, H., eds. *World Hunger and Moral Obligation.* Englewood Cliffs: NJ: Prentice-Hall, pp. 22–36.

A Human Rights Approach to World Hunger

JAMES W. NICKEL

James W. Nickel is professor of philosophy at the University of Colorado, Boulder. He is the author of *Making Sense of Human Rights* (Berkeley, University of California Press, 1987), and of many articles in moral and political philosophy.

This paper has three main themes. First, it criticizes ways of framing the problem of world hunger that see it as mainly a problem of famines that should be addressed by donations of food or money. A better way of framing the problem broadens the problem to include malnutrition and misery and emphasizes the importance of calling on the agency and responsibility not just of First World donors but also of the hungry and malnourished themselves and of local and national institutions. A second theme is the value of an international human rights approach to thinking about and dealing with hunger and malnutrition. Such an approach recommends the national and international recognition of a right to adequate food, but combines it with advocacy of other rights such as the right to education, due process rights, and rights of political participation, that protect and provide for the political and economic action of the hungry and malnourished and their political allies. The third theme is that a plausible approach to world hunger should be flexible, adaptable, and have multiple components so that it can deal with institutional failures, changing economic and political circumstances, and failures of key players to fulfill their responsibilities.

Framing the Problem of World Hunger

It is often assumed that it is easy to understand what the problem of hunger is and who should do something about it. Famines that lead to the starvation of thousands or millions are the main problem, and the key solution is for prosperous people in rich countries to recognize their ethical responsibilities to send food or money to those who are hungry.[1] I believe that this way of framing the problem of world hunger is deeply inadequate; it is far too narrow both in how it sees the problem and in what it envisions as its solution.

It is actually quite difficult to find adequate ways of understanding and addressing hunger and malnutrition around the world. First, these problems are likely to take different forms in different countries and regions. To understand the sources and likely remedies for hunger and malnutrition in Brazil—to take an example of a country that I know something about—one has to know a lot about Brazil's culture, history, regions, economy, and political system. Generic diagnoses of the problem of hunger and its possible remedies are sometimes helpful, but they are no substitute for detailed local knowledge.

Second, thinking of world hunger as mainly a problem of famines and starvation leads us to overlook many of the hungry and malnourished, the millions of people who experience hunger and malnutrition for extended periods but are not victims of famines. Rather, their abilities and economic circumstances make it very difficult for them to earn or produce the necessities of life in sufficient quantities. If our image of a hungry person is someone lying on the ground, already too weak to move, it will be obvious that someone should give this person food and silly to think that he or she can engage in self-help. But most people who experience hunger and malnutrition are functional, are getting water and a little food, and are capable of doing things to find food such as moving or seeking work. If we think of hungry and malnourished people as agents, albeit agents with limited capacities and options, we will avoid assuming that self-help is impossible and that only donated foreign food or money can address the problem. Further, viewing hungry people as agents is a more respectful stance that provides a barrier to the paternalistic attitude that it is mainly rich people from the First World who are competent to address problems of hunger in poorer countries. The purpose of reframing the problem of world hunger is not to get people in rich countries off the hook, but to have a better idea of which hook they should be on.

Third, we need to think hard about what hungry and malnourished people lack. "Food!" is too simple an answer. A better answer is that what is lacking is sufficient access to food and water that is nourishing and safe. Sufficient access is not guaranteed when a region or town has an adequate food supply; people can starve for lack of means to buy the food that is available but expensive. Sufficient access is a matter of being able to gain effective control over an adequate quantity of food and water. Notice also that my characterization of sufficient access mentions water as well as food, and introduces issues of nutrition and safety. The impact of a certain quantity of food and water on human health and flourishing isn't easily separated from how food and water are stored, prepared, and consumed, and from how human and other wastes are disposed. These are things that are normally done by locals, not by foreign donors. They involve patterns of acting and living. This suggests that a better role for foreign donors might be to fund education and infrastructure. Handouts of imported food may work as short term measures to relieve famine, but they are not a plausible solution to misery. A plausible normative approach to hunger should not, in my opinion, relieve normal adults of responsibility for self-provision. If it does, it will be financially unaffordable and will produce dependency that undermines dignity and makes people less capable of dealing with changing circumstances and institutional failures.

Finally, framing the problem of hunger and malnutrition as a matter of famines to be remedied by food shipments from abroad provides little or no role for action by local and national governments and nongovernment organizations (NGOs). Focusing on famine situations alone leads us to assume that local and national institutions are broken down, uncaring, or corrupt. This perpetuates the myth that only First World actors can be effective, or that there is no use in emphasizing the responsibilities of governments and other organizations in poor countries.

A Human Rights Approach to World Hunger

The approach to world hunger that I wish to advocate is distinctive not so much in its use of rights-talk as in its appeal to the norms and institutions of the international human rights movement. This approach, which has become familiar in most parts of the world in recent decades, appeals to moral and legal rights such as the right to freedom from torture, the right to a fair trial, and the right to freedom from racial discrimination to call for reforms in countries all around the world. Discussing social and political problems in terms of human rights has come to be seen as legitimate in most parts of the world, and serious attempts have been made to implement human rights norms internationally within the Council of Europe, the United Nations, and the Organization of American States. My present concern is not to justify the human rights approach, although I have attempted to do that elsewhere,[2] but rather to show how it supports a plausible and attractive approach to world hunger. Although the human rights approach finds inspiration in historic bills of rights such as the Magna Carta, the French Declaration of the Rights of Man and the Citizen, and the U.S. Bill of Rights, for specific normative guidance it looks to contemporary international bills of rights such as the Universal Declaration of Human Rights (1948), the European Convention on Human Rights (1953), the United Nations' Convention on Civil and Political Rights (1966), and Convention of Economic, Social, and Cultural Rights (1966).[3] Further, this movement attempts to create political and legal mechanisms at the international level to pressure governments to adopt and comply with these norms. Most human rights treaties establish institutions to monitor the performance of participating countries, receive complaints, and pressure governments to reform their practices.[4]

The rights of the contemporary human rights movement are not the grand, abstract rights to life, liberty, and property of philosophers such as Locke and Jefferson, but are rather specific rights that address abuses that are familiar in today's world. These specific rights include liberty rights such as freedom of movement, security rights such as rights against murder and torture, due process rights such as the right to a fair trial, equality rights such as equal protection of the law and freedom from discrimination, and welfare rights such as the right to education and the right to adequate food.

Governments are the main addressees (parties who have obligations and responsibilities) of international human rights, but not the only ones. The right to freedom from racial discrimination, for example, obligates other people in one's country, not just one's government, to refrain from discrimination. The Universal Declaration of Human Rights suggests a broad view of the addressees of human rights when it puts forward a list of rights as "a common standard of achievement for all peoples and all nations" and suggests that "every individual and every organ of society" should strive "by teaching and education to promote respect for these rights and freedoms" and use national and international measures to progressively secure "their universal and effective recognition and observance." Agencies that have played a prominent role in promoting human rights include national governments, international organizations such as the United Nations, the Council of Europe, and the Organization of American States, and NGOs such as Amnesty International or the International Commission of Jurists. Citizen action has also played an important role in promoting a return to respect for human rights in recent decades in countries such as Brazil, Argentina, and the Phillipines.

Contemporary human rights norms address hunger both directly and indirectly.[5] A direct approach in terms of a right to adequate food is found in the Universal Declaration and in the

International Covenant of Economic, Social, and Cultural Rights. Article 11 of this Covenant refers to a right to "adequate food" and to a "right of everyone to be free from hunger." Indirect approaches specify rights that do not mention food but that are useful to people both in seeking to avoid hunger and malnutrition and in organizing political campaigns to address hunger and malnutrition. For example, the right to freedom of movement is useful in protecting migrations in search of food or work, and the right to freedom of assembly is useful in protecting efforts to organize social or political action to combat hunger.

The Right to Adequate Food

Human rights documents deal directly with hunger and malnutrition by declaring a right to adequate food. International human rights documents typically follow the *Universal Declaration* in treating hunger and malnutrition as one dimension of a right to an adequate standard of living. But the United Nations *Covenant on Economic, Social, and Cultural Rights* goes beyond this to give separate attention to food.

11.1 The States Parties to the present Covenant, recognize the right of everyone to an adequate standard of living ... including adequate food, clothing, and housing....

11.2 The States Parties to the present Covenant, recognizing the right of everyone to be free from hunger, shall take ... measures ... which are needed:

(a) To improve methods of production, conservation, and distribution of food by making full use of technical and scientific knowledge, by disseminating knowledge of the principles of nutrition and by developing or reforming agrarian systems in such a way as to achieve the most efficient development and utilization of natural resources;

(b) ... [T]o ensure an equitable distribution of world food supplies in relation to need.[6]

Scope This section attempts to sketch a plausible account of the scope of the right to adequate food. To what does this right give one a claim? The previous text suggests that the answer is "adequate food," and I suggested earlier that this should be understood as a claim to food and water that is safe and sufficient for normal human functioning and health. People vary greatly in exactly how much food they need for health and normal functioning, so it isn't plausible to express this claim as, say, a minimal requirement of 1,500 calories a day. The vaguer language of "adequate" or "safe and sufficient" is better, even if it is harder to measure.[7]

It is more difficult to specify the terms on which one should have access to adequate food. Suppose that a healthy person who is perfectly capable of finding and preparing his own food doesn't do so but simply sits in the street demanding to be fed by others. This person's demand is not universalizable; if everyone expected to be fed by others there would be no one to do the feeding. A more plausible view of the scope of the right to adequate nutrition is that it does not relieve people of the responsibility to provide for themselves when their abilities and circumstances make it possible for them to do so. Those who advocate the right to adequate food are not so foolish as to hold that the appropriate response to a request for food is always to give people free food. Welfare rights such as the right to adequate food will be intolerably expensive and will undermine the productivity needed to fund a system of rights if everyone simply receives a free supply of all vital goods.

People who recognize their responsibility to provide for themselves and their families nevertheless may find that limited abilities, harsh circumstances, or a combination of both make it impossible for them to gain sufficient access to safe food and water. A drought may make it impossible to grow food, for example, or severe illness may make one unable to work, or the wages paid for working may be insufficient to buy adequate food. It is in these sorts of circumstances that one has a claim to assistance in gaining sufficient access to safe food and water. But this claim should not be thought of as always falling on governments or international organizations. At a minimum, it doesn't relieve families of the responsibility to provide for their members.

Addressees   This section sketches an account of who has what sorts of responsibilities for responding to the right to adequate food. This right will not be meaningful if it doesn't yield guidance as to who has the responsibility for ensuring that adequate food is available. People are often perplexed by the right to adequate food because they are not sure what it means for them. Does it mean that they have an obligation to feed some particular hungry person, or to feed some fair share of the world's hungry? As Onora O'Neill says, "it would be absurd to claim that everyone has an obligation to provide a morsel of food or a fraction of an income to each deprived person."[8] But this objection is wrong-headed in two ways. First, it wrongly assumes that the main thing the right to adequate nutrition requires is that people be *given* food or income, when in fact the steps needed to make food accessible to all are quite varied. Second, it wrongly assumes that the main way for a person to have a right to adequate nutrition is for everyone to have duties to that person, when in fact upholding the right to adequate nutrition calls for a division of labor.[9]

In my opinion the vocabulary of responsibilities is better than that of duties for describing the way in which human rights guide the behavior of their addressees. Very specific legal rights may identify very precise legal duties. Under a contract Jones may have a duty to deliver 1,000 neckties to Smith on a certain date, and Smith may have a duty to pay Smith a certain amount of money for those ties by a certain date. But political rights typically operate at a higher level of abstraction than this: they prescribe what must be done or not done in broader terms. For example, due process rights prescribe that governments provide fair trials to people that they arrest, but those rights don't specify exactly which government agency must do this or exactly how they must do it. They rather say that somebody in the government must somehow get this accomplished, while leaving the choice of whom and how to the government. Thus, our main job here is to identify the parties who have the responsibility to make sure that people are able to get adequate food, but not to specify exactly what it is that they must do to achieve this.

As I suggested earlier, the system of responsibilities that we elaborate in connection with the right to food should be capable of coping with the failure of key players to fulfill their responsibilities. We can't afford to put all of our eggs in one basket because if that basket breaks then we will go hungry (no need to mix metaphors here!). Thus, a system of shared responsibility is in order. If one of the parties sharing responsibility for ensuring the availability of food is unable or unwilling to perform, the other parties in the system will have their responsibilities increased. For example, if civil war makes it impossible for local political institutions to ensure the availability of food, individuals will have increased responsibilities (and liberties) to seek food, neighboring countries will have responsibilities to receive and provide for refugees, and international agencies and rich countries will have responsibilities to make food assistance available. Responsibilities will also fall on national and international NGOs. If adequate national or international institutions are unavailable, there is the option of reforming existing institutions or creating new ones.

This approach to assigning responsibilities for upholding the right to adequate food assigns primary responsibility to national governments, but recognizes that they may be unwilling or unable to meet their responsibilities. Every government has the duty to protect its people from hunger and starvation by adopting policies and creating institutions that make it possible for people to provide for themselves and their families, and to assist those who are unable to provide for themselves. Which government has the main responsibility to provide food assistance depends on which territory one is in. The people of a particular country share in the responsibility for the right to adequate food. They bear the responsibility of creating and maintaining an economic and political system that facilitates self-provision and adequately assists people unable to provide for themselves.

To show that this view of responsibilities is not cooked up just to deal with the right to adequate food, consider that something similar is true of a very different sort of human right, the right to freedom from torture. Suppose that during a period of political unrest paramilitary groups are kidnapping, torturing, and killing members of groups agitating for land reform. First and foremost, these paramilitary groups have the duty to refrain from using torture to advance their political goals (our example assumes that they are violating this duty). Second, the local government and its agencies have the responsibility to stop and prevent torture; they have the responsibility to bring these paramilitary groups under control. Every government has the responsibility to protect people within its territory from being tortured. The duties associated with the right to freedom from torture involve a division of labor. Third, foreign governments, international agencies, and NGOs such as Amnesty International have responsibilities to pressure local governments to fulfill their responsibilities to stop and prevent torture.

What sorts of measures can governments be expected to take to fulfill their responsibilities to ensure the availability of adequate food? Although this will vary with what the specific problems are and with available resources and institutions, the sorts of duties that governments have in regard to nutrition include the following:

- promote favorable conditions for the production and importation of food by providing an infrastructure of roads, markets, ports, storage, and credit,
- promote people's access to and efficient use of land and other productive resources,
- provide free public education to prepare people for their roles as producers and consumers, including education in nutrition, health, and family planning. Equal education for female children is especially important here,
- take measures, compatible with people's human rights, to keep population size proportional to the food resources that are likely to be available,
- monitor the availability of food and water to the poorer and more vulnerable parts of the populations,

- assist when necessary the poorer and more vulnerable parts of the population in obtaining food. This might be done by subsidizing the prices
  of basic commodities, or by distributing food stamps. Programs to
  import food, temporarily block exports, or store reserves of basic commodities may be needed here,
- combat the corruption and patronage that often plagues food programs.
  Here freedom of the press plays an important role.

What are the responsibilities of well-off foreigners under this
scheme? First, to work to ensure that their governments meet their
responsibilities to respect and promote the right to adequate nutrition, and other human rights, both at home and abroad. Second, to
work to ensure that their governments fulfill their responsibilities in
relation to food within international organizations such as the
United Nations and the Organization of American States. Third, to
support through membership and financial contributions organizations that are active and effective in combatting hunger and malnutrition through development work, education, and the provision of
emergency food assistance.

Indirect Human Rights Approaches to World Hunger

An indirect human rights approach to hunger and malnutrition
emphasizes that human rights other than the right to adequate food
provide important protections to actions that are necessary or helpful in dealing with problems of hunger and malnutrition. In this section I develop and defend such an approach. This defense is not
intended to make unnecessary or undermine the weight of the right
to adequate food. I will be concerned with civil and political rights
that protect self-help (e.g., freedom of movement), that protect efforts
to publicize problems of hunger and malnutrition (e.g., freedom of
the press), that protect political action (e.g., the right to assemble
peaceably), and that protect efforts to provide hunger relief and
development assistance (e.g., the right to security against violence).

   In this section I argue that hungry and malnourished people
have a substantial interest in having their civil and political rights
respected, even in situations where their right to adequate food is
not respected and implemented. This view is controversial since it
denies the proposition often asserted by Marxists that human rights
are of little value to people without food, and since it contradicts
Henry Shue's view that it is impossible to enjoy any rights in the
absence of guarantees of the availability of food.

   Shue holds that subsistence rights are "essential to the enjoyment of all other rights."[10] If this were true it would be impossible to
enjoy the right to freedom of movement if one didn't enjoy a right to

subsistence. But I submit that it is easy to find examples that show that this is not impossible. People leaving the Texas-Oklahoma "Dustbowl" in the thirties generally enjoyed a well-respected right to freedom of movement in the absence of an effectively implemented right to adequate food. The right to freedom of movement can be widely accepted by the public and by government officials, and many threats to this right blocked by legal measures, in the absence of an effectively implemented right to food. It is certainly true that having no food assistance programs in a famine situation can make it harder to migrate since it will be difficult to acquire food for and along the journey. But "harder" doesn't mean "impossible," especially if sure starvation is the price of staying put.

Respect for civil and political rights makes more available the kinds of actions that are needed in order to confront hunger and malnutrition. In some cases these are actions taken by the hungry and malnourished themselves (e.g., moving to locations where food is more available), and in other cases these are actions taken by the political allies of the hungry and malnourished, journalists, and relief workers. By facilitating the action of various parties to address hunger and malnutrition, respect for civil and political rights promotes flexibility in dealing with the failures of key institutions and actors to fulfill their responsibilities in respect of adequate food.

It would be easiest to argue this if it could be plausibly claimed that it is impossible to perform an action unless one has a well-respected right to perform that action. But this claim is false. People often succeed in doing things in the absence of well-respected rights to do those things. For example, people are often able to organize themselves politically in the absence of respect for rights to engage in political activity and in the presence of efforts to repress political activities. Because of this we will have to rely on a weaker claim, one that says that a well-respected right to do something makes it easier and cheaper to do that kind of action, thus making it more available as a means. For example, I will argue that well-respected rights to freedom of inquiry, communication, and publication make it easier for journalists and academics to publicize problems of hunger and malnutrition. Well-respected human rights serve the interests of the hungry and malnourished by making certain useful forms of action more available.

Rights That Facilitate Self-Help by the Hungry and Malnourished   The idea that the hungry and malnourished can engage in self-help may seem implausible, but in fact hunger and malnutrition are strong stimuli to action. As I suggested earlier, it is important to avoid stereotyping all hungry people with a television image from Somalia or Sudan in which an emaciated person is lying on the ground, too weak to move, and is certain to die soon if help is not provided. This is not a representative image since millions of hungry and malnourished people survive periods of famine and starvation, and indeed live for long periods thereafter. Many of the hungry and malnourished are capable of self-help. For both practical and moral reasons it is important not to deny the capacity for action of the hungry and malnourished, even though we must recognize that the strength of this capacity is often diminished.

Actions that allow the hungry and malnourished to engage in self-help include engaging in economic activities such as working, farming, and buying and selling, and moving to locations where food or economic opportunities are more available.[11] Let's focus on the latter. During the civil war and famine in Sudan during the mideighties, over a million people fled north to Khartoum.[12] Migrants are often inconvenient and burdensome to communities along the way, but to have a right to move is to have a right to be in places where one doesn't "belong." Threats to the ability to move include roadblocks and closed borders, as well as attacks, murder, and robbery along the way. Rights that, when respected, facilitate movement in search of food or other economic opportunities include rights to freedom of movement, communication, association, and assembly, to security against violence and murder, and to freedom to leave one's country and receive asylum or temporary refuge in other countries.[13]

Rights That Facilitate Efforts to Publicize Hunger and Malnutrition   Even when the responsibility to address problems of hunger and malnutrition is recognized by politicians, governmental and nongovernmental organizations, and ordinary people, specific areas of hunger and malnutrition need to be brought to their attention. When this responsibility is not recognized or met, publicity is needed to bring domestic and international attention and pressure to bear. Sen and others have suggested that free news media can and often do play an important role in bringing episodes of famine and starvation to the attention of the public and thereby pressuring governments to act. The freedoms in question are those of both local and foreign journalists.[14]

Actions typically requisite to calling attention to problems of hunger and malnutrition include investigating, communicating, traveling, and publishing or broadcasting. Threats to these actions may include government attempts to hide or minimize problems, to exaggerate what it is doing to help, to exclude journalists, academics, and activists from the area, and to censor the print and electronic media. Harsher threats may include violence, torture, and death to persons who call public attention to hunger and malnutrition. Specific rights that protect efforts to publicize problems of hunger and malnutrition include rights to freedom of the press, to freedom of inquiry, to freedom of movement, to security against violence, torture, and murder, and due process rights that protect journalists and academics from arbitrary arrest and phony charges.

Rights That Facilitate Political Action to Reduce Hunger and Malnutrition
Here we are concerned with actions intended to bring about governmental action to address hunger and malnutrition, as well as actions intended to stimulate action by civil society—by churches, community groups, companies, and national NGOs. The possibility of calling on civil society to address hunger and malnutrition is an important dimension of the capacity to adapt to failures of governmental institutions and to changing circumstances. Programs to address hunger and malnutrition are not limited to distributions of food, but may also include literacy programs, nutritional education, and the formation of organizations and cooperatives.

The threats to political action by and on behalf of the hungry and malnourished are familiar. They include the imprisonment, torture, and murder of political activists, the suppression of organizations and meetings, and the suspension of elections that might bring to power politicians committed to helping the hungry and malnourished. Rights of political activity and participation, when respected, help to block these threats. Security and due process rights are also important since they protect people against murder, torture, and arbitrary imprisonment. As I suggested earlier, an important goal of political participation in this context is to call on governmental agencies and NGOs to take steps and create programs that will make food, work, land, and education more available to the hungry and malnourished. This is difficult for the hungry and malnourished to do, but it is more feasible when they can act together with or through their political allies. These allies may be workers parties, the Catholic church, or other political entities that have a commitment to the impoverished.

A recent popular crusade against hunger in Brazil proceeded under the name, Citizenship Action Against Misery and For Life (Ação da Cidadania contra a Miséria e pela Vida). This movement, whose leader is the sociologist Herbert De Souza, has constantly emphasized the links between ending hunger and promoting citizenship and democratic participation.[15] On this view, democracy is not just a system of government in which citizens have the responsibility to vote in periodic elections but also a system in which citizens take responsibility to address important social and environmental problems through participation in nongovernmental organizations.

This movement presupposes that it is possible for people suffering from hunger and malnutrition to participate together with their political allies in struggles to improve their prospects. It recognizes that the capacity of these people to hold and exercise rights is impaired by their harsh circumstances, but suggests that often this capacity is not so impaired that it cannot be reinvigorated. The value of civil and political liberties and rights is reduced but not eliminated by hunger and malnutrition, and this value can be reclaimed through participation and self-help.

Rights That Facilitate Efforts to Provide Hunger Relief and Development Assistance   Hungry and malnourished people have an interest in the availability of help from national and international agencies and NGOs. Actions under this heading include importing, buying, transporting, and distributing food, organizing coops and work programs, creating schools, promoting education for women and girls and for members of minority groups, and seeking government tolerance and support of their activities. Familiar threats to such activities include denial of entry, refusal to allow transportation of food and other supplies, the theft of food and relief supplies, violence against relief and development workers, and corruption in the use of relief funds and supplies. Rights that facilitate relief and development work by protecting it from these sorts of threats include rights of freedom of movement, communication, association and assembly, and due process and security rights.

The possibility of calling on national and international NGOs to provide food and development assistance increases the flexibility of a system to address hunger and malnutrition. If a national government is unwilling to act, or unable to act because of civil war, lack of organization, or severe corruption, NGOs can shoulder the responsibility of addressing people's need for adequate food and water.

Avoiding War   A concluding thought on the value of respect for civil and political rights to the hungry and malnourished is that such respect makes it more likely that negotiation and democratic processes can be used successfully to defuse conflicts that would otherwise lead to civil war. War and violent conflict are great sources of famine and malnutrition, yet the hungry and malnourished, together with their sympathizers, often have strong reasons to engage in forms of protest and agitation that risk violent repression from the defenders of the status quo. If civil and political rights are respected, and the democratic processes they presuppose are available, peaceful political activity can function as a means of both protesting and defending the status quo. Thus, there is a better chance that accommodation can be reached without resort to large scale violence.

Conclusion

Respect for internationally recognized human rights is helpful in combating hunger and malnutrition in two ways. Most directly, the human right to adequate food calls for programs to ensure the availability of adequate food and water to persons unable to provide for themselves. Indirectly, various human rights are valuable to the hungry and malnourished by making more available actions that are essential to combating hunger. These rights include freedom of movement, freedom of the press, rights of political participation, and due process and security rights. By emphasizing a variety of rights that impose responsibilities on a range of addressees, this approach has the flexibility to deal with institutional failures, irresponsibility by key parties, and dynamic situations involving war and famine.

NOTES

1. This view is suggested by a number of the essays in the earlier edition of this anthology (William Aiken and Hugh LaFollette, eds. *World Hunger and Moral Obligation.* Englewood Cliffs, NJ: Prentice-Hall, 1977). This is particularly true of the essays by Peter Singer ("Famine, Affluence, and Morality") and William Aiken ("The Right to Be Saved from Starvation"). Even the cover shows an emaciated child sitting on a plot of barren earth.

2. James W. Nickel, *Making Sense of Human Rights,* Berkeley: University of California Press, 1987. See also Ronald Dworkin, *Taking Rights Seriously,* Cambridge, MA: Harvard University Press, 1977; Alan Gewirth, *Human Rights: Essays on Justification and Applications,* Chicago: University of Chicago Press, 1987; Loren Lomasky, *Persons, Rights, and the Moral Community,* New York: Oxford University Press, 1987; L. W. Sumner, *The Moral Foundations of Rights,* New York: Oxford University Press, 1987.

3. These documents can be found in Ian Brownlie, ed. *Basic Documents on Human Rights,* Oxford: Oxford University Press, 2nd ed. 1981. They are also available in James W. Nickel, *Making Sense of Human Rights,* Berkeley: University of California Press, 1987.

4. See the sections on the relevance of municipal and international law to world hunger in Philip Alston, "International Law and the Human Right to Food," in Philip Alston and K. Tomasevski, eds. *The Right to Food,* Martinus Nijhoff, 1984:9–67. See also Philip Alston, ed., *The United Nations and Human Rights: A Critical Appraisal,* Oxford: Oxford University Press, 1992.

5. See the comprehensive survey of how human rights norms treat hunger in Philip Alston, "International Law and the Human Right to Food."

6. See the extensive discussion of this clause in Philip Alston, "International Law and the Human Right to Food."

7. See Amartya Sen, "Food, Economics, and Entitlements," vol. 1: 38, in Jean Drèze and Amartya Sen, eds. *Hunger and Public Action,* 3 volumes: vol. 1, *Entitlement and Well-being;* vol. 2, *Famine and Prevention;* and vol. 3, *Endemic Hunger,* Oxford: Oxford University Press, 1990.

8. Onora O'Neill, "Hunger, Needs, and Rights," in Steven Luper-Foy, ed. *Problems of International Justice,* Boulder, Co: Westview Press, 1988:76.

9. See James W. Nickel, "How Human Rights Generate Duties to Protect and Provide," *Human Rights Quarterly* 15 (1993):77–86.

10. Henry Shue, *Basic Rights,* Princeton: Princeton University Press, 1980: 19. For criticisms of *Basic Rights* see James W. Nickel and Lizbeth Hasse, "Review of Basic Rights," *California Law Review* 69 (1981):1569–1586.

11. Paul Kennedy emphasizes the role of emigration in coping with food shortages in the first half of the nineteenth century, particularly in Ireland. See Paul Kennedy, *Preparing for the Twenty-First Century* New York: Random House, 1993:6–13.

12. A recent article in the *New York Times* claimed that more than three million people have moved to avoid fighting and hunger in Sudan: "650,000 people are internally displaced within the southern Sudan and 2 million in the north, and 400,000 have fled to neighboring countries." "Sudan's Long Civil War Threatening to Spread," *New York Times* November 22, 1994: A3.

13. A number of provisions in contemporary human rights documents are directed to the treatment of migrants and refugees. These provisions assert rights to leave any country, to return to one's own country, and to seek and enjoy asylum from persecution.

14. See N. Ram, "An Independent Press and Anti-hunger Strategies: The Indian Experience," in Drèze and Sen, *The Political Economy of Hunger,* vol. 1: 146.

15. Most of the characterization given here is based on newspaper accounts from *Folha de Sao Paulo.* More generally, see Herbert de Souza, *Escritos Indignados,* Rio de Janeiro: IBASE, 1991, and Vera Telles, "Cultura e Cidadania: Alianca contra a Miseria," in Christiane Costa and Valdo Franca, *Alternativas Alimentares: Solucoes Nutritivas, Baratas e Regionais para Combater a Fome,* Sao Paulo: Polis, 1993.

IV. JUSTICE AND DEVELOPMENT

*Goods and People**

AMARTYA SEN

Amartya Sen is Lamont University Professor and Professor of Economics at Harvard University. His recent books include *Ethics and Economics* (Blackwell), *Hunger and Public Action* (with Jean Drèze) (Oxford), and *Inequality Reexamined* (Harvard).

1 Introduction

Hugh MacDiarmid, the Scottish poet, wrote in his *Lament for Great Music*:

The struggle for material existence is over. It has been won.
The need for repressions and disciplines have passed.
The struggle for truth and that indescribable necessity,
Beauty, begins now, hampered by none of the lower needs.
No one now needs live less or be less than his utmost.[1]

While the necessity 'to live less or be less than his utmost' may indeed be over in some special sense, the tragic fact remains that the lives of most people of the world fall very far short of that ideal. In contrast with the expectation of life at birth of around the middle seventies in the rich countries, more than two-thirds of the "low-income" countries have life expectancy below 50 years.[2] The majority of people of the world do not have access to regular medical and hospital services, or to the security of safe water. Literacy rates are still shockingly low in most low-income countries. Even in the

*Reprinted by permission of the publishers from RESOURCES, VALUES, AND DEVELOPMENT by Amartya Sen, Cambridge, Mass.: Harvard University Press, Copyright ©1984 by Amartya Sen.

rich countries the relatively impoverished have to live a very constrained life in many respects.3 For a large part of the population of this globe there is no escape from the need to "live less or be less"–a great deal less–than their "utmost."

This paper is concerned with some foundational issues in development analysis. It is argued here that the process of economic development is best seen as an expansion of people's 'capabilities'. This approach focuses on what people can *do* or can *be*, and development is seen as a process of emancipation from the enforced necessity to 'live less or be less'. The capabilities approach relates to, but fundamentally differs from, characterizing development as either (1) expansion of *goods and services*, or (2) increase in *utilities*, or (3) meeting *basic needs*. These contrasts are taken up first in the next three sections.

Another foundational issue concerns understanding the process of economic expansion and structural change through which capabilities can be expanded. This involves focusing on the 'entitlements' of people, representing the command of households over commodity bundles. These issues are briefly discussed in Sections 5 and 6. That question also requires us to look into the *use* of entitlements and the factors governing it, e.g., division of commodities within the family, use of commodities to generate capabilities. The *conversion* of entitlements into capabilities raises many difficult economic and social problems, a few of which are takenup in Section 7.

In Section 8 the so-called "world food problem" is discussed in the light of the approach of *capabilities*, and related to it, *entitlements* and *conversion*. The paper ends with some "Concluding Remarks" (Section 9).

2 Commodities and Capabilities

It is not uncommon to think of economic development as expansion of the availability of goods and services in the country in question. The focus on the growth of GNP per head is an especially simple version of that general approach. There are some obvious merits in taking that approach. It is, for example, a good antidote to the temptation to build castles in the air–overlooking the commodity basis of prosperity.

But while goods and services are valuable, they are not valuable in themselves. Their value rests on what they can do for people, or rather, what people can do with these goods and services.4 This question is an important one to emphasize because 'commodity fetishism'—to borrow an expression from Marx (1887)—is a widespread phenomenon, and the important role that the exchange of commodities plays in modern society tends to sustain that fetishism.

If the capabilities of each person were uniquely (and positively) related to the national availability of goods and services, then there would have been perhaps no great harm in focusing on the total supply of goods and services. But that assumption is a nonstarter. There is not only the problem of the division of the national output between families and individuals,[5] but also the fact that the conversion of commodities into capabilities varies enormously with a number of parameters, e.g. age, sex, health, social relations, class background, education, ideology, and a variety of other interrelated factors.

Take the case of food and nutrition. The nutrition of people depends not merely on the availability of food per head in the community, but also on distribution considerations, on the one hand, and on the other on such factors as (i) the person's age and sex (and if a woman, whether pregnant or lactating); (ii) metabolic rates and body size; (iii) activity levels; (iv) medical conditions (including presence or absence of stomach parasites); (v) climatic conditions; (vi) the social needs of entertainment and communal relations (including offering and partaking of food); (vii) education in general, and in particular, knowledge of nutritional and health matters; (viii) access to medical services and the ability to use them, and so on. The capability of a person to be well nourished cannot be identified or linked in a straightforward way with the national supply of food, or even with his or her own individual access to food. The object of the exercise in dealing with the "food problem" is to expand the ability to be well nourished and also to expand other related capabilities such as eliminating hunger, enjoying food and social intercourse, and so on. To focus on food as such without looking beyond would be a mistake.

The same applies to commodities in general. Development is not a matter, ultimately, of expanding supplies of commodities, but of enhancing the capabilities of people. The former has importance only in an instrumental and strongly contingent way, traceable to the real importance of the latter.

3 Capabilities and Utilities

It might be tempting to think that the above line of reasoning must lead to focusing on utilities as the standard of value, which is what traditional welfare economics tend to do. But confining attention to utilities amounts to seeing people in a highly limited way. Happiness or desire-fulfilment represents only one aspect of human existence. It can be argued that capabilities are valued ultimately because they reflect freedom, including, *inter alia*, the freedom to achieve happiness. It is a question of the command that people have over their lives.[6] Hunger, starvation, and famines are awful social phenomena not just because they cause disutility. An elementary failure of freedom is involved in this, and we do not judge the seriousness of the situation by the precise extent of the unhappiness, or dissatisfaction.

It is inevitable that on a fundamental subject like this there would be differences of approach. It is not my purpose in this essay to present detailed arguments as to why the utilitarian basis of traditional welfare economics is fundamentally flawed. I have discussed this question more extensively elsewhere,[7] and will not further pursue the debate here. But there is a practical issue related to this question that has not been much discussed in the literature and which happens to be very important in evaluating and assessing development and structural change. Judging importance by the mental metric of happiness or desire-fulfillment can take a deeply biased form due to the fact that the mental reactions often reflect defeatist compromises with harsh reality induced by hopelessness. The insecure sharecropper, the exploited landless laborer, the overworked domestic servant, the subordinate housewife, may all come to terms with their respective predicaments in such a way that grievance and discontent are submerged in cheerful endurance by the necessity of uneventful survival.[8] The hopeless underdog loses the courage to desire a better deal and learns to take pleasure in small mercies. The deprivations appear muffled and muted in the metric of utilities.

In such situations discontent and disutility, instead of being tragic outcomes (as in utilitarian assessment), would have constituted a positive assertion of creative potentiality. Since economic development has much to do with making structural changes to conquer the inequities and exploitations that characterize the world, the importance of questioning the utilitarian method of accounting cannot be overemphasized.

The ability to achieve happiness is, of course, of importance on its own, and it can certainly be seen as one of many capabilities of relevance to development. The difference with utilitarianism arises in the insistence of the latter that everything—including all other capabilities—be judged exclusively in the metric of utilities. Judging the importance of anything is thus identified with measuring the utilities associated with it. Removal of starvation, poverty, inequity, exploitation, illiteracy, and other deprivations, is seen as unimportant in itself and rendered important only if—and to the extent that—there is a net utility gain through that removal. It is this utility-based narrow vision of traditional welfare economics that is fundamentally inadequate as a basis for evaluating action and policy, in general, and development and structural change, in particular.

4 Capabilities and Basic Needs

The approach of meeting "basic needs,"[9] which has played an important part in recent literature on economic development, has some similarities with the capabilities approach. As Paul Streeten (1981) has pointed out, "the basic needs concept is a reminder that the objective of the development effort is to provide all human beings with the *opportunity* for a full life" (p. 21). It involves the rejection of both utility-based welfare economics and commodity-based growth calculus. These characteristics are shared by the basic needs approach with the capabilities approach, and more specifically the focus on "nutrition, health, shelter, water and sanitation, education, and other essentials" in the basic needs approach makes it directly concerned with a number of important capabilities.

There are, however, significant differences as well. First, the "basic needs" are defined in terms of commodities (in Streeten's (1981) words, "particular goods and services required to achieve certain results"), even though attention is paid to differences in the commodities needed by different persons to satisfy the same human requirements. Thus the focus remains on commodities even though the contingent nature of commodity requirements is fully acknowledged. Often commodity requirements may not be at all derivable from a specified set of capabilities, since the relation between commodity bundles and capability bundles may quite plausibly be a *many-one* correspondence, with the same capabilities being achievable by more than one particular bundle of goods and services. (For example, different combinations of food and health services may produce the same level of nutrition.) Operating on the commodity space rather than directly on the space of capabilities involves additional problems.

Second, the commodity requirements for specific capabilities may not be independently decidable for each person, due to social interdependence. For example, such capabilities as the ability to appear in public without shame (discussed by Adam Smith, 1776), or taking part in the life of the community (discussed by Peter Townsend, 1979), depends on the consumption of others. This has not merely the consequence that *absolute* deprivation in capabilities may take the form of *relative* deprivation in terms of commodities and incomes (see Sen, 1983a), but also that the needs of commodities may not be absolutely specifiable at all.

Third, basic needs are "interpreted in terms of *minimum* speci-fied quantities" of particular commodities, and the implicit frame-work is that of reaching a *minimum* level of capabilities (see Streeten, 1981, pp. 25–26). The capability approach, in contrast, is not con-fined to that use only, and indeed can be used for judging individual "advantage" at any level.[10] In this sense the basic needs approach involves one particular application of the capabilities framework. The capabilities approach is applicable in judging advantage and depri-vation in rich countries as well as poor ones (Sen, 1983a), and it can also be used for such other purposes as judging the real extent of inequality (Sen, 1980).

Fourth, "needs" is a more passive concept than "capability," and it is arguable that the perspective of positive freedom links natural-ly with capabilities (what can the person *do*?) rather than with the fulfillment of their needs (what can be *done for* the person?). The per-spective of fulfilling needs has some obvious advantages in dealing with dependents (e.g., children), but for responsible adults the for-mat of capabilities may be much more suitable in seeing what is involved and in linking it with the issue of freedom. This distinction is really a matter of outlook and emphasis, but it can be quite impor-tant in analyzing general objectives of development.

The controversies on the use of the basic needs approach has tended to be concerned with strategic issues rather than with foun-dational ones. It has, for example, been argued that concentrating on basic needs may interfere with building a solid material basis of eco-nomic prosperity. However, economic prosperity is not sought for its own sake, and the concern with it can be seen to be based ultimate-ly on worry about capabilities in the future, which might not be achievable in the absence of economic expansion. The debate can thus be cast in terms of the conflicts between immediately enhanc-ing capabilities now (reflected in meeting *basic needs*) and long-term expansion of capabilities in the future (*through* economic prosperity). Thus analyzed, the debate can be seen to be of the traditional form— familiar in the literature on planning[11]—of capabilities now *versus* a bigger expansion of capabilities in the future. Though the object of value is changed here from the traditional concentration on utilities (utilities now versus more utilities later), the intertemporal conflict must be seen to be of the familiar type.

Another criticism of the basic needs approach arises from the worry that a concentration on just the minimum requirements may lead to a softening of the opposition to inequality in general. "Minimum needs and no more" is a familiar—and unfair—caricature. But if the basic needs approach is seen as just one application of the capabilities approach, it would be clear that other issues related to capabilities (including that of the *equality* of capabilities, see Sen, 1980), is not prejudiced by the special concern with basic needs at a certain stage of development.

What is needed is to take the basic needs approach out of the arbitrarily narrow box into which it seems to have got confined. To see it as just one part of the capabilities approach—to which it is motivationally linked—would do just that. All the standard issues of efficiency, equality, etc. can be seen as arising within the capabilities approach.[12] (The contribution of that approach is mainly to make the metric of advantage and achievement avoid both the fetishism of the commodity focus and the subjectivism of the utility focus, rather than to lead to undue concentration on minimality or immediacy.) The basic needs approach would cease to appear one-sided and distracting if it is seen to be a part of a more general approach and if that recognition is allowed to have its due impact in policy formulation.

5 Entitlements, Famines, and Hunger

The capabilities of persons depend, among other things, on the bundles of commodities over which they can establish command. In each society there are rules that govern who can have the use of what, and people pursue their respective objectives subject to these rules. For example, in a private ownership economy, use depends on ownership and exchange. The set of all bundles of commodities from which a person can choose one bundle can be called the person's "entitlement."[13]

To illustrate, suppose person i owns initially 20 units of commodity 1 and 30 units of commodity 2. This can be called his endowment vector. He can stick to that bundle if he so chooses, but he can also exchange that bundle into another through trade or production. Any other bundle of goods that would cost no more than what 20 units of commodity 1 and 30 units of commodity 2 would fetch in the market is included in his entitlement set. So is every other bundle within that budget constraint. And so are other bundles that he can acquire through production ('exchange with nature'), or a mixture of production and trade. The trade and production possibilities are summarized by an 'exchange entitlement mapping,' which specifies, for each endowment bundle, all the different bundles any one of which he can command (e.g., through the use of trade or production).[14] A person's endowment vector and the exchange entitlement mapping together determine his over-all entitlement, representing the actual opportunity of acquiring commodity bundles in his particular situation.

The entitlement of a person also includes what can be obtained through claims against the state, e.g. the entitlement to unemployment benefit (if the person fails to find a job), or to social subsidy (if his income falls below a certain minimum figure). In many economies these entitlements are substantial enough to provide a person with a good deal of security, but in others they are tiny or just absent. In situations of distress, e.g., a slump, the existence of such claims against the state might well be vital for survival.

The entitlement approach concentrates on relating a person's or a household's actual command over goods and services to the rules of entitlement in that system and the person's or household's actual position in the system (e.g., the initial ownership or endowment). This way of approaching the issue contrasts with approaches that avoid the question of command by making some general assumption about the overall availability of goods for distribution among the population. This includes theories (such as Malthusian population theory) that concentrate on average food output per head as the key indicator determining famines and other disasters,[15] as well as those that explicitly assume a given unequal pattern of distribution without going into the causation of that distribution. Since these distributions have been known to change sharply over a short period (and not only over the longer run), the case for a causal analysis of the type demanded by the entitlement approach seems to be strong.

Whether a person is able to establish command over, say, enough food to avoid starvation depends on the nature of the entitlement system operating in the economy in question and on the person's own position in that society. Even when the overall ratio of food to population is high, particular occupation groups can perish because of their inability to establish command over enough food. To see the food problem in terms of, say, the Malthusian focus on food output or supply per head can be a deadly mistake—literally so.[16]

To illustrate this point, I shall make brief references to a number of particular experiences of hunger and famine in the modern world, based on some of the detailed case studies that I have presented elsewhere (Sen, 1981a; see also Essay 18 in this volume).

(1) In the Great Bengal Famine of 1943, in which about 3 million people died, food availability per unit of population was not particularly low and was, in fact, about 9 per cent higher than in 1941 when there was no famine. The famine victims (e.g., landless rural labourers, fishermen) suffered a drastic decline in their market entitlements due to their wages and money earnings not keeping up with the rise in food prices, resulting from demand-fed inflationary pressure in a war-boom economy (with urban expansion being supplemented by exclusively urban food rationing at controlled prices, largely insulating urban purchasers from the rise in food prices in the rest of the economy).[17]

(2) During the Ethiopian famine in Wollo of 1972, the food availability per head in Ethiopia as a whole was normal. Though the food output in Wollo itself was much lower due to drought, food did not move much into Wollo from elsewhere in the country, and some food actually moved *out* of Wollo, which experienced a famine with largely stationary prices (since the ability of the Wollo population to buy food had fallen along with the decline of agricultural output).[18]

(3) In the Ethiopian famine in Harerghe in 1974, the most-affected victim-group, viz. the pastoralists, were hit not merely by the loss of animals due to drought, but also—quantitatively more importantly—by the change in the relative prices of animals and animal products vis-à-vis foodgrains, which affected their basis of subsistence in the form of selling animals and animal products to buy normally cheaper calories in foodgrains. The market mechanism played a decimating role in this famine, through the general fall in incomes (agricultural and pastoral) making consumers shift from richer animal products to basic foodgrains, driving up the relative price of the latter.[19]

(4) In the Bangladesh famine in 1974 the food availability per head was higher than in any other year during 1971–75. Rural labourers were affected by the loss of employment due to floods, which later affected output to be harvested, but which had an immediate and devastating impact on the entitlement of the wage laborers. Rise in rice prices due to general inflationary pressure also made the market entitlements go down.[20]

The cases of famines bring out dramatically the importance of variations of entitlements in matters of life and death—a role that cannot be taken over by such variables as the index of food availability or of food output per head. The relevance of entitlements is, however, much more pervasive than might appear from these examples. For example, in determining the causation of endemic malnutrition in many developing economies, such as India, the entitlement system provides a helpful format for analysing the mechanism of the failure to establish command over an adequate bundle of food on the part of many occupation groups. For example, for landless labourers the only endowment worth the name is labour power, and their fortunes depend crucially on the working of the labour market. For sharecroppers, in contrast, there is also the issue of the right to cultivate the land in question, and the substance of entitlements related to it depends on the legal and practical status of that right and the economic circumstances governing them.

6 Incomes and Entitlements

Since food is bought and sold in the market in a straightforward way, and since much of the income of the poor is expended on food, it may be helpful to see the entitlement to food in terms of *incomes*. Indeed, it has become quite widely recognized in recent years that hunger is very often caused by shortage of incomes rather than by the over-all shortage of food. This rather simple way of seeing the entitlement problem is a bit incomplete since income has to be earned and the causes of the inability to earn enough income would have to be studied, investigating endowments (including labor power) and exchange possibilities (including employment and wages). Nevertheless the level of income is a crucial variable in understanding the entitlement to food and can be treated as such without losing the essentials of a more complete approach.

The commanding power of incomes depends, naturally, on prices, and as such we have to look at some notion of "real income" (that is, corrected for prices). The real income is, of course, a weight-based index, and much depends on what weights are chosen. In dealing with food command in distress situations it may be appropriate to put a greater weight on food, and indeed in some contexts it is useful to get a straightforward estimate of the total amount of food command if all income were expended on food.[21] Since the weight of food is in any case very high in the budget of the poor in the developing countries, the issue of weighting is not such a complex one in dealing specifically with the entitlement to food in that context.

However, for other goods and services (e.g., education, health services, transport), real income may provide quite a distant way of viewing entitlement. The expenditure on these commodities may not be a large part of the total budget so that their weight on the price index may be relatively small. A change in the price or availability of these goods and services may not thus be strongly reflected in the real-income index. Further the existence of quantity restrictions make the income-based view very opaque. If there is no hospital in the neighborhood or no school within easy reach—or if there are hospitals and schools but with highly limited capacity—the income of the would-be purchaser may not give much of an idea as to whether the person can or cannot acquire these commodities.

Entitlements have to be studied in a more elaborate way in these cases and the short-cut of making do with an income-based picture will give little clue as to what people can or cannot acquire. In examining the enormous differences in the access to health services, medicine, education, etc., in different poor countries, the approach of entitlement has to be more fully applied (see Sen, 1983c).

This problem may not be very serious for the *entitlement to food*, but it can be nevertheless extremely serious for the *capability to be well nourished*, which—as was discussed earlier—is the real concern in being interested in the entitlement to food. The capability to be well nourished depends, among other things, on the medical condition of the people (e.g., the presence or absence of parasitic diseases in the stomach),[22] and it depends also on nutritional education and knowledge. The entitlements to these other goods and services (e.g., health and educational services) are not well approximated by over-all indices of real income. Thus, when it comes to the capability to be well nourished, income ceases to be an adequate parameter of analysis, and considerations of food entitlement have to be supple-mented by those of entitlements to complementary goods and ser-vices. This is an important qualification to bear in mind while applauding the fact that in recent years the importance of income shortage in hunger has—rightly—come to be widely recognized.

7 Intra-family Distribution and Capabilities

Capability to be nourished, as was argued in the last section, is not a matter of entitlement to food only, but depends also on entitle-ments to other goods and services such as health services, medicine, and education. In fact, even when the entitlements to all these com-modities have been fully taken into account, there remain other sources of variation of the capability to be nourished, as was dis-cussed in Section 2.

One issue concerns the distribution of food and other com-modities *within* the family. While we have been talking of entitle-ments of *persons*, the usual procedures of production and exchange apply to *households* only, with the distribution within the household being determined by other procedures.[23] It is the entitlements of households that have to be then translated into actual consumption of members of the household. There is a good deal of evidence that in poor countries in different parts of the world, food is often dis-tributed very unequally within the family (see, for example, the sur-veys by den Hartog (1973) and Schofield (1975)).

An important difficulty in studying this problem arises from the fact that the relationship between consumption of food and capabil-ity to be well nourished varies with age, sex, activity level, pregnan-cy, lactation, and other variables. For example, an observed lower intake of food by women vis-à-vis men has often not been taken as evidence of sex bias, on the ground that the calorie requirements of men are also higher. However, the so-called "calorie requirements" specified by the FAO/WHO Expert Committee (1973) are extremely arbitrary both in general methodology (relying simply on body size and activity level) and in the particular way activity levels are speci-fied (especially underestimating the energy use in home-based work).[24] The fact that the lower food intake of women may appear to be more than counterbalanced by the lower "requirements" of women is thus not as definitive evidence of the absence of anti–female bias in household allocation as it has sometimes been taken to be.

In fact, as was argued in the context of discussing the "basic needs" approach (Section 4), the idea of commodity "requirements" for particular "capabilities" is itself unsustainable. There are possibilities of "multiple equilibria" of energy and work, and also considerable variations in these relations between one person and another.[25] There are "many-one" correspondences between commodity bundles (food, health, education, etc.) and nutritional levels. The simple formulas of "requirements" are less scientific than they might look, and they have sometimes simply helped to justify systematic biases in the treatment of different groups, such as men and women.

In judging the well-being of different groups and the deal they get in the society, it would be more sensible to go directly towards observing achievements rather than commodity consumption. For example, it is more sensible to look for medical signs of undernourishment and nutrition-related morbidity and mortality, than to estimate, first, personal food intake, and then, see how that relates to the assumed requirements.

In terms of the capabilities approach, observing morbidity or undernourishment is clearly the right direction to go, since our ultimate concern is not with who eats how much, but largely with the capabilities of nourishment that the persons in question enjoy. Two objections can, however, be raised. First, the capabilities can be difficult to measure, and it can be argued that they are not as straightforward as intakes of food. This is, up to a point, a sustainable objection. However, observational problems in ascertaining who eats how much are also very serious. To get accurate data on the intake of calories and other nutrients of each member of the family, it would be necessary not only to *see* who is eating how much in a family meal, but also to *weigh* exactly all the food items consumed by each, and it is a little difficult to assume that the eating activities would be unaffected by such interference. Ascertaining nutritional characteristics and getting morbidity and mortality data may be a *relatively* simpler operation.[26]

The second objection takes the form of pointing out that observing nutritional characteristics may not tell us much about inequalities in the distribution of food. That is indeed so, but since ultimately interest in food consumption largely rests in its effects on nutrition and its consequences, the loss may not be very great.[27] The essence of the capabilities approach is to see commodity consumption as no more than a means to generating capabilities, and if the capabilities and their use can be directly ascertained, the absence of detailed information on commodity consumption may not be much regretted.

It should be conceded that when dealing with less elementary capabilities than the ability to be well nourished, the observational problems may be more serious. Indeed, it will sometimes be the case that commodity inputs may be much easier to observe than capabilities and their use, and there may then be some practical advantage in using adjusted commodity data as "proxy" for capabilities (see Sen, 1983b). However, that is a tactical issue and does not overturn the basic fact that it is capabilities that we are interested in, and even in these cases, observing commodity consumption would be motivated by treating it as a possibly convenient indicator of capabilities.

The importance of entitlements rests in the role they play in the determination of capabilities. From the point of view of policy this role can be sometimes crucial, and in dealing with such extreme problems as famines, an almost exclusive concentration on entitlements and their variations may sometimes make sense. On the other hand, in dealing with less extreme problems, e.g., endemic malnutrition, high morbidity and mortality, it is important to remember that entitlements constitute no more than one part of the story. It is, to be sure, a part that undoubtedly deserves serious attention, especially in dealing with policy issues related to land reform, employment policy, social security, food for work programmes, etc., but the incompleteness of the entitlement picture has to be kept in view for a more comprehensive attack on deprivation (and on the enforced necessity of people to "live less or be less" than what society can organize).

8 Remarks on the Food Problem

Malthusian pessimism has had a great revival in recent decades, and the so-called "world food problem" has become a subject of great concern. Model-based reasoning has outlined various scenarios of collapse of "material existence" on this planet,[28] and the prospect of worldwide starvation has been forcefully portrayed. These analyzes have had a great impact on the way the food problem and the future of the world are viewed by the general public, fed by hair-raising reports in the media, blowing up and distorting the pronouncements of specialist experts. As I write this paper, *The Times* of Friday, 17, June, 1983, reports under the eye-catching heading, 'Starvation Threat to 65 Nations": "More than half of the world's developing nations will be unable to feed their people by the end of this century, according to a United Nations survey, published today.' We are told: "Data about soils and climate in 117 lands was fed into a complex computer program to produce the "grim conclusion," according to the UN Fund for Population Activities which sponsored the survey in collaboration with the UN Food and Agriculture Organisation" (p. 5).

It is right that worries about the economic future of the world should engage serious attention. However, serious attention has not typically confirmed the pessimism. Models of collapse are not, of course, difficult to construct (with or without 'a complex computer program'!). But most of the serious studies of long-run prognostication (including the FAO report *allegedly* summarized by *The Times*) have not prophezied such a coming doom, and have indicated much greater scope for decisive policy response.[29] There are obvious scopes for disagreement on various assumptions used in these models, but the case for Malthusian pessimism looks far from plausible.

The neo-Malthusian resurgence does, in fact, seriously misguide economic thinking in two important ways. First, by focusing on such misleading variables as food output per unit of population, the Malthusian approach profoundly misspecifies the problems facing the poor in the world, as was discussed in Section 5 above. The question of entitlements in general and food entitlements in particular get submerged in the crude picture of supply and availability. It is often overlooked that what may be called 'Malthusian optimism' has actually killed millions of people. Focusing attention on the Malthusian variable of food output per head, the food situation has often appeared to be comfortable even when there have been good economic grounds for expecting terrible troubles for particular occupational groups, and in such circumstances public policy based on smugness (related to food output per head) has tended to permit the development of a widespread famine when it could have been easily averted.

Second, by concentrating attention on the alleged long-run decline in the future, neo-Malthusianism distracts attention from the already existing sufferings and miseries in the world. The need for a positive advance gets overshadowed by an imagined need for countering a hypothetical future decline. The real problem is not that the world will *turn* beastly, but that it *is* beastly already; and it has been so throughout history, with human life being nasty, brutish, and short.

Food output per head has been steadily rising in the world as a whole. It has, however, been falling in particular countries, most of them in parts of Africa. In itself this is not a pointer to disaster. Not every country has to grow all the food it eats—many of the rich ones (e.g., Britain) do not. The real problem is that the decline in food output per head in many of these countries is going hand in hand with a decline in real income per head, and the entitlement to food is also slipping for many of the occupational groups in these countries. Such an occurrence can and does take place in many countries through the decline of *other* economic variables such as nonfood crops, industrial output and employment, and mining activities. What is really worrying about the so-called "African food problem" is this decline in economic power to *command* goods and services, especially food. The fact that in many of these countries this economic decline is associated with a decline in food output per head is not *in itself* of overwhelming significance.

This way of looking at the problem in terms of entitlements also suggests that in deciding on policy response there is no *a priori* reason to pursue expansion of food output only, and it is rather a matter of deciding what type of economic expansion would lead to a steady rise of real income in general and that for poor and vulnerable groups in particular. The seriousness of the problem of survival and nutrition should not turn us all into Physiocrats.

The question of food output is, however, of importance in itself in two particular respects, within the entitlement approach. First, the relative prices of food will depend on the supply, and if there is a decline in the world food output this would be reflected in prices being higher than what would have otherwise been the case. But this line of reasoning points not to the necessity that every country should grow its own food, but that the world supply should keep in line with world demand, which is a very different type of requirement. Indeed, given the fact that incomes are rising in many poor countries leading to an increase in food consumption per head, the issue of demand and supply calls for a substantially *faster* rate of expansion of food output in the world than the growth of population.

The second direct role of food output as such relates to the fact that given inefficiencies and the uncertainties of the market mechanism, particular occupation groups may be safer by growing their own food than by depending on income from other sources.[30] This is a matter of economic judgment, and the issue once again is not the size of food output as such but the minimum food command that vulnerable groups might be able to secure.[31]

The question of food entitlements represents one side of the food problem, and in this, food production has an important, though contingent, role. But as was argued earlier, the capability to be well nourished does not depend on food entitlement only. There is also the question of entitlement to complementary goods and services such as health services and education, and furthermore the problem of distribution of food within the family. The success of some countries in eliminating endemic malnutrition and the related morbidities and mortality (e.g., China and Sri Lanka) has been based on a policy package in which a more equal access to food has been supplemented by widespread access to health services and elementary education. Policies of free or subsidized food distribution have been supplemented by an active public policy of health and education. I have discussed these questions elsewhere (Sen, 1981c, 1983c), and here I shall only note that on the basis of these policies China and Sri Lanka have been able to achieve levels of health and longevity that are much higher than in countries with comparable GNP per head (such as Pakistan or India), and at least as high as many countries that are many times richer in terms of GNP per head (such as Brazil or Mexico).

The part of the food policy that is most difficult to deal with concerns the issue of distribution of food within the family. Evidence of a systematic bias against women, and even against girls vis-à-vis boys, is quite strong in many developing countries, especially in Asia.[32] This applies to observed differences in capability failure with respect to nutrition,[33] and seems also to relate to the fact that despite the biological advantages of the female in survival, in many of these countries women have lower longevity (and higher mortality at most ages).

The problem is particularly acute in Asia. It is interesting to note that while the ratio of female to male population is 1.02 in Africa and 1.05 in Europe and North America, that ratio is 0.99 in Latin America, 0.96 in East Asia (including China), 0.96 in Southwest Asia, and 0.93 in South Asia (including India).[34] There are a number of complex causal factors in this contrast, but the relative neglect of the female in intrafamily distribution (involving both food and health services) is possibly an important influence.[35] Just as there might be a special "African food problem," with persistent production problems, there might even be a peculiarly "Asian food problem," involving intra-family biases in the distribution of food (and of complementary goods and services).[36]

The policy issues related to this Asian food problem are very complex, since changing the modes of family behavior is no mean task. The role of education, especially *political* education, is important in the long-run solution of the problem, as is the question of female employment and economic power.[37] In the short run there might be considerable scope for reducing the extent of the discrimination against little girls through supplementary feeding of children in direct nutritional intervention (through school meals and other programs of public feeding of children). There is, in fact, some evidence that such intervention might reduce the excess female undernourishment and morbidity, aside from reducing undernourishment in general.[38]

There is no one "world food problem." There are many distinct–though interrelated–problems of food entitlement and the capability to be nourished. The policy issues include, among others:

(1) generating and guaranteeing entitlement to food of households in different occupational groups (involving not merely issues of food production, but also of income security, employment policy, public distribution, land reform, and related structural changes in the economy).

(2) generating and guaranteeing entitlement to complementary goods and services (especially health services and education, possibly through public policy).

(3) working towards the elimination of biases against women and children where they exist (involving long-run economic, political, and social change, and in the short-run possibly various types of feeding programs, especially of children).

9 Concluding Remarks

In this paper there has been an attempt to discuss the case for, and the implications of, seeing development as expansion of capabilities of people. This perspective differs from taking a commodity-centred view, of which concentration on GNP and its growth rate is an especially simple case (Section 2). It also involves the rejection of a utility-based view, common in welfare economics (Section 3). Further, it differs from the "basic needs" approach, though it facilitates seeing that approach in a wider perspective (Section 4). It is important to go into these foundational issues for understanding and analyzing the requirements of development, including the nature of the structural changes that are called for.

The generation of capabilities relates to entitlements, in the form of command over goods and services. Economic analyses based on such gross variables as food availability per head, or GNP per head, can be very misleading in understanding starvation and hunger, and deprivation in general. Entitlement systems and the positions of particular occupational groups in such systems deserve careful analysis (Section 5).

While *income* is a good intermediate variable in studying food entitlement, it often provides an unhelpful perspective in dealing with entitlements to other goods and services, including those complementary to food. It can also be very misleading as a basis for causal analysis of nutritional differences (Section 6).

The problem of distribution of food within the household raises a particularly complex set of questions. Given the firm evidence of sex bias in some parts of the world, especially in much of Asia, the policy issues can be particularly serious. Sex bias is best analyzed in terms of differences of capabilities and nutritional achievements rather than in terms of differences in consumption (including food intake). The former relates better to the ultimate objectives and it also avoids the absurdly difficult problem of observing individual consumption in a joint family meal (Section 7).

While the "world food problem" has attracted, in recent decades a lot of attention the nature of the difficulties has often been mis-specified. There are several distinct 'food problems' that require sep-arate, but not independent, analysis. Some remarks have been made on these problems (Section 8), including that of food entitlements, entitlements of complementary goods and services (such as health services, medicine and education), and conversion of household enti-tlements into personal capabilities (including the important problem of distribution within the family).

The process of development is not primarily one of expanding the supply of goods and services but of enhancing the capabilities of people. Focusing on capabilities forces us to see the theoretical ques-tions and policy issues in a particular light. There is a need to pay specific attention to the generation and security of entitlements and their conversion into capabilities. Some of the underlying policy issues are as complex as the basic approach is simple. That, of course, is not unusual in economics.

NOTES

1. Hugh MacDiarmid, 1967. *Collected Poems* London: MacGibbon & Kee.

2. *World Development Report 1982*, Table 21. The "low-income" coun-tries are defined as those with GNP per head less than $410. See also Singer and Ansari (1977), Grant (1978), and Morris (1979).

3. See, for example, Jencks (1972), Atkinson (1975), Beckerman (1979), Townsend (1979). Paper presented at the opening Plenary Session of the Seventh World Congress of the International Economic Association, Madrid, 1983.

4. Arguments for focusing on "capabilities" in analyzing well-being, equality, living standard, and positive freedom have been presented in Sen (1979a, 1980, 1982a, 1983b). The capabilities approach can be traced back at least to Adam Smith and Marx, as is discussed in Sen (1983a, 1983b).

5. The distributional question raises interesting problems in the char-acterization of real national income; see Sen (1976b).

6. The roots of this approach go back at least to Smith (1776) and Marx (1887).

7. See Sen (1970, 1979a, 1979b, 1982b). See also Rawls (1971), Williams (1973) and Sen and Williams (1982). For defenses of the utility-based approach, see Ng (1981) and the papers by Hare, Haranyi, and Mirrless in Sen and Williams (1982), in which you also see the antiutilitarian arguments presented by Dasgupta, Elster, Hahn, Hammond, Hampshire, Rawls, Scanlon, Taylor, and others.

8. See Sen (1981b, 1982c), Crocker in this volume, and Eister (1982).

9. See Pant and colleagues (1962), Haq (1976), Herrera and colleagues (1976), ILO (1976), Ghai and colleagues (1977), Griffin (1978), Streeten and Burki (1978), Chichilnisky (1980), Streeten (1981), for various ways of characterizing basic needs.

10. This can be done through vector comparisons (yielding a partial order) or through weighting and indexing (leading to a more complete ordering). The underlying technical issues as well as some empirical problems are discussed in my forthcoming monograph *Commodities and Capabilities*, Hennipman Lecture, Sen (1983b).

11. See Chakravarty (1970), Heal (1973), Dasgupta (1982).

12. This includes problems of incentives and the conflicts between efficiency and equality. How important these conflicts are is an empirical question that is both important and complex and this question has to be faced just as much within the capabilities approach as under the more traditional approaches.

13. The concept of entitlements has been more fully presented, explored, and used for analysis in Sen (1977b, 1981a). See also Arrow (1982).

14. Formally, if x is a person's endowment vector and $f(*)$ a net-valued function specifying for each endowment vector a set of vectors over which he can establish command, then $f(x)$ is the person's endowment set. The characteristic of the exchange entitlement mapping $f(*)$ in different economic systems and circumstances have been explored in Appendices A and B in Sen (1981a).

15. Malthus (1798). However, see also Malthus (1800), in which he outlines an entitlement system, albeit in a rudimentary form; on this see Sen (1981a), pp. 174–179.

16. On related issues, see Aziz (1975, 1982), Taylor (1975), Lipton (1977), Griffin (1978), Sinha and Drabek (1978), Ghose (1979), Parikh and Rabar (1982), Oughton (1982), Srinivamn (1982), Ravallion (1983).

17. See Sen (1981a, Chapter 6). There were other factors supplementing this picture, for example, powerful speculative rises in food prices partly engineered by a few traders, and totally inept government policy adding to panic rather than providing relief.

18. See Sen (1981a, Chapter 7). Food "counter-movement," that is, food moving *out of* the famine areas, has also been observed in other famines, for example, the Irish famines of 1840s and the Bangladesh famine of 1974. It is characteristic of certain types of famines in which the effective demand falls more than the supply of food (Sen, 1981a, pp. 160–162).

19. See Sen (1981a, Chapter 7). The market-oriented development of commercial agriculture also contributed to the decline by affecting the availability of good grazing grounds for the Ethiopian pastoralists to use.

20. See Sen (1981a, Chapter 9). See also Alamgir (1980); also Islam (1977). A further adverse development was the decision of the

United States government to discontinue food aid to Bangladesh (because of Bangladesh's trade with Cuba) precisely when it was most needed—with a famine threatening and food stocks in the public distribution system being very low (on this see McHenry and Bird, 1977, and Sobhan, 1979). The introduction of public relief, creating entitlements against the state, was delayed crucially as a result.

21. See Sen (1981a, pp. 63–70, 104–111, 145–150).

22. See, for example, Scrimashaw (1977).

23. The theory that argues that nonmarket transactions can be fruitfully seen in terms of *as if* market exchanges has a long way to go to be convincing either in theory or in empirical application, even though it has provided some useful insights on some particular issues (see Becker, 1981).

24. See Chen, Huq, and D'Souza (1980) and Sen (1981c), among others.

25. See Sukhatme (1977), Davidson, Passmore, Brock, and Truswell (1979), and Srinivasan (1982).

26. It should, however, be emphasized that assessing capability, which represents a set of possibilities, is not identical with assessing the actual use that is made of the capabilities, reflected in the particular outcome. In the case of avoiding serious undernourishment or high morbidity or mortality, the problem may be less difficult than it is in other cases. On this general question, see Sen (1983b).

27. Note, however, the ability to enjoy consuming food or using it for various social purposes can also be quite an important capability, and this cannot be identified with nutrition. See Douglas and Isherwood (1979). But nor is the quantity of food consumed in itself a good indicator of these functional uses of food. A more sophisticated analysis is called for capabilities.

28. See, for example, Forrester (1971), Meadows and colleagues (1972), Mesarovic and Pastel (1974), Brown and Eckholm (1974).

29. See Parikh and Rabar (1981), and also Leontief and colleagues (1977), Herrera and colleagues (1976), Interfutures (1979), Linnemann (1981). See also Aziz (1975, 1982), Taylor (1975), Griffin (1978), Simhs and Drabek (1978), Swaminathan (1983).

30. See Chapters 7, 8, and 10 in Sen (1981a).

31. See Sinka and Drabek (1978) and Aziz (1982).

32. See, for example, Bentham (1974), den Hartog (1973), Schofield (1975), Chen, Huq, and D'Souza (1980), Mitra (1980), Sen (1981a), Kyach and Sen (1982).

33. See Kynch and Sen (1982) and Sen and Sengupta (1983).

34. See United Nations, *Demographic Year book 1981*. New York: UN, 1982. The latest Chinese census seems to suggest an even lower female-male ratio for China, just over 0.94.

35. See Kynch and Sen (1982).

36. It should be mentioned, however, that nutritional sex bias seems to be less present in Southeast Asia. Also, the female–male ratio in

Southeast Asia is, in fact, around 1.01—much higher than in the rest of Asia.

37. See Sen (1983d, 1984).

38. See Sen and Sengupta (1983), for a case study.

REFERENCES

Alamgir, M., 1980. *Famine in South Asia–Political Economy of Mass Starvation in Bangladesh*. Cambridge, MA: Oelgeschlager, Gunn and Hain.

Arrow, K. J. 1982. "Why People Go Hungry," *New York Review of Books*, 29 (15 July).

Atkinson, A. B., 1975. *The Economics of Inequality*. Oxford: Clarendon Press.

Aziz, S., ed. 1975. *Hunger, Politics and Markets: The Real Issues in the Food Crisis*. New York: New York University Press.

——, ed. 1982. "The Fight Against World Hunger," Special number of *Development*, 4.

Bardhan, P., 1974. "On Life and Death Questions," *Economic and Political Weekly* (4 September).

Becker, G., 1981. *A Treatise on the Family*. Cambridge, MA: Harvard University Press.

Beckerman, W., 1979. *The Impact of Income Maintenance Programmes on Poverty in Four Developing Countries*. Geneva: International Labour Office.

Bentham, J., 1974. *Principles of Morals & Legislation*. Oxford: Oxford University Press.

Brown, L. R., and Eckholm, E. P., 1974. *By Bread Alone*. Oxford: Pergamon Press.

Chakravarty, S., 1970. *Capital and Development Planning*. Cambridge, MA: MIT Press.

Chen, L. C., Huq, E., and D'Souza, S., 1980. "A Study of Sex-Biased Behaviour in the Intra-family Allocation of Food and the Utilization of Health Care Services in Rural Bangladesh," Harvard School of Public Health.

Chichilnisky, G., 1980. "Basic Needs and Global Models: Resources, Trade and Distribution," *Alternatives*, VI.

Dasgupta, P., 1982. *The Control of Resources*. Oxford: Blackwell.

Davidson, S., Passmore, R., Brock, J. F., and Truswell, A. S., 1979. *Human Nutrition and Dietectics*. Edinburgh: Churchill Livingstone.

den Hartog, A. P., 1973. "Unequal Distribution of Food within the Household," *FAO Newsletter*, 10(4) (October–December).

Douglas, M., and Isherwood, B., 1979. *The World of Goods*. New York: Basic Books.

Elster, J., 1982. "The Sour Grapes," Sen, A. K., and Williams, B., eds. *Utilitarianism and Beyond.* Cambridge: Cambridge University Press.

FAO/WHO Expert Committee, 1973. *Energy and Protein Requirements* (Rome: FAO).

Forrester, J. W., 1971. *World Dynamics.* Cambridge, MA: Wright-Allen.

Ghai, D., Khan, A. R., Lee, E., and Alfthan, T. A., 1977. *The Basic Needs Approach to Development.* Geneva: International Labour Office.

Ghose, A., 1979. *Short Term Changes in Income Distribution in Poor Agrarian Economies.* Geneva: International Labour Office.

Gorman, W. M., 1956: "The Demand for Related Goods," *Journal Paper J3129,* Iowa Experimental Station, Ames, Iowa.

Grant, J. P., 1978. *Disparity Reduction Rates in Social Indicators.* Washington, DC: Overseas Development Council.

Griffin, K., 1978. *International Inequality and National Poverty.* London: Macmillan.

—— and Khan, A. R., 1977: *Poverty and Landlessness in Rural Asia.* Geneva: International Labour Office.

Haq, Mahbubul, 1976. *The Poverty Curtain.* New York: Columbia University Press.

Heal, G. M., 1973. *The Theory of Economic Planning.* Amsterdam: North Holland.

Herrera, A. O. et al. 1976. *Catastrophe or New Society? A Latin American World Model.* Ottawa: International Development Research Centre.

ILO, 1976. *Employment, Growth and Basic Needs: A One-World Problem.* Geneva: International Labour Office.

Interfutures, 1979. *Facing the Future.* Paris: Organization for Economic Cooperation and Development.

Islam, N., 1977. *Development Planning in Bangladesh: A Study in Political Economy.* London: Hurst.

Jencks, C., 1972. *Inequality.* New York: Basic Books.

Kynch, J., and Sen, A., 1982. "Indian Women: Well-being and Survival," mimeographed. Forthcoming in *Cambridge Journal of Economics.* 7, pp. 363–83.

Lancaster, K. J., 1966. "A New Approach to Consumer Theory,"*Journal of Political Economy,* 74.

Leontief, W., 1977. *The Future of the World Economy.* New York: Oxford University Press.

Linnemann, H., 1981. *MOIRA: A Model of International Relations in Agriculture.* Amsterdam: North-Holland.

Lipton, M., 1977. *Why Poor People Stay Poor*. London: Temple Smith.

MacDiarmid, Hugh, 1967. *Collected Poems*. London: MacGibbon & Kee.

McHenry, D. F., and Bird, K., 1977. "Food Bungle in Bangladesh," *Foreign Policy*, no. 27 (Summer).

McNicoll, G., and Nag, M., 1982. "Population Growth: Current Issues and Strategies," *Population and Development Review* 8.

Malthus, T. R., 1798. *Essay on the Principle of Population*. London.

—— 1800. *An Investigation of the Cause of the Present High Price of Provisions*.

Marx, K., 1887. *Capital: A Critical Analysis of Capitalist Production*. Translated by S.

Moore, S., and Aveling, E., Engels, F., ed. London: Sonnenschein.

—— 1977. *Karl Marx: Selected Writings*, McLellan, D., ed. Oxford: Oxford University Press.

Meadows, M., Meadows, D., Ronders, L. Behrens, W. 1972. *The Limits to Growth*. Washington, DC: Potomac.

Mesarovic, M., and Pestel, E., 1974. *Mankind at Turning Point*. New York: Dutton.

Mitra, A., 1980. *Implications of Declining Sex-Ratio in India's Population*. Bombay: Allied Publishers.

Morris, M. D., 1979. *Measuring the Conditions of the World's Poor: The Physical Quality of Life Index*. Oxford: Pergamon Press.

Ng, K., 1981. "Welfarism: A Defense Against Sen's Attack," *Economic Journal* 91.

Oughton, E., 1982. "The Maharashtra Drought of 1970–73: An Analysis of Scarcity," *Oxford Bulletin of Economics and Statistics*, 44.

Pant, P. et al., 1962. "Perspective of Development: 1961–1976, Implications of Planning for a Minimum Level of Living," Perspective Planning Division, Planning Commission of India, New Delhi.

Parikh, K., and Rabar, F., eds. 1981. *Food For All in a Sustainable World*. Laxenberg: International Institute for Applied Systems Analysis.

Rao, V. K. R. V., 1982. *Food, Nutrition and Poverty in India*. Brighton: Harvester Press.

Ravallion, M., 1983. "The Performance of Rice Market in Bangladesh during the 1974 Famine," mimeographed, Oxford University.

Rawls, J., 1971. *A Theory of Justice*. Cambridge, MA: Harvard University Press.

Schofield, S., 1975. *Village Nutrition Studies: An Annotated Bibliography*. Brighton: Institute of Development Studies, University of Sussex.

Scrimshaw, N. S., 1977. "Effect of Infection on Nutrient Requirements," *American Journal of Clinical Nutrition*, 30.

Sen, A. K., 1970. *Collective Choice and Social Welfare.* San Francisco: Holden-Day; Amsterdam: North-Holland.

— 1976a. "Real National Income," *Review of Economic Studies,* 43 (reprinted in Sen (1982a)).

— 1976b. "Poverty: An Ordinal Approach to Measurements," *Econometrica* 44 (reprinted in Sen (1982a)).

— 1977a. "On Weights and Measures: Informational Constraints in Social Welfare Analysis," *Econometrica,* 45 (reprinted in Sen (1982a)).

— 1977b. "Starvation and Exchange Entitlement: A General Approach and Its Application to the Great Bengal Famine," *Cambridge Journal of Economics,* 1.

— 1979a. "Personal Utilities and Public Judgment: Or What's Wrong with Welfare Economics?" *Economic Journal,* 89 (reprinted in Sen (1982a)).

— 1979b. "Utilitarianism and Welfarism," *Journal of Philosophy,* 76.

— 1980. "Equality of What?" McMurrin, S., ed. *Tanner Lectures on Human Values,* vol. I. Cambridge: Cambridge University Press, (reprinted in Sen (1982a)).

— 1981a. *Poverty and Famines: An Essay on Entitlement and Deprivation.* Oxford: Clarendon Press.

— 1981b. "Family and Food: Sex-Bias in Poverty?" in *Resources, Value, & Development,* Cambridge, MA: Harvard University Press.

— 1981c. "Public Action and the Quality of Life in Developing Countries," *Oxford Bulletin of Economics and Statistics,* 43.

— 1982a. *Choice, Welfare and Measurement.* Oxford: Blackwell; and Cambridge, MA: MIT Press.

— 1982b. "Rights and Agency," *Philosophy and Public Affairs,* 11.

— 1982c. "Food Battles: Conflicts in the Access to Food," Coromandel Lecture, 12 December; reprinted in *Mainstream* (8 January 1983).

— 1983a. "Poor, Relatively Speaking," *Oxford Economic Papers* 35., pp. 153–69.

— 1983b. *Commodities and Capabilities,* North-Holland, Amsterdam.

— 1983c. "Development: Which Way Now?" *Economic Journal,* 93, pp. 745–62.

— 1983d. "Economics and the Family," *Asian Development Review,* 1, pp. 3–16.

— 1984. "Women, Technology and Sexual Divisions," Working Paper, Technology Division, UNCTAD, Geneva.

— ,and Sengupta, S., 1983. "Malnutrition of Rural Children and the Sex Bias," mimeographed. Forthcoming *Economic and Political Weekly,* 18, pp. 855–64.

— ,and Williams, B., eds., 1982. *Utilitarianism and Beyond.* Cambridge: Cambridge University Press.

Singer, H., and Ansari, J., 1977. *Rich and Poor Countries.* London: Allen & Unwin.

Sinha, R., and Drabek, A. G., 1978. *The World Food Problem: Consensus and Conflict.* Oxford: Pergamon Press.

Smith, Adam, 1776. *An Inquiry into the Nature and Causes of the Wealth of Nations.*

Sobhan, R., 1979. "Politics of Food and Famine in Bangladesh," *Economic and Political Weekly*, 14.

Srinivasan, T. N., 1982. "Hunger: Defining It, Estimating Its Global Incidence and Alleviating It," mimeographed. To be published in D. Gale Johnson and E. Schuh, eds. *Role of Markets in the World Food Economy*, Boulder, CO: Wesview Press.

Streeten, P., 1981. With S. J. Burki, Mahbubul Haq, N. Hicks, and F. Stewart. *First Things First: Meeting Basic Needs in Developing Countries.* New York: Oxford University Press.

—— and Burki, S., 1978. "Basic Needs: Some Issues," *World Development*, 6.

Sukhatme, P. V., 1977. *Nutrition and Poverty.* New Delhi: Indian Agricultural Research Institute.

Swaminathan, M. S., 1983: "Agricultural Progress: Key to Third World Prosperity," Third World Lecture, Third World Foundation.

Taylor, L., 1975: "The Misconstrued Crisis: Lester Brown and World Food," *World Development*, 3.

Townsend, P., 1979. *Poverty in the United Kingdom.* Harmondsworth: Penguin.

United Nations, 1982. *Demographic Year Book 1981.* New York: United Nations.

Williams, B., 1973. "A Critique of Utilitarianism," Smart, J., and Williams, B., eds. *Utilitarianism: For and Against.* Cambridge: Cambridge University Press.

Hunger, Capability, and Development

DAVID A. CROCKER[1]

David A. Crocker is a visiting senior research scholar at the Institute for Philosophy and Public Policy and a visiting professor at the School of Public Affairs, University of Maryland-College Park. Crocker has taught philosophy at Colorado State University since 1966 and has twice been a Fulbright scholar at Central American universities. He is a founding member and current president of the International Development Ethics Association (IDEA).

World Hunger and Moral Obligation (WH),[2] the predecessor of the present volume, illustrated and advanced the new philosophical movement called *applied ethics*. The anthology's focus was salutary. The essays addressed the question: "What moral responsibility affluent nations (or those people in them) have to the starving masses?" Among those arguing that nations do have a positive obligation to aid distant and hungry people, there were efforts to explore the nature, foundation, and limits of this obligation. It is now apparent, however, that this initial moral problematic issue needs to be recast and enlarged.

I argue that the philosophical discussion in WH, and innumerable subsequent texts and anthologies in applied ethics, committed what Whitehead called "the fallacy of misplaced concreteness."[3] Philosophers abstracted one part—famine and food aid—from the whole complex of hunger, poverty, and development, and proceeded to consider that part in isolation from other dimensions. We now need to redirect and then broaden our attention with respect to the complex causes, conditions, and cures of hunger. Otherwise, we will have an incomplete and distorted picture of both the facts and the values involved. Instead of philosophical preoccupation with the moral basis for aid from rich countries to famine victims in poor countries, emphasis should be shifted: (1) from moral foundations to interpretative and strategic concepts, (2) from famine to persistent malnutrition, (3) from remedy to prevention, (4) from food availability to food entitlements, (5) from food and food entitlements to capabilities and a capabilities-based model of development. Overall, the progression I favor will take us from an ethics of aid to an ethics for development.

From Moral Foundations to Interpretative and Strategic Concepts

The moral problem of world hunger and the ethics of famine relief were among the first practical issues that philosophers tackled after John Rawls's pivotal 1971 study, *A Theory of Justice*,[4] convinced them that reflection on normative issues was part of the philosopher's task. Although Rawls himself limited ethical analysis to abstract principles of distributive justice, applied philosophical ethicists addressed the ethical and conceptual aspects of a variety of practical problems and policies. In the same year that Rawls's volume appeared, Peter Singer first wrote about famine in East Bengal (now Bangladesh)[5] and, more generally, about "the obligations of the affluent to those in danger of starvation."[6] In his 1974 *New York Times Magazine* article, "Philosophers are Back on the Job,"[7] Singer championed the philosophical turn to applied ethics, employing the ethics of famine relief as a leading example.

Philosophers were back on the job because, as John Dewey had urged 50 years earlier, "philosophy recovers itself when it ceases to be a device for dealing with the problems of philosophers and becomes a method, cultivated by philosophers, for dealing with the problems of men."[8] One of these human problems in the midseventies was whether or not affluent states and their citizens were in any way morally obligated to send food to famine victims in other countries. Is such aid morally required, permissible, or impermissible?

More than two decades later, however, many perceive the problem of "world hunger and moral obligation" differently. When we see pictures—whether in the media or on the cover of WH—of a starving child crouching on infertile soil, the question "Do we have a duty to help?" seems to many beside the point. Of course we should help, provided that such help will do genuine and sustainable good.[9] We should not take seriously those who insist that no action be taken until an argument is found to justify the view that the rich in the North should help the poor in the South. To be sure, there is a place for moral debate with respect to *how much* assistance morality requires us to give distant people, in light of our concomitant obligations to aid our families, friends, and compatriots.[10] And in some contexts—university seminar rooms, for instance—it can be valuable to consider whether we owe the foreign poor anything at all. But usually we see no good reason to doubt that we owe them *something*, if we can be reasonably sure that our help will alleviate their immediate misery and improve their long-term prospects. What challenges aid to distant peoples is not so much skepticism concerning moral foundations as pessimism about practical results.

Unfortunately, preoccupied as they were with the task of justifying aid to distant people, most philosophers evinced scant interest in institutional and practical issues. They seemed to believe that if they could resolve the foundational questions, the rest would be easy; the rational—on its own—would become real. Thus, although WH's editors did challenge their readers to consider, "If one ought to help the hungry, how should one help?" (WH, p.10), the volume's essays almost completely failed to address the best ways to diagnose and remedy the problem of world hunger.

It might be objected that analysis of the causes and cures of world hunger is a purely factual, empirical, or technical matter to which ethicists cannot contribute. Yet I would argue that facts and values cannot be so easily kept separate, for we discern ethically salient features of facts on the basis of our moral values.[11] Ethical reflection, whether the work of philosophers or nonphilosophers, plays not only a critical and guiding role but also an interpretative role in relation to social reality and change. An ethic proposes norms for assessing present social institutions, envisaging future alternatives, and assigning moral obligations. An ethic, finally, provides a basis for deciding how agents should act in particular circumstances. What is equally important and frequently neglected, however, is that a normative vision also informs the ways we discern, describe, explain, and forecast social phenomena. How we "read" the situation, as well as how we describe and classify it, will be a function of our value commitments and even our moral sensitivities.[12] For instance, if we ask, "How is India doing?" we are seeking an empirical analysis of what is going on in that country. Yet alternative ethical perspectives will focus on distinct, though sometimes overlapping, facts: hedonistic utilitarianism attends to pleasures and pains, preference utilitarianism selects preference satisfactions and dissatisfactions (or per capita productivity and consumption), human rights approaches emphasize human rights compliances and violations, and contractarians investigate the distributions of "social primary goods" such as income, wealth, liberties, and opportunities. In each case the ethic structures determine what counts as morally relevant information. One value of dialogue between different ethical perspectives is that we learn to see the world in new and different ways. Moreover, as Sherman says, "how to see becomes as much a matter of inquiry (*zetêsis*) as what to do."[13]

Amartya Sen, Martha Nussbaum, Jean Drèze, and others offer the capabilities ethic as the result of an inquiry about understanding and combating world hunger and other deprivations. Capabilities theorists employ this ethic to appraise social institutions and guide policy-formation and actions.[14] To accomplish this task they defend explicit ethical principles and assign moral responsibilities.[15] The capabilities perspective, however, also yields distinctive ways of perceiving world hunger and understanding its empirical causes and attempted cures. With its emphasis on "the commodity commands [entitlements] and basic capabilities that people enjoy" (HPA, p. 273), the capabilities ethic interprets and supplies a rationale for broadening the investigative focus from food aid for famine victims to the most important (and modifiable) causes, conditions, consequences, and remedies of endemic hunger and other privations.[16] As Drèze and Sen argue, "seeing hunger as entitlement failure points to possible remedies as well as helping us to understand the forces that generate hunger and sustain it" (HPA, p. 24). In this essay I emphasize the interpretative contribution of the capabilities ethic and argue that this normative perspective helps justify a broader approach to world hunger.

In the mid-1990s, philosophical reflection on world hunger remains important. After Ethiopia, Kampuchea, Sudan, Somalia, and Rwanda, however, philosophers are appropriately less concerned with morally justifying aid to the distant hungry and more concerned with the conceptual and ethical dimensions of understanding hunger and with policies for successfully combating it.

From Famine to Persistent Malnutrition

Philosophers, like policymakers and the public, typically pay excessive attention to famine and insufficient attention to persistent malnutrition.[17] Both famine and endemic malnutrition are forms of hunger in the sense of "an inadequacy in dietary intake relative to the kind and quantity of food required for growth, for activity, and for maintenance of good health."[18] Famine and chronic hunger, however, differ in character, causes, consequences, and cures. Famine is dramatic, "involving acute starvation and sharp increase in mortality" (HPA, p. 7). It makes a sensational topic for the evening news or fund-raising rock concerts. Chronic hunger, "involving sustained nutritional deprivation on a persistent basis," has deeper causes than famine and is less visible. Moreover, persistent hunger affects many more people[19] and is harder to eradicate than famine. The consequences of persistent hunger—severe incapacitation, chronic illness and humiliation—may be worse than death. And chronic hunger is itself a killer, since weak or sickly persons are especially prone to deadly diseases. If we are concerned about the misery and mortality caused by famine, we should be even more exercised by the harms caused by persistent malnutrition.

Strategies to combat famine and persistent malnutrition also differ.

> To take one example [of diverse strategies in responding to transitory and endemic hunger], in the context of famine prevention the crucial need for speedy intervention and the scarcity of resources often call for a calculated reliance on existing distributional mechanisms (e.g., the operation of private trade stimulated by cash support to famine victims) to supplement the logistic capability of relief agencies. In the context of combating chronic hunger, on the other hand, there is much greater scope for slower but none the less powerful avenues of action such as institution building, legal reforms, asset redistribution or provisioning in kind (HPA, pp. 7–8).

Famine and chronic malnutrition don't always go together. Nations—for instance, India since independence and Haiti in 1994—can be free of famine and yet beset by endemic malnutrition. A country such as China can achieve a reasonably high level of nutritional well-being and yet be stricken by terrible famines. To be exclusively preoccupied with famine is to ignore food deprivation and misery in countries not prone to famine.

As important as is the distinction between these two types of hunger, we must neither exaggerate the differences nor fail to recognize certain linkages. Not only are famine and chronic malnutrition both forms of hunger, but they have certain causes and remedies in common. Both can be understood as what Drèze and Sen call "entitlement failures" and "capability failures" (of which more presently).

As with many other problems, a nation with the right sort of basic political, economic, and social institutions—for instance, stable families, infrastructure, certain kinds of markets, a democratic government, a free press, and nongovernmental organizations—can prevent and remedy both sorts of hunger, while a society without the right set of interlocking institutions is likely to experience one or the other if not both. Moreover, some of the best short-term and long-term approaches to famine prevention—remunerated public employment and, more generally, sustainable development—build on and often intensify effective efforts to address persistent malnutrition (HPA, p. 158). In contrast, the most common emergency action to combat famine—the herding of people into relief camps in order to dole out free food—jeopardizes long-term solutions by disrupting normal economic activities, upsetting family life, and creating breeding grounds for infectious diseases.

From Remedy to Prevention

Whether concerned with abrupt or chronic hunger, almost all the essays in WH emphasized the moral response to *existing* hunger problems rather than the prevention of *future* ones. Only Onora O'Neill clearly addressed the question of prefamine as well as famine policies (WH, pp. 161–164). On the basis of an expanded conception of the duty not to kill others, O'Neill argued that we have a duty to adopt prefamine policies that ensure that famine is postponed as long as possible and is minimized in severity. Such prefamine policies must include both a population policy and a resources policy, for "a duty to try to postpone the advent and minimize the severity of famine is a duty on the one hand to minimize the number of persons there will be and on the other to maximize the means of subsistence" (WH, p. 163).

O'Neill's approach, however, unfortunately assumes that famines cannot be prevented altogether, only postponed and minimized. This supposition flies in the face of recent historical experience. Drèze and Sen summarize their findings on this point when they observe, "There is no real evidence to doubt that all famines in the modern world are preventable by human action;...many countries—even some very poor ones—manage consistently to prevent them" (HPA, p. 47). Nations that have successfully prevented impending famines (sometimes without outside help) include India (after independence), Cape Verde, Kenya, Zimbabwe, and Botswana (HPA, Chapter 8).

It is also possible to prevent and reduce if not eliminate chronic hunger. We must combat that pessimism—a close cousin of complacency—that assures us that the hungry will always be with us—at least in the same absolute and relative numbers.[20] One of the great achievements of Drèze and Sen is to document, through detailed case studies of successes in fighting hunger, that "there is, in fact, little reason for presuming that the terrible problems of hunger and starvation in the world cannot be changed by human action" (HPA, p. 276). What is needed is a forward-looking perspective for short-term and long-term prevention of both types of hunger.

From Food Availability to Food Entitlements

Moral reflection on the prevention and relief of world hunger must be expanded from food productivity, availability, and distribution to what Sen calls food "entitlements." Popular images of famine relief emphasize policies that, in Garrett Hardin's words, "move food to the people" or "move people to food" (WH, p. 19). In either case, the assumption is that hunger is principally caused by lack of food. Chronic hunger, it is often believed, will be solved by greater agricultural productivity, and famine "relief" consists in getting food and starving people together. Much hunger, however, occurs even when people and ample food—even peak supplies—are in close proximity. For a starving person may have no access to or command over the food that is right next door.

In a country, region, and even village stricken by famine, there is often more than enough food for everyone to be adequately fed. Recent research makes it evident that since 1960 there has been sufficient food to feed all the world's people on a "near-vegetarian diet" and that "we are approaching a second threshold of improved diet sufficiency"[21] in which 10 percent of everyone's diet could consist of animal products. Accordingly, it is often said that the problem is one of distribution. This term, however, is ambiguous. Purely spatial redistribution is insufficient and may not be necessary. Sen reminds us that "people have perished in famines in sight of much food in shops."[22] What good distribution of food should mean is that people have effective access to or can acquire the food (whether presently nearby or far away). Hence, it is better to say that the problem of hunger, whether transitory or persistent, involves an "entitlement failure" in the sense that the hungry person is not able to acquire food or lacks command over food. What is crucial is not the mere food itself, nor the amount of food divided by the number of people in a given area, nor even the food transported to a stricken area. What is decisive is whether particular households and individuals have operative "entitlements" over food. The distinction between households and individuals is important, for households as units may have sufficient food for the nourishment of each family member, yet some members—usually women or female children—may starve because of entitlement failures.

We must be careful here, for Sen's use of the term "entitlement" has caused no little confusion and controversy. Unlike Robert Nozick's normative or prescriptive use of the term, Sen employs "entitlement" in a descriptive way—relatively free of moral endorsement or criticism—to refer to a person's actual or operative command, permitted by law (backed by state power) or custom, over certain commodities.[23] A person's entitlements will be a function of: (1) that person's endowments, for instance, what goods or services he or she has to exchange for food, (2) exchange opportunities, for instance, the going rate of exchange of work for food, (3) legal claims against the state, for instance, rights to work, food stamps, or welfare, and (4) nonlegal but socially approved and operative rules, for instance, the household "social discipline" that mandates that women eat after and less than men.[24]

Generally speaking, an entitlement to food would be the actual ability, whether *morally* justified or not, to acquire food by some legally or socially approved means—whether by producing it, trading for it, buying it, or receiving it in a government feeding program. A Hutu child separated from its family may be morally justified in stealing a meal from a Tutsi food supply center, but has no legal claim or other social basis for effective access to the food. In Sen's sense, then, the child lacks an entitlement to that food.

To view hunger as an entitlement failure does not commit one to the position that hunger is never caused by a lack of food nor that it is always explained by the same set of causes. Rather, the entitlement theory of hunger directs one to examine the various links in a society's "food chain"—production, acquisition, and consumption— any of which can be dysfunctional and thereby result in an entitlement failure. A production failure caused by drought or pests will result in an entitlement failure for those peasants "whose means of survival depend on food that they grow themselves."[25] Even when food is abundant and increasing in an area, landless laborers may starve because they have insufficient money to buy food, no job to get money, nothing of worth to trade for food, or no effective claim on their government or other group.

Conceiving hunger as an entitlement failure also yields ways of preventing impending famines and ways of remedying actual famines. What is needed is not only food but institutions that protect against entitlement failure and restore lost entitlements. Moving food to hungry people may not be necessary, for the food may already be physically present. The problem is that some people cannot gain access to it. Even worse, increasing food availability in a given area may increase the hunger problem. For instance, direct delivery of free food can send market food prices plummeting, thereby causing a disincentive for farmers to grow food. The result is a decline not only in their productivity but also in their own food entitlements. Moreover, even when necessary, food by itself is not sufficient to prevent or cure famine if people never had entitlements to food or lost what they had previously. And it may be that the best way to ensure that people have the ability to command food is not to give them food itself, but rather cash relief or cash for work. Such cash "may provide the ability to command food without directly giving the food."[26] It may also have the effect of increasing food availability, for the cash may "pull" private food traders into the area in order to meet the demand.

One deficiency of the "food availability" approach to hunger is that it is purely aggregative, that is, concerned solely with the amount of food in a given area summed over the number of people. Thus, it has inspired a simplistic and inconclusive debate between "Malthusian optimists," those who think that *the* answer to the "world food problem" is more food, and "Malthusian pessimists," those who think that the answer is fewer people.[27] Another—more deadly—consequence is that data concerning food output and availability often lull government officials and others into a false sense of food security and thereby prevent them from doing what they might to prevent or mitigate famine: "The focus on food per head and Malthusian optimism have literally killed millions."[28] In contrast, Sen's approach is disaggregative with respect to command over food on the part of vulnerable occupation groups, households, and, most important, individuals (see HPA, pp. 30–31). It recognizes that although food is indispensable for famine prevention and remedy, much more than food is needed. According to the capabilities ethic, an approach to hunger that attended exclusively to food and entitlements to food would stop short of the fundamental goal—to reduce human deprivation and contribute to human well-being.

From Food and Food Entitlements to Capabilities and Development

Different moral theories understand human well-being and the good human life in diverse ways. Capabilities theorists choose valuable human "functionings" and capabilities to so function as the basis of their ethical outlook. They argue that these moral categories are superior to other candidates for *fundamental* concepts, such as resources or commodities, utilities, needs, or rights. Although these latter concepts do have a role in a complete moral theory and approach to world hunger, they refer to "moral furniture" that is in some sense secondary. Commodities are at best *means* to the end of valuable functions and abilities to so function. Utilities are only one among several good functionings and may "muffle" and "mute" deprivations. Rights are not free-standing but are best defined in relation to valuable human functions and abilities to so function.[29]

What do capabilities theorists mean by the term *functionings*? A person's functionings consist of his or her physical and mental states ("beings") and activities ("doings"). The most important of these functionings, the failure of which constitutes poverty and the occurrence of which constitutes well-being, "vary from such elementary physical ones as being well-nourished, being adequately clothed and sheltered, avoiding preventable morbidity, and so forth, to more complex social achievements such as taking part in the life of the community, being able to appear in public without shame, and so on."[30] A person's *capabilities* are that set of functionings open to the person, given the person's personal characteristics ("endowment") as well as economic and social opportunities. An alternative formulation is that the general idea of capability refers "to the extent of freedom that people have in pursuing valuable activities or functionings" (HPA, p. 42).

Drèze and Sen give four reasons for expanding the perspective on hunger to include capabilities as well as food and entitlements: (1) individual variability, (2) social variability, (3) diverse means to nourishment, (4) nourishment as a means to other good goals. Let us briefly consider each.

Individual Variability The capabilities approach recommends itself because it makes sense of and insists on the distinction between food intake and being nourished or capable of being nourished. The focus is not on food in itself nor food as merely ingested, but food as a means to being well-nourished and being able to be well-nourished. Exclusive attention to food, food entitlement, and food intake neglects importantly diverse impacts that the same food can have on different human beings and on the same individual at different times. A particular woman at various stages of her life "requires" different amounts and types of food, depending on her age, her reproductive status, and her state of health. Generally, higher food intake at one time may compensate for lower or no intake at other times without it being true that the person is ever suffering from nutritional distress or malfunctioning.

Instead of identifying hungry people simply by a lack of food intake and mechanically monitoring individuals or dispensing food to them according to nutritional requirements, the focus should be on nutritional functioning and those "nutrition-related capabilities that are crucial to human well-being" (HPA, p. 14). A person's energy level, strength, weight and height (within average parameters that permit exceptions), the ability to be productive, and capacities to avoid morbidity and mortality—all valuable functionings or capabilities to function—should supplement and may be more significant with respect to nutritional well-being than the mere quantity of food or types of nutrients (HPA, p. 41).[31]

Social Variability In addition to differences in individual or communal biological or physical characteristics, the capabilities approach is sensitive to differences in socially acquired tastes and beliefs with respect to foods. That is, it recognizes that these tastes and beliefs can also block the conversion of food into nutritional functioning. Attempts to relieve hunger sometimes fail because hungry people are unable, for some reason, to eat nutritious food. Hungry people sometimes won't eat because the taste of available grain is too different from that to which they are accustomed. There is evidence that people who receive extra cash for food sometimes fail to improve their nutritional status, apparently because they choose to consume nutritionally deficient foods. If food is to make a difference in people's nutritional and wider well-being, it must be food that the individuals in question are generally willing and able to convert into nutritional functioning.[32] This is not to say that food habits cannot be changed. Rather, it underscores the importance of nutritional education and social criticism of certain food consumption patterns. Even nutritious food to which people are entitled, however, will not by itself protect or restore nutritional well-being.

Diverse Means to Being Well-Nourished If one goal of public action is to protect, restore, and promote nutritional well-being, we must realize that food is only one means of reaching this goal (HPA, p. 267). A preoccupation with food transfers as the way to address impending or actual hunger ignores the many other means that can serve and may even be necessary to achieve the end of being (able to be) well-nourished. These include "access to health care, medical facilities, elementary education, drinking water, and sanitary facilities" (HPA, p. 13).

To achieve nutritional well-being, a hungry parasite-stricken person needs not only food but also medicine to kill the parasites that cause the malabsorption of consumed food. A disease-enfeebled person who is too weak to eat requires medical care as well as food. A Rwandan youngster separated from its family in a refugee camp may be ignorant of what to eat and what not to eat. Without clean water, basic sanitation, and health education, recipients of nutritious food aid may succumb to malaria, cholera, dysentery, and typhoid before having the chance to be adequately nourished.

In particular situations, the best way to combat famine may not be to dispense food but to supply jobs for those who can work and cash for those who can't (HPA, p. 121). The evidence is impressive that an increase in the purchasing power of hungry people often pulls food into a famine area, as private traders find ways of meeting the increased demand (HPA, pp. 88–93). Finally, famine and chronic hunger are prevented and reduced by long-term development strategies that protect and promote entitlements and valuable capabilities. In the next section, we will return to the hunger-fighting role of national development strategies and international development. At this juncture, the crucial point is that direct food delivery is only one means, and often not the best means, for fighting world hunger. The capabilities approach helpfully interprets and underscores that point when it insists that public action can and should employ an array of complementary strategies to achieve the end of nutritional well-being for all.

Food as a Means to Other Components of Well-Being   The capabilities approach helps widen our vision to see that the food that hungry people command and consume can accomplish much more than give them nutritional well-being. Nutritional well-being is only one element in human well-being; the overcoming of transitory or chronic hunger also enables people and their governments to protect and promote other ingredients of well-being. Being adequately nourished, for instance, contributes to healthy functioning that is both good in itself and indispensable to the ability to avoid premature death and fight off or recover from disease. Having nutritional well-being and good health, in turn, is crucial to acquiring and exercising other valuable capabilities such as being able to learn, think, deliberate, and choose as well as be a good pupil, friend, householder, parent, worker, or citizen.

Because adequate food and food entitlements can have so many beneficial consequences in people's lives, creative development programs and projects find ways in which people can link food distribution/acquirement to other valuable activities. Pregnant and lactating women (and their infants) acquire food supplements in health clinics, for nutritional deficiencies affect fetal and infant development. Schoolchildren eat free or subsidized lunches at school, for hungry children don't learn as well and certain nutritional deficiencies result in visual and cognitive impairment.[33]

Nutritional well-being, then, is both constitutive of and a means to human well-being and personal development. And human development is the ultimate purpose of societal development. Hence, a more ample perspective on world hunger must include socioeconomic development as part of the cure. Just as the right kind of development is a large part of the answer to the various problems of population, so it is crucial to resolving the diverse problems of world hunger.[34]

In the capabilities approach to international development, the linkage between hunger alleviation and development is spelled out in the language of valuable capabilities and functionings. In this approach, a society's development is conceived as a process of change that protects, restores, strengthens, and expands people's valued and valuable capabilities.[35] Being able to be well nourished and other nutrition-related capabilities are among the most important capabilities. Hence, a society striving to be developed will search for, establish, and maintain institutions and policies that attack and try to eradicate all forms of hunger and the poverty that causes hunger.[36] Even emergency measures to prevent, relieve, or extirpate famine must not undermine and, if possible, should contribute to long-term strategies that "may be used to reduce or eliminate failures of basic capabilities" (HPA, p. 16). Economic, political and other institutions, such as schools and the family, must be modified and development strategies elected in the light of the effect such changes will have on what all persons will be able to do and be.

From the Ethics of Aid to an Ethics for Development

Finally, the ethics of famine relief should be incorporated into an ethics for development. International development ethics evaluates the basic goals and appropriate strategies for morally desirable social change. No longer fixated on the stark options of earlier debates—food aid versus no food aid, aid as duty versus aid as charity—it asks instead what kind of aid is morally defensible and, even more fundamentally, what sort of national and international development aid should foster.

As early as the midfifties, development economists had been examining the developmental impact of different kinds of food aid and trying to design famine relief that would contribute to rather than undermine long-term development goals.[37] Yet in the seventies, philosophers and others, such as Garrett Hardin, failed to refer to the nuanced debate that had been going on for more than 20 years. Furthermore, as one expert on food aid remarks, "many of them did not feel it important to become more than superficially familiar with the technical or institutional aspects of food production, distribution, or policy."[38] As happens all too often, the owl of Minerva—Hegel's image for the philosopher—"spreads its wings only with the falling of dusk" and comes on the scene too late to give "instruction as to what the world ought to be."[39]

Moreover, when philosophers did try to analyze development, they usually emphasized development *aid* that rich countries provided to poor countries, rather than the development *goals* that poor countries set and pursued for themselves. By the mideighties, however, ethicists became increasingly aware that they could not talk about morally justified or unjustified development aid from the outside without first talking about the recipient nation's own development philosophies, goals, strategies, leadership, and will.[40] One marked advantage of the capabilities ethic is that it puts its highest priority on a nation's intellectual and institutional capability for *self-development* without denying the role of international theoretical and practical help (see HPA, p. 273 and "Goods and People").

With respect to morally defensible "development paths," a new discipline—international development ethics—has emerged.[41] Development ethicists ask several related questions. What should count as development? Which should be the most fundamental principles to inform a country's choice of development goals and strategies? What moral issues emerge in development policymaking and practice? How should the burdens and benefits of good development be distributed? What role—if any—should more affluent societies and individuals play in the self-development of those less well off? What are the most serious national and international impediments to good development? Who should decide these questions and by what methods? To what extent, if any, do moral skepticism, political realism, and moral relativism pose a challenge to this boundary-crossing ethical inquiry?

This new discipline is being practiced in ways that sharply distinguish it from the earlier ethics of famine relief. First, development ethics is international in the triple sense that ethicists from diverse societies are trying to forge an international consensus about solutions to global problems. It has become evident that policy analysts and ethicists—whether from "developing" countries or "developed" countries—should not simply accept the operative or professed values implicit in a particular country's established development path. Rather, both cultural insiders and outsiders[42] should engage in an ongoing and critical dialogue that includes explicit ethical analysis, assessment, and construction with respect to universal development ends and generally appropriate means of national, regional, and planetary change. Rather than being predominantly if not exclusively the work of white North American males, as was the case in the initial ethics of famine relief, international development ethics is an inquiry that includes participants from a variety of nations, groups, and moral traditions seeking an international consensus about problems of international scope.[43]

Second, development ethics is interdisciplinary rather than exclusively philosophical. It eschews abstract ethical reflection and relates values to relevant facts in a variety of ways. Development ethicists, as we have seen in Drèze and Sen's work on hunger, evaluate: (1) the normative assumptions of different development models, (2) the empirical categories employed to interpret, explain, and forecast the facts, and (3) development programs, strategies, and institutions.[44]

Finally, development ethics straddles the distinction between theory and practice. Its practitioners include, as well as engage in dialogue with, policymakers and development activists. Instead of conducting a merely academic exercise, development theorists and development practitioners together assess the moral costs and benefits of current development policies, programs, and projects, and articulate alternative development visions.[45]

Famine, food aid, and the ethics of famine relief remain—as they were in the midseventies—pressing personal, national, and international challenges. Philosophers can play a role in meeting these challenges and thereby reducing world hunger. This goal is best achieved, however, when the questions of world hunger and moral obligation are reframed and widened. Since the best long-term cure for hunger is national and international development, we must put emergency food aid in a developmental perspective and incorporate an ethics of famine relief into an international development ethics. To avoid the fallacy of misplaced concreteness is not to eschew abstractions but to place them in their proper relations to each other and to the concrete world of facts and values.

NOTES

1. I owe thanks to my colleagues at the Institute for Philosophy and Public Policy and the School of Public Affairs for illuminating discussions of these issues. Will Alken, Arthur Evenchik, Hugh LaFollette, and James W. Nickel made valuable comments on earlier versions of the essay. I gratefully acknowledge support for this research from the National Endowment for the Humanities (NEH) Grant #R0-22709-94 and from the Global Stewardship Initiative of the Pew Charitable Trusts. The views expressed are mine and not necessarily those of NEH or the Pew Charitable Trusts.

2. William Aiken and Hugh La Follette, eds. *World Hunger and Moral Obligation*, Englewood Cliffs, NJ: Prentice-Hall, 1977. Hereafter I cite this volume as WH.

3. Alfred North Whitehead, *Science and the Modern World*, New York: Macmillan, 1925, p. 200.

4. John Rawls, *A Theory of Justice*, Cambridge, MA: Belknap Press of Harvard University Press, 1971.

5. Peter Singer, "Famine, Affluence, and Morality," *Philosophy and Public Affairs* 1, 1972, pp. 229–243. Singer's initial essay, reproduced with a new "Postscript" in WH, was written in 1971 and first appeared in *Philosophy and Public Affairs* in 1972, the initial year of publication of what was to become the premier philosophical journal in applied ethics.

6. Peter Singer, "Reconsidering the Famine Relief Argument," in Peter G. Brown and Henry Shue, eds., *Food Policy: The Responsibility of the United States in the Life and Death Choices*, New York: Free Press, 1977, p. 36.

7. The *New York Times Magazine*, July 7, 1974, pp. 17–20.

8. "The Need for Recovery of Philosophy" Bernstein, Richard J., ed., *John Dewey: On Experience, Nature and Freedom*, New York: The Liberal Arts Press, 1960, p. 67.

9. A 1995 study by the Program on International Policy Attitudes shows that 80 percent of those polled agreed that "the United States should be willing to share at least a small portion of its wealth with those in the world who are in great need." This belief does not seem to stem solely from a view of national interest. However, 67 percent agreed that "as one of the world's rich nations, the United States has a moral responsibility toward poor nations to help them develop economically and improve their people's lives" and 77 percent rejected the idea that the United States should give aid only when it serves the national interest. Although 87 percent believe that waste and corruption is rife in foreign aid programs, 55 percent said they would be willing to pay more taxes for foreign aid if they knew that "most foreign aid was going to the poor people who really need it rather than to wasteful bureaucracies and corrupt governments." Steven Kull, "Americans and Foreign Aid: A Study of American Public Attitudes," Program on International Policy Attitudes, Center for the Study of Policy attitudes and Center for International and Security Studies at Maryland, School of Public Affairs, University of Maryland, March 1, 1995. pp. 3, 16, 21.

10. See, for example, Catherine W. Wilson, "On Some Alleged Limitations to Moral Endeavor," *Journal of Philosophy* 90 (1993), 275–289. It is beyond the scope of this paper to consider the best way to think about our general duty to assist others and our particular duty to aid the foreign needy.

11. I owe the idea of perceiving or discerning "ethical salience," to Nancy Sherman, *The Fabric of Character: Aristotle's Theory of Virtue*, Oxford: Clarendon Press, 1989, pp. 28–44. See also Martha Nussbaum, *Love's Knowledge: Essays on Philosophy and Literature*, New York, Oxford: Oxford University Press, 1990, especially Chapters 2 and 5.

12. For a discussion of how ethical principles constrain what counts as relevant and irrelevant factual information, see Amartya Sen, "Well-being, Agency, and Freedom: The Dewey Lectures 1984." *Journal of Philosophy* 82 (1985), pp. 169–184. Sherman discusses the way in which the agent's "reading of the circumstances" may be influenced by his or her moral or immoral character; see *Fabric* p. 29.

13. Sherman, *Fabric* p. 30.

14. See for example, recent volumes in The World Institute for Development Economics Research (WIDER) series *Studies in Development Economics*: Jean Drèze and Amartya Sen, *Hunger and Public Action*, Oxford: Clarendon Press, 1989, hereafter cited in the text as HPA; Jean Drèze and Amartya Sen, eds., *The Political Economy of Hunger. Entitlement and Well-Being*, 3 volumes: Vol. 1, *Entitlement and Well-being*; Vol. 2, *Famine and Prevention*; Vol. 3, *Endemic Hunger*, Oxford: Clarendon Press, 1990; Martha C. Nussbaum and Amartya Sen, eds., *The Quality of Life*, Oxford: Clarendon Press, 1993. See also Keith Griffin and John Knight, eds., *Human Development and the International Development Strategy for the 1990s*, London: Macmillan, 1989. For a bibliography of Sen and Nussbaum's extensive writings and an analysis of the "capabilities ethic" as a feature of the "capabilities approach" to development, see my essays: "Functioning and Capability: The Foundations of Sen's and Nussbaum's Development Ethic," *Political Theory* 20 (November 1992), pp. 584–612; "Functioning and Capability: The Foundations of Sen's and Nussbaum's Development Ethic, Part 2," in Martha C. Nussbaum and Jonathan Glover, eds., *Women, Culture, and Development*, New York: Oxford University Press/Clarendon Press, 1995. For an article that anticipates many of my arguments, but that I did not have an opportunity to read until after the present essay was completed, see George R. Lucas, Jr., "African Famine: New Economic and Ethical Perspecitves," *Journal of Philosophy*, 87 (November 1990): 629–641.

15. See Amartya Sen, "The Right Not to Be Hungry," in G. Floistad, ed., *Contemporary Philosophy: A New Survey*, Vol. II, The Hague: Martinus Nijhoff, 1982, pp. 343–360.

16. Just as one's focus can be too narrow, it can also be so broad as to be disabling. Blaming or praising such large formations as capitalism, socialism, or industrialism commits fallacies of hasty generalization and deters us from examining causes that are both specific and alterable in the short and medium run. I owe this point to James W. Nickel.

17. The editors of WH did distinguish the two types of hunger (WH, p. 1), but they themselves and the anthology's other contributors almost exclusively attended to the plight of famine victims rather than that of the chronically hungry.

18. Sara Millman and Robert W. Kates, "Toward Understanding Hunger," in Lucile F. Newman, ed., *Hunger in History: Food Shortage, Poverty, and Deprivation*, Cambridge, MA: Basil Blackwell, 1990, p. 3.

19. In the fall of 1994, it is estimated that while 800 million people suffer from malnutrition, none suffer from famine. See *Hunger 1995: Causes of Hunger*, Silver Spring, MD: Bread for the World Institute,

1994, p. 10. However, serious potential for famine exists in Rwanda and Afghanistan, and the United States presence in Haiti has averted famine in a country with severe and widespread malnutrition.

20. Studies show that the number of chronically malnourished people in the world decreased from 976 million people in 1975 to 786 million in 1990 and that in the same period, because of a population increase of 1.1 billion, the proportion of hungry people in the developing world declined from 33 percent to 20 percent. See *Hunger 1995: Causes of Hunger*, pp. 10–11.

21. Robert W. Kates and Sara Millman, "On Ending Hunger: The Lessons of History," in *Hunger in History*, p. 404.

22. Amartya Sen, "The Food Problem: Theory and Practice," *Third World Quarterly*, 3 (July 1982); 454.

23. Sen states that "the entitlement of a person stands for the set of different alternative commodity bundles that the person can acquire through the use of the various legal channels of acquirement open to someone in his position" ("Food, Economics and Entitlements," in Drèze and Sen, *The Political Economy of Hunger*, Vol. 1, *Entitlement and Well-Being*, Oxford: Clarendon Press, 1990, p. 36).

24. See HPA, pp. 10–11; Amartya Sen, *Inequality Reexamined*, New York: Russell Sage Foundation; Cambridge: Harvard University Press, 1992, pp. 149–150 and "Goods and People" (in this volume). Charles Gore shows that Sen has gradually expanded his concept of entitlement to include nonlegal—primarily household—rules, but that Sen needs to go further in recognizing the ways in which "socially approved moral rules" may be extra-legal and even antilegal. See Charles Gore, "Entitlement Relations and 'Unruly' Social Practices: A Comment on the Work of Amartya Sen," *Journal of Development Economics* 29 (1993), pp. 429–460.

25. Amartya Sen, "Food Entitlements and Economic Chains," in *Hunger in History*, p. 377.

26. Amartya Sen, "Food, Economics and Entitlements," in *The Political Economy of Hunger*, Vol. 1, *Entitlement and Well-Being*, p. 43.

27. Sen, "The Food Problem," pp. 447–451. Cf. HPA, pp. 24–25 and "Food, Economics, and Entitlements," pp. 35–36.

28. Amartya Sen, "The Food Problem," p. 450. Cf. Amartya Sen, *Poverty and Famines: An Essay on Entitlement and Deprivation*, Oxford: Clarendon Press, 1981, and "Goods and People" (this volume).

29. For a clarification and defense of these claims, see Sen and Nussbaum's writings and my analysis and evaluations of them in the essays referred to in number 14.

30. Sen, *Inequality Reexamined*, p. 110.

31. For a more detailed and technical discussion of these issues by nutritionists who are sympathetic with the capabilities approach, see S.R. Osmani, ed., *Nutrition and Poverty*, Oxford: Clarendon Press, 1992. See also Paul Streeten, *Thinking about Development*, Cambridge: Cambridge University Press, 1995.

32. A new strain of "miracle" rice, which promises enormous productivity gains, will be hybridized with local rice varieties in order to make it acceptable to regional tastes in different parts of the world.

33. Cf. John Osgood Field and Mitchel B. Wallerstein, "Beyond Humanitarianism: A Developmental Perspective on American Food Aid," in *Food Policy*, pp. 234–258.

34. See Amartya Sen, "Population: Delusion and Reality," *New York Review of Books*, 61 (September 22, 1994), pp. 62–71, and "Goods and People" (this volume).

35. See Amartya Sen, "Goods and People" (this volume); "Development: Which Way Now?" in *Resources, Values and Development*, Oxford: Blackwell; Cambridge, MA: Harvard University Press, 1984, pp. 485–508; "The Concept of Development," in Hollis Chenery and T.N. Srinivasan, eds., *Handbook of Development Economics*, vol. 1, Amsterdam: North Holland, 1988, pp. 9–26; "Development as Capability Expansion," in Griffin and Knight, eds., *Human Development and the International Development Strategy for the 1990s*, pp. 41–58; Crocker, "Functioning and Capability," pp. 584–588. See also United Nations Development Programme, *Human Development Report 1994*, New York and Oxford: Oxford University Press, 1994 p. 13: "The purpose of development is to create an environment in which all people can expand their capabilities, and opportunities can be enlarged for both present and future generations.

36. For a detailed examination of intitutions and policies—both national and international—that have proven successful in alleviating hunger and reducing poverty, see HPA and Streeten, *Thinking about Development*.

37. For a good account, with full references, of controversies in the fifties, sixties, and seventies concerning U.S. food aid and development policy, see Anne O. Krueger, Constantine Michalopoulos, and Vernon W. Ruttan, *Aid and Development* Baltimore and London: Johns Hopkins University Press, 1989; Vernon W. Ruttan, ed., *Why Food Aid?* Baltimore and London: Johns Hopkins University Press, 1993, especially pp. 37–129.

38. Ruttan, ed., *Why Food Aid?* p. 66.

39. Georg W.F. Hegel, *Hegel's Philosophy of Right*, trans. T.M. Knox, Oxford: Oxford University Press, 1952, pp. 12–13.

40. See especially, Nigel Dower, *World Poverty: Challenge and Response*, York, UK: Ebor Press, 1983; Onora O'Neill, *Faces of Hunger: An Essay on Poverty, Justice, and Development*, London: Allen & Unwin, 1986; Jerome M. Segal, "What is Development?" Working Paper, DN-1, College Park, MD: Institute for Philosophy and Public Policy, October 1986.

41. For philosophical accounts of development ethics, see David A. Crocker, "Toward Development Ethics," *World Development* 19, no. 5 (1991):457–483, and "Development Ethics and Development Theory-Practice," Discussion Paper CBPE 93-2, College Station:

Center for Biotechnology Policy and Ethics, Texas A&M University, 1993; and Nigel Dower, "What is Development?—A Philosopher's Answer," Centre for Development Studies Occasional Paper Series, 3, Glasgow: University of Glasgow, 1988.

42. David A. Crocker, "Insiders and Outsiders in International Development Ethics," *Ethics and International Affairs* 5 (1991): 149–173.

43. See Godfrey Gunatilleke, Neelen Tiruchelvam, and Radhika Coomaraswamy, eds., *Ethical Dilemmas of Development in Asia*, Lexington, MA: Lexington Books, 1988; Kwame Gyekye, *The Unexamined Life: Philosophy and the African Experience*, Legon: Ghana Universities Press, 1988; Martha Nussbaum, "Aristotelian Social Democracy," in R. Bruce Douglass, Gerald R. Mara, and Henry S. Richardson, eds., *Liberalism and the Good*, New York and London: Routledge, 1990, pp. 203–252; and Luis Camacho, *Ciencia y tecnologia en el subdesarrollo*, Cartago: Editorial Tecnológica de Costa Rica, 1993.

44. Since the early sixties, Denis Goulet has been addressing the ethical and value dimensions of development theory and practice. His new book, *Development Ethics: A Guide to Theory and Practice*, New York: Apex Books, 1995, treats development ethics from the perspective of a policy analyst and activist. Economist Paul Streeten, an architect of the basic human needs strategy and currently a consultant with UNDP, has persistently addressed ethical issues in his work; see, for example, *Strategies for Human Development: Global Poverty and Unemployment*, Copenhagen: Handelshjskolens Forlag, 1994.

45. An early anticipation of an integrated approach to world hunger is Peter G. Brown and Henry Shue, eds., *Food Policy: The Responsibility of the United States in the Life and Death Choices*, New York: Free Press, 1977. This anthology, which appeared in the same year as WH, shared WH's deficiencies with respect to minority and international participation. *Food Policy's* contributors, however, included policy analysts and policymakers as well as a variety of academics. Moreover, the volume displayed an excellent balance— as a whole and in several individual essays—of moral, empirical, institutional, political, and policy analysis.

Combining Justice with Development: Rethinking Rights and Responsibilities in the Context of World Hunger and Poverty

RADHIKA BALAKRISHNAN and UMA NARAYAN

Radhika Balakrishnan received her B.A. in Economics at the University of Illinois at Champagne. She received her M.A. and Ph.D in Economics at Rutgers University. She has worked at Wellesley College and at the Ford Foundation, and is presently teaching at Wagner College, New York.

Uma Narayan received her B.A. in Philosophy from Bombay University, and her M.A. in Philosophy at Poona University, India. She received her Ph.D. in Philosophy at Rutgers University and is presently teaching at Vassar College. Her areas of interest are Social and Political Philosophy, Philosophy of Law, Applied Ethics, and Feminist Philosophy.

Introduction

Both our respective disciplines, Economics and Philosophy, have made significant contributions to public awareness about, and policy debates on, world hunger and poverty. We are both however deeply concerned about mistaken assumptions that pervade much of the discussion on world hunger and poverty within our respective disciplines. An accurate understanding of a problem is crucial to arriving at reasonable solutions to it. Misdescriptions of an issue are dangerous in that they urge commitment to misguided solutions. The first section of this essay is an explication and critique of several problematic assumptions that are commonplace in the discourse on world hunger and poverty.

In the second section, we will explore some of the ways in which everyday hunger, malnourishment, and poverty are the consequences of economic choices and development policies, paying particular attention to how women are affected by these policies in gender-specific ways. We end this section by arguing that the central focus of our moral concern should be everyday poverty and resilient hunger, and not the episodic crises of famines. The final section of the essay ends by arguing that moral obligations to end world hunger are obligations of justice, and not merely obligations of charity. In so doing, we say that the persons and institutions who are responsible for and have benefited from such choices bear the brunt of the moral obligation to alleviate the poverty and hunger that result from these choices. We conclude by arguing that citizens in democratic societies have an obligation to exercise their political rights to support national and international policies that will secure both basic political rights as well as basic subsistence rights for all human beings.

Distancing Hunger

Disagreement on answers to complex practical and moral issues such as those raised by world hunger is not surprising. What is surprising is the degree to which one particular question seems to frame academic and policy-oriented discourse on world hunger. The "central question" about world-hunger often tends to be posed in terms of "What, if anything, do those in the affluent nations owe the starving peoples of the Third World?"[1] We think the centrality of this question is neither obvious nor innocuous, since it fosters a number of misconceptions.

This question tends to suggest that *all* the hungry people of the world live in Third World countries, and eclipses the existence of hunger and malnutrition in western countries such as the United States. In so doing, stereotypes of Third World poverty are reinforced, while a comforting blindness to problems of hunger and poverty in the western world is fostered. It is worth reminding ourselves that "*world* hunger" is distinctly a *global* problem, and that "Third World hunger" is only *one* of its facets. Those who go hungry in western countries tend to be members of marginalized groups such as the homeless and the severely poor. Increasingly, most of those who suffer from hunger and poverty in western countries tend to be single mothers and their children. Lack of attention to hunger and poverty in western contexts then becomes yet one more instance of a chronic tendency to ignore problems that primarily affect women, and especially women who are additionally marginalized because of their race and class backgrounds.[2]

Lack of attention to the presence of poverty and hunger in western countries might be rooted in a belief that there is moral and political consensus in these countries about providing for the needs of their poor and destitute people. Focusing on obligations to distant others may be assumed to be more urgent because of greater uncertainty about what is owed, and because of our greater blindness or indifference to the suffering of distant others. However, we would argue that this perspective is mistaken. It fails to attend to the existence of extensive political apathy and active antipathy to the poor and hungry in western contexts, where the public attitudes and political response to the poor, such as homeless people or welfare mothers, is often denunciation and victim-blaming rather than political concern to ameliorate their problems.[3]

There are, after all, many kinds of distance other than geographical ones; and the distance between the privileged and the destitute in western contexts is only exacerbated by social structures that contribute to the segregation of many of the western poor in projects, in inner cities, and in poor neighborhoods, out of the literal and imaginative sight of their privileged fellow citizens. Many people in western contexts unquestioningly assume that their societies have sufficient institutionalized means for providing for the needs of their poor, and are likely to be surprised at the grim textures of the lives led by their homeless and destitute fellow citizens, movingly depicted for instance in Jonathan Kozol's book, *Rachel and Her Children.*[4] Kozol reports, among other things, several instances of soup kitchens running out of food before all the waiting hungry are fed, and that many of the hungry routinely did not receive enough food to sustain them for a full day. We could not reiterate more strongly the need to focus the attention of western citizens not only on distant hunger but on the hunger and poverty in their midst, in contexts where their concern stands the greatest chance of being efficacious.

Another group of persons entirely missing from many discussions of world hunger are the privileged elites of Third World countries. Just as persons in western countries are not uniformly affluent, there are significant groups of privileged individuals in Third World countries whose lives are as free from hunger and malnutrition as the lives of privileged citizens of the western world. Ignoring the existence of affluent groups in the Third World creates a false picture of a uniformly affluent western world and a uniformly poor and hungry Third World. The problems involved in ignoring the afflu-

ent of the Third World goes far beyond the reinforcing of such stereotypes. The affluent elites of the Third World are often *largely* responsible for economic and political decisions in their countries that contribute to creating, and to failing to ameliorate, problems of hunger,
poverty, and malnutrition.[5] Not attending to their agency amounts to
ignoring the active role these elites play in generating situations that
contribute to widespread poverty and hunger, leading to an analysis
that is both normatively and causally inadequate. The military, economic, and political decisions of these elites, that often contribute to
hunger and poverty in their national contexts, are frequently made
with the support, assistance and collaboration of western states,
corporations and development agencies, which often play an important role in training these elites. Ignoring the roles of nonwestern
elites therefore indirectly facilitates ignoring the associated roles of
western nations and institutions in contributing to the creation of
world hunger and poverty. Ignoring the role of Third World elites also
amounts to ignoring the highly efficacious roles some sections of
such elites play in generating famine relief efforts in their national
contexts. For instance, Amartya Sen has argued that the coverage
extended by the news media as well as pressures from opposition
political parties when famine conditions threatened, have significantly contributed to the prevention of famines in India.[6] The roles
that Third World elites play, in creating as well as in ameliorating
hunger in their national contexts must be given serious attention in
any policy recommendations designed to reduce or eradicate world
hunger.

Ignoring the presence of the poor in western countries, and of
the affluent in Third World countries, contributes to the perceived
validity of what we shall call the "two life-boats" metaphor, one that
frequently haunts philosophical discussions of world hunger. In this
metaphor, the population of the earth is envisioned as inhabiting two
different life-boats. The populations of the affluent nations are seen
as occupying a well-stocked and uncrowded life-boat, while the
wretched masses of the Third World occupy an under-stocked lifeboat, in imminent danger of capsizing because of their prolific rate
of reproduction.[7] A variety of arguments are then often offered to
support the view that those in the well-stocked life-boats ought not
to assist those in the under-stocked life-boat. We will proceed to analyze the various problems with this metaphor, and argue that this
metaphor is far more full of leaks than its imagined Third World lifeboat.

Part of what is wrong with the two-lifeboats metaphor is, as our
previous discussion points out, that the world simply does not correspond to two areas, one characterized by uniform affluence, and

the other by uniform deprivation. Many countries in the Western world and in the Third World correspond to life-boats within which some individuals own and control a vast quantity of existing provisions, while others have little access to adequate means of subsistence. The relative numbers of the affluent and the destitute might well differ from country-to-country, but the overall picture we have drawn, of inequalities *within* life-boats, is a far more accurate representation than the two-lifeboats metaphor. The two-lifeboats metaphor is misleading in other important ways. It often suggests, for instance, that it is simply a *contingent* fact that one life-boat happens to be well-stocked while the other is not. This picture overlooks the possibility that the provisions on the affluent lifeboat might be in part a result of unjust transactions that depleted the provisions available on the poor lifeboat. The two-lifeboats scenario avoids considering the many ways in which the affluent elites of western and nonwestern nations have helped to cause and to maintain the poverty and hunger of others. Questions about the moral obligations of the affluent toward the poor and hungry are not simply questions about what the former might possibly owe those who just *happen* to be poor. We believe that since poverty and chronic hunger often *result* from the economic and political decisions of national governments, foreign governments and international development agencies, the *responsibility* for alleviating these problems must be accepted by a number of countries and institutions.

The Causes and Gendered Impact of Global Poverty and Hunger

In this section, we will briefly describe some of the ways in which chronic hunger and poverty are the historically constituted and ongoing results of development policies and economic decisions at the national and international level. We will also point to some to the ways in which world hunger and poverty have gender-specific impacts on the well-being of women. The economic history of colonialism, as well as the global economic patterns of the postcolonial era arguably provide many examples of economic patterns and transactions between the affluent western nations and impoverished Third World countries that have contributed to world hunger and poverty. An illustration of the devastating economic impact of colonialism is provided by the following:

> Bengal (today's Bangladesh and the West Bengal state of India), the first territory the British conquered in Asia, was a prosperous

province with highly developed centers of manufacturing and trade, and an economy as advanced as any prior to the industrial revolution. The British reduced Bengal to poverty through plunder, heavy land taxes and trade restrictions that barred competitive Indian goods from England, but gave British goods free entry into India. India's late Prime Minister Nehru commented bitterly, "Bengal can take pride in the fact that she helped greatly in giving birth to the Industrial Revolution in England."[8]

Those who think that blaming a "long-past" colonialism for the current economic problems of former colonies is unconvincing would do well to remember that many of these countries were colonies well past the middle of this century. It is also worth noting that some of the economic patterns set up during colonialism persist to this day.[9] The economies of many former colonies continue to be dependent on a single agricultural crop, such as cocoa, coffee or bananas, an outcome of a colonial history where particular colonies were reduced to suppliers of specific commodities for the colonizer's markets, a pattern that not only makes these countries highly vulnerable to the shifting global prices of their particular cash-crop commodity, but makes them economically and politically dependent on the affluent countries that purchase the product they supply. The shift to producing cash crops for western markets also adversely affected the production and availability of foods consumed by local populations, as large areas of land were converted to growing cash crops rather than food crops. Recent development policies that stress large-scale mechanized farming to produce crops for export have further undermined female farming systems that were central to food-sufficiency in many Third World countries, where female farmers now have access only to small marginalized plots of land.[10] Many of these women now have to work on "green revolution" farms to supplement family income to buy sufficient food, in addition to doing subsistence farming and taking care of their families. National and international development policies have thus contributed to increasing the vulnerability to poverty and hunger of several groups of people, including many women who can no longer fully function as subsistence farmers.[11] Marginalized subsistence farmers are forced to re-use their plots over and over without crop rotation. Corporate farms do not use crop-rotation either, and use farming methods that destroy the topsoil. These practices lead to widespread desertification, adversely affecting people's quality of life.[12]

The account we have sketched of some of the causes of global poverty and hunger is very different from the one that informs the "two-lifeboats metaphor" we previously discussed, one that sees world hunger and poverty as primarily an effect of "overpopulation." The Malthusian assumption that world hunger is a result of over-population is fairly common in philosophical and economic dis-course as well as in ordinary understanding. It remains central to the vision of many who make global and national decisions about economic development, and is often used as an explanation for poverty by both Third World and western elites. Contemporary eco-nomic policy discourse retains the pervasive assumption that both famine and chronic poverty are the results of overpopulation. Contemporary policy discourse on hunger and world development is marked by a debate between two schools of thought. One is com-mitted to the view that the central task of global development is to draw more of the world's population into increased efficiency market production, thus creating new jobs and productive opportunities. This, it is argued, will alleviate both poverty and the population problem, since those who are less poor will have an incentive to have fewer children. The other school of thought emphasizes population control as the primary goal of development policies, since they see growing populations as an impediment to many countries initiating sufficient economic development to reap the demographic benefits of a falling birth rate. The latter seems to be the dominant perspective in contemporary economic policy discourse. However, both perspec-tives see overpopulation as a root cause of poverty and underdevel-opment.

We would like to call attention to the problematic gendered implications of such perspectives. First, locating chronic poverty in overpopulation targets women's bodies as the central site of the problem. Attributing hunger and poverty to overpopulation rein-forces stereotypes about the irrational, out-of-control fertility of backward and ignorant Third World women. These images of the out-of-control fertility of poor Third World women mirror stereotypes about the out-of-control fertility of welfare mothers, within western contexts. Both groups of women are seen as virtually parthenogen-tic reproducers, who have vast quantities of children without ratio-nality or regard to the general social good. While we leave open the possibility that some countries may have legitimate demographic concerns, we believe that the overwhelming emphasis on overpopu-lation as the *central* cause of poverty and hunger conveniently dis-places attention from numerous economic structures and develop-ment decisions that are far more important causes of endemic pover-ty and hunger.

The picture of overpopulation as the central cause of world hunger leads to support for policies that give greater priority to population control than to women's health and empowerment.[13] Such policies tend to be designed without respect for women's reproductive rights, and without concern for how these policies will affect women's economic roles. The target of these coercive population policies are generally poor third world women and women of color in the industrialized western nations.[14] We need to be critical of both of views that attribute poverty and hunger to simple overpopulation and of views that regard a rise in per capita income as *the* solution to curbing population growth. The population of the state of Kerala in South India has been stabilized at zero even though per capita incomes are very low, much lower than in other parts of India and in other Third World countries that continue to have much higher rates of population growth.[15] High-literacy rates among women, low infant mortality because of good health care and adequate nutrition, legal recognition of women's property rights, and noncoercive access to a variety of affordable birth control techniques, seem to be the major causes of Kerala's success.[16] We believe that the case of Kerala provides concrete empirical proof that the social empowerment of women is more central to a fall in population growth rates than rise in per capita incomes, and that development policies that promote women's rights can secure the demographic results of low population growth. Therefore, coercive populations policies that violate women's reproductive rights cannot be justified on the grounds that they are "necessary evils" that must be resorted to in order to "solve the population crisis."

Women are adversely affected not only by the Malthusian assumptions that pervade current thinking about development, but also by the increasingly popular view that the growth of market economies is *the key* to development. The end of the Cold War has resulted in much of the world being drawn into a global market economy. Women are particularly adversely affected by development policies that focus on developing market economies, and this is often not an *accidental* side-effect of these policies, as we pointed out in our discussion of cash-cropping and mechanized agriculture. Women's roles and ensuing costs to women are *structurally taken into account* in many ongoing development policies which assume that women's exploited labor in the marketplace, as well as increased burdens on them in terms of their contributions to their families and communities, are acceptable costs of "development." In the 1980s many Third World countries were pressured by the International Monetary Fund (IMF) to adopt "structural adjustment" or austerity programs, in order to qualify for development loans. These programs "require countries to increase productivity and exports while decreasing government spending on social welfare...forcing working women to perform the caretaking for which the public sector is abandoning responsibility."[17] The structural adjustments made in the drive to develop market economies assumes women's increasing time and labor in the maintenance of human resources, and assumes that women will carry the burden of safety nets that are cut by government. Women's increased labor is counted on to compensate for ecological devastation that makes clean water and fuel hard to obtain in areas where "land is lost to corporate farms and water sources are polluted by agricultural runoff from fertilizers and pesticides."[18] Hence, women not only bear the brunt of developing these market economies (as vulnerable cheap labor), but also bear the brunt of compensating for the adverse effects of the market economy on others in the community.[19]

Our discussion thus far has focused on some of the causes of everyday poverty and hunger, rather than on hunger in the context of famine situations. In contrast, philosophical discussions of moral obligations to the hungry have tended to focus on situations of famine rather than on chronic poverty and hunger. We believe that this emphasis on famine situations is problematic. Famines, by their "crisis" nature often generate media attention and international action. The everyday effects of continuing poverty and malnutrition, that contributes to the early death and debilitation of millions, is so commonplace that it invites less concern, attention, or action. However, the effects of chronic poverty and malnutrition are as devastating in their way as those of famine, and require us to focus on our obligations to conceive of *long-term* solutions, rather than on *episodic* obligations in times of famine "crises." We would therefore like to conclude this section by insisting that chronic poverty and everyday hunger, rather than famines, should be the central focus of moral concern in discussions of world hunger.

World Hunger and Poverty as Matters of Justice

The moral obligations we have to alleviate chronic poverty and hunger are more appropriately considered obligations of rights and justice than obligations of charity. Obligations of charity are often seen as matters of what we ought to do to promote the *good* of, or alleviate the suffering of, others, and not as matters of their moral entitlements. On the other hand, rights "are not mere gifts or favors, motivated by love or pity" but something that "can be demanded or insisted on without embarrassment or shame."[20] Philosophical discussions about poverty and world hunger often pose the moral question at issue as one of charity—as matters of what the privileged should do to assist unfortunate others, rather than as matters of the rights and entitlements of the poor and the hungry.

We believe that charity provides an inadequate moral framework in which to think about obligations to alleviate world hunger and poverty for several reasons. A number of moral frameworks regard obligations to charity as less stringent than obligations of justice. In such frameworks, although one has moral obligations to be charitable, agents have leeway in deciding on which occasions will elicit their charity. Agents have no such leeway in respecting the rights of others, since we have obligations to respect the rights of others at all times. Many moral frameworks also consider moral omissions with respect to charity (i.e., failures to respond to the suffering of others) as less blameworthy than the failure to respect people's rights. We will argue that obligations to alleviate chronic poverty and hunger are centrally matters of justice, matters of respecting people's rights, and not obligations of mere charity.

We have obligations to ensure that all human beings are guaranteed "basic welfare rights," rights to the material means to satisfy their basic needs and to secure a decent level of subsistence. We concur with Henry Shue in including rights to "...unpolluted air, unpolluted water, adequate food, adequate clothing, adequate shelter and minimal preventive public health care" among such basic subsistence rights.[21] Many discussions of rights have tended to focus overwhelmingly on "negative rights," rights to freedom from intrusion and interference in important realms of human choices. Most of the rights constitutionally guaranteed to citizens in liberal democratic societies, such as rights to free speech or to privacy, tend to be "negative rights" of this sort. There has been reluctance to extend the notion of rights to include "positive rights" to the material means to secure one's basic subsistence needs. State provision of such means has often been regarded in terms of "charitable assistance to the needy" rather than centrally as a matter of protecting the rights of individuals. We believe that this view is misguided, and that when the moral project of protecting individual rights is properly understood, we can see that the reasons for recognizing positive rights to the basic means of subsistence are not fundamentally dissimilar to the reasons for recognizing negative rights to freedom from intrusion in important areas of human life.

Guaranteeing *both basic negative and positive rights* is crucial to any moral framework that endorses the dignity and worth of all individuals. Human dignity is at risk when human beings are left without protection for important human vulnerabilities. Thus, human dignity is compromised when people are rendered vulnerable to serious intrusions on their capacities for autonomy and choice.

The guarantee of negative rights to freedom from such intrusions is therefore one important component of preserving human dignity. However, human dignity is also at risk when human beings are left vulnerable as a result of lacking adequate means for the satisfaction of their basic needs. The guarantee of positive rights to the means for securing one's basic subsistence needs is therefore an equally important component of preserving human dignity.

Both negative and positive rights can therefore be seen as guaranteeing basic dignity, respect and worth to human beings, and as existing to protect them from being rendered vulnerable in ways that adversely affect their dignity. If we understand rights in this way, we can see an underlying unity between the roles of "negative" and "positive" rights. Meaningful exercise of one's choices as well as the adequate satisfaction of one's needs are both vital components of human dignity and worth. Failures to guarantee either basic negative or positive rights to individuals is tantamount to declaring that their fate and future do not matter, and to be treated as creatures whose vital interests do not matter is to be reduced to the moral status of a creature who is accorded no dignity, respect or worth. Thus, any moral framework that is committed to seeing all humans as bearers of dignity and worth needs to guarantee all individuals not merely important negative rights to noninterference, but positive welfare rights to the basic means of subsistence. Understanding our moral obligations to alleviate chronic poverty and hunger as a matter of securing basic welfare rights to all individuals helps us to see that our obligations to eradicate acute poverty and hunger *in all parts of the world* are connected, since such poverty and hunger are corrosive of human dignity and respect whether they occur in western contexts or in Third World contexts. Further, if our obligations to alleviate chronic poverty and hunger are seen as matters of securing welfare rights to all individuals, these obligations turn out to be obligations of justice rather than of charity, since the protection of rights is centrally a matter of justice.

We believe that recognizing the connected roles of both negative and positive rights as important dimensions of justice is a matter of great urgency and importance. The Cold War context tended to polarize human rights discourse. Western nations such as the United States tended to emphasize political and civil rights, while resisting equal emphasis on economic and social rights. Henry Shue points out that "much official U.S. Government rhetoric routinely treats all 'economic rights,' among which basic subsistence rights are buried amidst many nonbasic rights, as secondary and deferrable...."[22] On the other hand, nondemocratic Third World regimes, and their western supporters, often argued that economic subsistence rights were of paramount importance to their citizens, and that such subsistence rights could only be guaranteed by "trade-offs" with political and democratic rights.[23] The end of the Cold War has generated a space in which there seems to be greater global willingness to reject such "trade-offs" between economic and political rights, to consider the connectedness of these various human rights, and to face the challenges that securing both sorts of human rights pose in the current global context. Human rights concerns seem to be gaining increasing attention among economic and development policy makers. We believe that such a unified theoretical vision of the roles played by both negative and positive rights is especially pertinent, given that human rights and their role in development are being subject to active rethinking.[24]

Although both negative rights and basic welfare rights are matters of justice, we recognize that there is an important difference between the ways in which the obligations to protect these two different kinds of rights may function. An individual's negative rights entail obligations on the part of every other individual and institution to refrain from intrusion and interference. It is less clear who bears the brunt of the obligation to protect positive welfare rights, since every individual or institution may not have the means or ability to guarantee these rights to other individuals. The primary responsibility of guaranteeing the basic welfare rights of all individuals falls on the national and international institutions—economic institutions, nation states, and international bodies—whose policies and choices are responsible for the occurrence of world hunger and poverty, and who have the means to act so as to guarantee these rights. We would argue that national and international institutions that have primary responsibility for many economic decisions and development policies need to recognize that the provision of basic economic and social welfare rights to all is a binding moral and political obligation, one that cannot be overridden for reasons of economic convenience.

We think that there are good reasons to believe that the affluence of those who are affluent (whether they are Third world elites or the well-off citizens of western nations) is neither a simple result of their special merits (such as hard work or enterprise) nor merely a consequence of fortunate contingencies such as their having been born in a context rich in natural resources. Patterns of global affluence, and of global poverty, are results of complex historical economic relationships between nations, and between different classes of people within nations. They are complex results of the unequal economic and political relationships that have been characteristic of relationships between affluent and poorer nations, and between the affluent and the poor within nation states. We are arguing that the moral obligation of the affluent to alleviate world hunger and poverty is rooted in the fact that they have often both perpetrated and benefited from this historical process.[25]

World hunger and poverty are increasingly *foreseeable and foreseen effects* of development polices, national and international. These policies have a lot to do with the creation and maintenance of poverty and everyday hunger in many countries. If world hunger and poverty are understood to be effects of national and international economic policies, political leaders and economic policy-makers in particular need to learn to think about how to combine justice with development. We are not suggesting that the task of combining justice with development is an easy one, nor do we have a blueprint for how this should be done. Our task is a more modest one. We think there is an urgent need for questions about justice and questions about development to be *linked together in on-going ways* in the making of development policies. What would this involve?

It would require considering difficult questions about what sorts of development costs (environmental as well as human) are morally acceptable, and accepting moral obligations to repair some of the worst effects of development. It would involve not allowing the market alone to define people's entitlements, as it often currently does, but recognize moral responsibilities toward groups of people whose lives are adversely affected by the market forces unleashed by national and international economic policies. It would involve attending to the special adverse impacts of economic policies on women, and refusing to dismiss them as acceptable consequences of development. Market economies generate inequalities. Many people are marginalized or excluded from the market economy because of structural unemployment. Structural changes in the economy often destroy or render obsolete previous ways of making a living, without being able to absorb those displaced in new sectors of development. Many people are likely to be temporarily or permanently barred from participation in market-driven development because they are too old or young or ill or unskilled, or because the skills they possess have become obsolete as a result of rapid technological change. Market-driven development, in both western and Third World contexts, often results in groups of people being economically excluded, marginalized, and exploited. On the other hand, there is reason to believe that economic development, even development that relies heavily on market forces, can be combined with a commitment to creating societies that respect the basic welfare rights of individuals and promote their flourishing.

Jean Drèze and Amartya Sen have argued that the elimination of everyday hunger and undernourishment requires extensive public provisioning of healthcare, education, clean water, and basic sanitation, as well as of food. They point out that some countries with a fast growth of real national income (such as South Korea, Hong Kong, Singapore, and Kuwait) have "used the fruits of that growth to expand the basic entitlements to food, healthcare, and elementary education for all."[26] They also point out that some other countries (such as China, Costa Rica, Chile, and Cuba) have promoted entitlements to these goods without waiting for national income to rise to a high level. On the other hand, countries like Brazil and Oman have experienced fast economic growth, but have failed to ensure public support programs to guarantee these goods to all sectors of the population.[27] These variations suggest that policy decisions at the national level substantially affect the degree to which the agenda for economic development is combined with a commitment to social justice and to policies that can alleviate the worst aspects of poverty and everyday hunger. These examples suggest that countries can make a substantial commitment to combining justice with development, if they choose to do so.

While we have argued that the brunt of the moral obligations to alleviate poverty and hunger fall on national and international policy making institutions, we would also argue that the existence of widespread hunger and poverty creates certain obligations on the part of individual citizens. We have in mind here obligations of a different sort than might be fulfilled by contributing to charitable organizations such as Oxfam. Those of us who are citizens of democratic political systems have an obligation to use our political rights to support national and international policies that are conducive to alleviating, rather than exacerbating, hunger and poverty at home and abroad. We have obligations to be active and concerned citizens who support not only the sorts of economic policies that would be conducive to securing the basic welfare rights of all individuals, but also to encourage the growth and survival of democratic regimes in other parts of the world. The securing of substantive political rights to those who suffer from poverty and hunger is crucial to empowering them so that they are able to call attention to their problems, and to participate in the complex endeavor of developing policies that would change their situations for the better. As Senator Diokno of the Philippines put it:

> Development is not just providing people with adequate food, clothing and shelter; many prisons do as much. Development is also people deciding what food, clothing, and shelter are adequate, and how they are to be provided.[28]

We believe that the separation between disciplines and forms of expertise is particularly worrying in the context of world hunger and poverty. Economists and development policy makers are often trained not to think about moral questions of social justice, and are thus encouraged to think in terms of development and efficiency without heed to moral questions. Philosophers who are trained in moral theory are often profoundly ignorant of economic realities and theories, and thus liable to misunderstand the causes of world poverty and hunger, and misconstrue the nature of the moral obligations such problems generate. The difficult question of how to combine justice with development needs to be of central concern to development policy makers and philosophers, as well as be an important issue for concerned citizens.

NOTES

1. The introduction to the first edition of this volume provides a clear example when it describes the central question explored as, "What moral responsibility do affluent nations (or those people in them) have to the starving masses?"

2. For interesting discussions on the treatment of poor women in the context of the United States, see the essays in *Women, the State and Welfare*, edited by Linda Gordon, Madison, WI: University of Wisconsin Press, 1990.

3. Nancy Fraser and Linda Gordon describe a number of "icons" or stereotypes of dependency that have permeated the historical and present discourses of our society. They conclude that "Postindustrial culture has called up a new personification of dependency: the Black, unmarried, teenaged, welfare-dependent mother. This image has usurped the symbolic space previously occupied by the housewife, the pauper, the native, and the slave, while absorbing and condensing their connotations." See Nancy Fraser and Linda Gordon, "'Dependency' Demystified: Inscriptions of Power in a Keyword of the U.S. Welfare State," forthcoming in *Reconstructing Political Theory: Feminist Perspectives*, Mary L. Shanley and Uma Narayan (eds), Cambridge: Polity Press.

4. Jonathan Kozol, *Rachel and Her Children: Homeless Families in America*, New York: Crown Books, 1988.

5. For an interesting discussion of the role of Third World elites and the professionalization of development, see Arturo Escobar, "Power and Visibility: Development and the Invention of Management of the

Third World," *Cultural Anthropology*, vol. 3 (4), November 1988: 428–443.

6. Amartya Sen, "Property and Hunger," in *Social and Political Philosophy*, edited by John Arthur and William Shaw, Prentice Hall, 1992, pp. 222–230.

7. Two examples of discussions on world hunger where this picture is clearly at work are Joseph Fletcher, "Give If It Helps but Not If It Hurts," and Garrett Hardin, "Lifeboat Ethics: The Case Against Helping the Poor," both in *World Hunger and Moral Obligation*, W. Aiken and H. LaFollette, eds. Englewood Cliffs, NJ: Prentice-Hall, 1977.

8. Arthur Simon, *Bread for the World*, New York: Paulist Press, 1975, p. 41. Quoted in Robert N. Van Wyck, "Perspectives on World Hunger and the Extent of Our Positive Duties," *Public Affairs Quarterly*, 1988, 2:75–90.

9. For an interesting discussion, see Chakravarti Raghavan, *Recolonization: GATT, the Uruguay Round and the Third World*, London and New Jersey: Zed Books, 1990.

10. V. Spike Peterson and Anne Sisson Runyon, *Global Gender Issues*, Boulder, CO: Westview Press, 1993, p. 94.

11. For analyses of how transnational and national economic policies affect the production of food consumed by the poor, see Richard J. Barnet and Ronald E. Miller, Global Reach, *The Power of the Multinational Corporations*, New York: Simon and Schuster, 1974; and Jeffrey M. Paige, *Agrarian Revolution: Social Movements and Export Agriculture in the Underdeveloped World*; New York: Free Press, 1975.

12. V. Spike Peterson and Anne Sisson Runyon, *Global Gender Issues*, Boulder, CO: Westview Press, 1993, p. 108

13. See Ruth Dixon-Mueller, *Population Policy and Women's Rights: Transforming Reproductive Choice*, Westport, CT: Praeger, 1993.

14. See Brenda Wyss and Radhika Balakrishnan, "Making Connections: Women and the International Economy," in *Creating a New World Economy: Forces of Change and Plans for Action*, Gerald Epstein, Julie Graham and Jessica Nembhard, eds. Philadelphia: Temple University Press, 1993.

15. Albert Gore, "A Global Marshall Plan," in *Earth Ethics*, James Sterba, ed. Englewood Cliffs, NJ: Prentice Hall, 1995, p. 385.

16. See Radhika Balakrishana, *Access to Property and Its Relationship to Sex-Ratios in India*, Ph.D. Thesis, Rutgers University, 1990.

17. V. Spike Peterson and Anne Sisson Runyon, *Global Gender Issues*, Boulder, CO: Westview Press, 1993, p. 104.

18. V. Spike Peterson and Anne Sisson Runyon, *Global Gender Issues*, Boulder, CO: Westview Press, 1993, p. 106.

19. See Diane Elson, "Male-Bias in Macro Economics: The Case of

Structural Adjustment," in Diane Elson, ed. *Male-Bias in the Development Process*, Manchester, UK: Manchester University Press.

20. Joel Feinberg, *Social Philosophy*, Englewood Cliffs, NJ.: Prentice-Hall, 1973, p. 59.

21. Henry Shue, *Basic Rights: Subsistence, Affluence and U.S. Foreign Policy*, Princeton, NJ: Princeton University Press, 1980, p. 23.

22. Henry Shue, Basic Rights: Subsistence, *Affluence and U.S. Foreign Policy*, Princeton, NJ: Princeton University Press, 1980, p. 35.

23. A work justifying the trade-off of political liberty for development is Samuel P. Huntington and Joan M. Nelson, *No Easy Choice: Political Participation in Developing Countries*, Cambridge, MA: Harvard University Press, 1976.

24. Recent discussions at the NGO Forum and at the official conference at the U.N. World Summit for Social Development in Copenhagen, Denmark suggest that policy makers and activists are attempting to concretely relate to development issues the arguments about human rights made at the earlier U.N. Human Rights Conference in Vienna.

25. Our notion of "helping to perpetrate" is fairly wide. It covers not only direct engagement in economic transactions based on unequal economic and political power between nations, but includes providing political support for the global economic and political policies of one's nation, by means of the exercise of the powers of citizenship.

26. Jean Drèze and Amartya Sen, *Hunger and Public Action*, Oxford: Clarendon Press, 1989, p. 268.

27. Jean Drèze and Amartya Sen, *Hunger and Public Action*, Oxford: Clarendon Press, 1989, pp. 266–270.

28. Jose W. Diokno, untitled lecture, International Council of Amnesty International, Cambridge, 1978. Quoted in Henry Shue, *Basic Rights: Subsistence, Affluence and U.S. Foreign Policy*, Princeton, NJ: Princeton University Press, 1980, p. 66.

V. HUNGER AND THE ENVIRONMENT

Feeding People versus Saving Nature?

HOLMES ROLSTON III

Holmes Rolston III is University Distinguished Professor of Philosophy at Colorado State University. He is the author of five books, including: *Science and Religion: A Critical Survey* (Random House and McGraw-Hill); *Philosophy Gone Wild* (Prometheus); *Environmental Ethics* (Temple University Press); *Conserving Natural Value* (Columbia University Press).

When we must choose between feeding the hungry and conserving nature, people ought to come first. A bumper sticker reads: Hungry loggers eat spotted owls. That pinpoints an ethical issue, pure and simple, and often one where the humanist protagonist, taking high moral ground, intends to put the environmentalist on the defensive. You wouldn't let the Ethiopians starve to save some butterfly, would you?

"Human beings are at the centre of concerns for sustainable development." So the *Rio Declaration* begins. Once this was to be an *Earth Charter*, but the developing nations were more interested in getting the needs of their poor met. The developed nations are wealthy enough to be concerned about saving nature. The developing nations want the anthropocentrism, loud and clear. These humans, they add, "are entitled to a healthy and productive life in harmony with nature," but there too they seem as concerned with their entitlements as with any care for nature.[1] Can we fault them for it?

We have to be circumspect. To isolate so simple a trade-off as hungry people versus nature is perhaps artificial. If too far abstracted from the complex circumstances of decision, we may not be facing any serious operational issue. When we have simplified the question, it may have become, minus its many qualifications, a different question. The gestalt configures the question, and the same question reconfigured can be different. So we must analyze the general matrix, and then confront the more particular people-versus-nature issue.

Humans win? Nature loses? After analysis, sometimes it turns out that humans are not really winning, if they are sacrificing the nature that is their life support system. Humans win by conserving nature—and these winners include the poor and the hungry. "In order to achieve sustainable development, environmental protection shall constitute an integral part of the development process and cannot be considered in isolation from it."[2] After all, food has to be produced by growing it in some reasonably healthy natural system, and the clean water that the poor need is also good for fauna and flora. Extractive reserves give people an incentive to conserve. Tourism can often benefit both the local poor and the wildlife, as well as tourists. One ought to seek win-win solutions wherever one can. Pragmatically, these are often the only kind likely to succeed.

Yet there are times when nature is sacrificed for human development; most development is of this kind. By no means all is warranted, but that which gets people fed seems basic and urgent. Then nature should lose and people win. Or are there times when at least some humans should lose and some nature should win? We are here interested in these latter occasions. Can we ever say that we should save nature rather than feed people?

Feed People First? Do We? Ought We?

"Feed people first!" That has a ring of righteousness. The *Rio Declaration* insists, "All States and all people shall cooperate in the essential task of eradicating poverty as an indispensable requirement."[3] In the biblical parable of the great judgment, the righteous had ministered to the needy, and Jesus welcomes them to their reward. "I was hungry and you gave me food, I was thirsty and you gave me drink." Those who refused to help are damned (Matthew 28:31–46). The vision of heaven is that "they shall hunger no more, neither thirst any more" (Revelation 7.16), and Jesus teaches his disciples to pray that this will of God be done on earth, as it is in heaven. "Give us this day our daily bread" (Matthew 5.11). These are such basic values, if there is to be any ethics at all, surely food comes first.

Or does it? If giving others their daily bread were always the first concern, the Christians would never have built an organ or a sanctuary with a stained glass window, but rather always given all to the poor. There is also the biblical story of the woman who washed Jesus' feet with expensive ointment. When the disciples complained that it should have been sold and given to the poor, Jesus replied, "you always have the poor with you. She has done a beautiful thing." (Matthew 26.10-11). While the poor are a continuing concern, with whom Jesus demonstrated ample solidarity, there are other commendable values in human life, "beautiful things," in Jesus' phrase. The poor are always there, and if we did nothing else of value until there were no more poor, we would do nothing else of value at all.

Eradicating poverty is an indispensable requirement! Yes, but set these ideals beside the plain fact that we all daily prefer other values. Every time we buy a Christmas gift for a wife or husband, or go to a symphony concert, or give a college education to a child, or drive a late model car home, or turn on the air conditioner, we spend money that might have helped to eradicate poverty. We mostly choose to do things we value more than feeding the hungry.

An ethicist may reply, yes, that is the fact of the matter. But no normative ought follows from the description of this behavior. We ought not to behave so. But such widespread behavior, engaged in almost universally by persons who regard themselves as being ethical, including readers of this article, is strong evidence that we in fact not only have these norms but think we ought to have them. To be sure, we also think that charity is appropriate, and we censure those who are wholly insensitive to the plight of others. But we place decisions here on a scale of degree, and we do not feel guilty about all these other values we pursue, while yet some people somewhere on earth are starving.

If one were to advocate always feeding the hungry first, doing nothing else until no one in the world is hungry, this would paralyze civilization. People would not have invented writing, or smelted iron, or written music, or invented airplanes. Plato would not have written his dialogues, or Aquinas the *Summa Theologica*; Edison would not have discovered the electric light bulb or Einstein the theory of relativity. We both do and ought to devote ourselves to various worthy causes, while yet persons in our own communities and elsewhere go hungry.

A few of these activities redound subsequently to help the poor, but the possible feedback to alleviating poverty cannot be the sole justification of advancing these multiple cultural values. Let us remember this when we ask whether saving natural values might sometimes take precedence. Our moral systems in fact do not teach us to feed the poor first. The Ten Commandments do not say that; the Golden Rule does not; Kant did not say that; nor does the utilitarian greatest good for the greatest number imply that. Eradicating poverty may be indispensable but not always prior to all other cultural values. It may not always be prior to conserving natural values either.

Choosing for People to Die

But food is absolutely vital. "Thou shalt not kill" is one of the commandments. Next to the evil of taking life is taking the sustenance for life. Is not saving nature, thereby preventing hunting, harvesting, or development by those who need the produce of that land to put food in their mouths, almost like killing? Surely one ought not to choose for someone else to die, an innocent who is only trying to eat; everyone has a right to life. To fence out the hungry is choosing that people will die. That can't be right.

Or can it? In broader social policy we make many decisions that cause people to die. When in 1988 we increased the national speed limit on rural Interstate highways from 55 to 65 miles per hour, we chose for 400 persons to die each year.[4] We decide against hiring more police, though if we did some murders would be avoided. The city council spends that money on a new art museum, or to give the schoolteachers a raise. Congress decides not to pass a national health care program that would subsidize medical insurance for some now uninsured, who cannot otherwise afford it; and some such persons will, in result, fail to get, timely medical care and die of preventable diseases.

We may decide to leave existing air pollution standards in place because it is expensive for industry to install new scrubbers, even though there is statistical evidence that a certain number of persons will contract diseases and die prematurely. All money budgeted for the National Endowment for the Humanities, and almost all that budgeted for the National Science Foundation, could be spent to prevent the deaths of babies that die from malnutrition. We do not know exactly who will die, but we know that some will; we often have reasonable estimates how many. The situation would be similar, should we choose to save nature rather than to feed people.

U.S. soldiers go abroad to stabilize an African nation, from which starving refugees are fleeing, and we feel good about it. All those unfortunate people cannot come here, but at least we can go there and help. All this masks, however, how we really choose to fight others rather than to feed them. The developed countries spend as much on military power in a year as the poorest two billion people on Earth earn in total income. The developed countries in 1990 provided 56 billion dollars in economic aid to the poorer countries but they also sold 36 billion dollars worth of arms to them. At a cost of less than half their military expenditures, the developing countries could provide a package of basic health care services and clinical care that would save 10 million lives a year. World military spending in 1992 exceeded 600 billion dollars. U.S. military spending accounted for nearly half this amount, yet in the United States one person in seven lives below the poverty line and over 37 million people lack any form of health care coverage.[5] These are choices that cause people to die, both abroad and at home.

But such spending, a moralist critic will object, is wrong. This only reports what people do decide, not what they ought to decide. Yes, but few are going to argue that we ought to spend nothing on military defense until all the poor are fed, clothed, and housed. We believe that many of the values achieved in the United States, which place us among the wealthier nations, are worth protecting, even while others starve. Europeans and others will give similar arguments. Say if you like that this only puts our self-interest over theirs, but in fact we all do act to protect what we value, even if this decision results in death for those beyond our borders. That seems to mean that a majority of citizens think such decisions are right.

Wealthy and poverty-stricken nations alike put up borders across which the poor are forbidden to pass. Rich nations will not let them in; their own governments will not let them out. We may have misgivings about this on both sides, but if we believe in immigration laws at all, we, on the richer side of the border, think that protecting our lifestyle counts more than their betterment, even if they just want to be better fed. If we let anyone who pleased enter the United States, and gave them free passage, hundreds of millions would come. Already 30 percent of our population growth is by immigration, legal and illegal. Sooner or later we must fence them out, or face the loss of prosperity that we value. We may not think this is always right, but when one faces the escalating numbers that would swamp the United States, it is hard not to conclude that it is sometimes right. Admitting refugees is humane, but it lets such persons flee their own national problems and does not contribute to any long-term solutions in the nations from which they emigrate. Meanwhile, people die as a result of such decisions.

Some of these choices address the question whether we ought to save nature if this causes people to die. Inside our U.S. boundaries, we have a welfare system, refusing to let anyone starve. Fortunately, we are wealthy enough to afford this as well as nature conservation. But if it came to this, we would think it wrong-headed to put animals (or art, or well-paid teachers) over starving people. Does that not show that, as domestic policy, we take care of our own? We feed people first—or at least second, after military defence. Yet we let foreigners die, when we are not willing to open our five hundred wilderness areas, nearly 100 million acres, to Cubans and Ethiopians.

Hunger and Social Justice

The welfare concept introduces another possibility, that the wealthy should be taxed to feed the poor. We should do that first, rather than cut into much else that we treasure, possibly losing our wildlife, or wilderness areas, or giving up art, or underpaying the teachers. In fact, there is a way greatly to relieve this tragedy, could there be a just distribution of the goods of culture, now often so inequitably distributed. Few persons would need to go without enough if we could use the produce of the already domesticated landscape justly and charitably. It is better to try to fix this problem where it arises, within society, than to try to enlarge the sphere of society by the sacrifice of remnant natural values, by, say, opening up the wilderness areas to settlement. Indeed, the latter only postpones the problem.

Peoples in the South (a code word for the lesser developed countries, or the poor) complain about the overconsumption of peoples in the North (the industrial rich), often legitimately so. But Brazil has within its own boundaries the most skewed income distribution in the world. The U.S. ratio between personal income for the top 20 percent of people to the bottom 20 percent is 9 to 1; the ratio in Brazil is 26 to 1. Just one percent of Brazilians control 45 percent of the agricultural land. The biggest 20 landowners own more land between them than the 3.3 million smallest farmers. With the Amazon still largely undeveloped, there is already more arable land per person in Brazil than in the United States. Much land is held for speculation; 330 million hectares of farm land, an area larger than India, is lying idle. The top 10 percent of Brazilians spend 51 percent of the national income.[6] This anthropocentric inequity ought to be put "at the center of concern" when we decide about saving nature versus feeding people.

Save the Amazon! No! The howler monkeys and toucans may delight tourists, but we ought not save them if people need to eat. Such either-or choices mask how marginalized peoples are forced onto marginal lands; and those lands become easily stressed, both because the lands are by nature marginal for agriculture, range, and life support, and also because by human nature marginalized peoples find it difficult to plan for the long-range. They are caught up in meeting their immediate needs; their stress forces them to stress a fragile landscape.

Prime agricultural or residential lands can also be stressed to produce more, because there is a growing population to feed, or to grow an export crop, because there is an international debt to pay. Prime agricultural lands in southern Brazil, formerly used for growing food and worked by tenants who lived on these lands and ate their produce, as well as sent food into the cities, have been converted to growing coffee as an export crop, using mechanized farming, to help pay Brazil's massive debt, contracted by a military government since overthrown. Peoples forced off these lands were resettled in the Amazon basin, aided by development schemes fostered by the military government, resettled on lands really not suitable for agriculture. The integrity of the Amazon, to say nothing of the integrity of these peoples, is being sacrificed to cover for misguided loans. Meanwhile the wealthy in Brazil pay little or no income tax that might be used for such loan repayment.

The world is full enough of societies that have squandered their resources, inequitably distributed wealth, degraded their landscapes, and who will be tempted to jeopardize what natural values remain as an alternative to solving hard social problems. The decision about social welfare, poor people over nature, usually lies in the context of another decision, often a tacit one, to protect vested interests, wealthy people over poor people, wealthy people who have exploited nature already, ready to exploit anything they can. At this point in our logic, en route to any conclusion such as let-people-starve, we regularly reach an if-then, go-to decision point, where before we face the people-over-nature choice we have to reaffirm or let stand the wealthy-over-poor choice.

South Africa is seeking an ethic of ecojustice enabling five million privileged whites and twenty nine million exploited blacks (as well as several million underprivileged "Coloureds") to live in harmony on their marvelously rich but often fragile landscape.[7] Whites earn nearly ten times the per capita income of blacks. White farmers, 50,000 of them, own 70 percent of farmland; 700,000 black farmers own 13 percent of the land (17% other). Black ownership of land was long severely restricted by law. Forced relocations of blacks and black birth rates have combined to give the homelands, small areas carved out within the South African nation, an extremely high-average population density. When ownership patterns in the homelands are combined with those in the rest of the nation, land ownership is as skewed as anywhere on Earth. Compounding the problem is that the black population is growing, and is already more than ten times what it was before the Europeans came.

The land health is poor. South African farmers lose twenty tons of topsoil to produce one ton of crops. Water resources are running out; the limited wetlands in an essentially arid nation are exploited for development; water is polluted by unregulated industry. Natal, one of the nation's greenest and most glorious areas, is especially troubled with polluted winds. Everywhere, herbicides float downwind with adverse human, vegetative, and wildlife effects on nontarget organisms.

With an abundance of coal, South Africa generates 60 percent of the electricity on the African continent, sold at some of the cheapest rates in the world, although less than a third of South Africans have electricity. The Eskom coal-burning power plants in the Transvaal are the worst offenders in air pollution, leaving the high veld as polluted as was Eastern Germany, also threatening an area producing 50 percent of South Africa's timber industry and 50 percent of the nation's high potential agricultural soils. As a result of all this, many blacks go poorly nourished; some, in weakened condition, catch diseases and die.

What is the solution? South Africa also has some of the finest wildlife conservation reserves in Africa. Some are public; some are private. They are visited mostly by white tourists, often from abroad. One hears the cry that conserving elitist reserves, in which the wealthy enjoy watching lions and wildebeest, cannot be justified where poor blacks are starving. What South Africa needs is development, not conservation. In an industry-financed study, Brian Huntley, Roy Siegfried, and Clem Sunter conclude: "What is needed is a much larger cake, not a sudden change in the way it is cut."[8] One way to get a bigger cake would be to take over the lands presently held as wildlife reserves.

But more cake, just as unequally cut, is not the right solution in a nation that already stresses the carrying capacity of its landscape. Laissez-faire capitalists propose growth so that every one can become more prosperous, oblivious to the obvious fact that even the present South African relationship to the landscape is neither sustainable nor healthy. They seem humane; they do not want anyone to starve. The rhetoric, and even the intent, is laudable. At the same time, they want growth because this will avoid redistribution of wealth. The result, under the rubric of feeding people versus saving nature, is in fact favoring the wealthy over the poor.

What is happening is that an unjust lack of sharing between whites and blacks is destroying the green. It would be foolish for all, even for white South Africans acting in their own self-interest, fur-

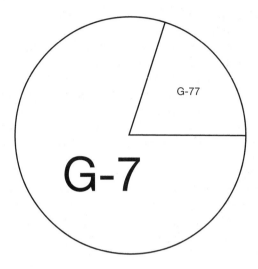

Figure 1   Proportionate Production and Consumption among Nations.

ther to jeopardize environmental health, rather than to look first and resolutely to solving their social problems. It would not really be right, if South Africans were to open their magnificent wildlife reserves, seemingly in the interests of the poor, while the cake remains as inequitably divided as ever. Fortunately, many South Africans have realized the deeper imperative, and the recent historic election there, and efforts toward a new constitution, promise deep social changes. This, in turn, will make possible a more intelligent conservation of natural values.[9]

In the more fortunate nations, we may distribute wealth more equitably, perhaps through taxes or minimum wage laws, or by labor unions, or educational opportunities, and we do have in place the welfare systems referred to earlier, refusing to let anyone starve. But lest we seem too righteous, we also recall that we have such policies only domestically. The international picture puts this in a different light. There are two major blocs, the G-7 nations (the Group of 7, the big nations of North America, Europe, and Japan, "the North"), and the G-77 nations, once 77 but now including some 128 lesser developed nations, often south of the industrial north. The G-7 nations hold about one fifth of the world's five billion persons, and they produce and consume about four fifths of all goods and services. The G-77 nations, with four fifths of the world's people, produce and consume one fifth. (See figure 1.) For every person added to the population of the North, twenty are added in the South. For every dollar of economic growth per person in the South, 20 dollars accrue in the North.[10]

The distribution problem is complex. Earth's natural resources are unevenly distributed by nature. Diverse societies have often taken different directions of development; they have different governments, ideologies, and religions; they have made different social choices, valued material prosperity differently. Typically, where there is agricultural and industrial development, people think of this as an impressive achievement. Pies have to be produced before they can be divided, and who has produced this pie? Who deserves the pie? People ought to get what they earn. Fairness nowhere commands rewarding all parties equally; justice is giving each his or her due. We treat equals equally; we treat unequals equitably, and that typically means unequal treatment proportionately to merit. There is nothing evidently unfair in the pie diagram, not at least until we have inquired about earnings. Some distribution patterns reflect achievement. Not all of the asymmetrical distribution is a result of social injustice.

Meanwhile, it is difficult to look at a distribution chart and not think that something is unfair. Is some of the richness on one side related to the poverty on the other? Regularly, the poor come off poorly when they bargain with the rich; and wealth that originates as impressive achievement can further accumulate through exploitation. Certainly many of the hungry people have worked just as hard as many of the rich.

Some will say that what the poorer nations need to do is to imitate the productive people. Unproductive people need to learn how to make more pies. Then they can feed themselves. Those in the G-7 nations who emphasize the earnings model tend to recommend to the G-77 nations that they produce more, often offering to help them produce by investments which can also be productive for the G-7 nations. Those in the G-77 nations do indeed wish to produce, but they also see the exploitation and realize that the problem is sharing as well as producing. Meanwhile the growth graphs caution us that producing can be as much part of the problem as part of the solution. One way to think of the circular pie chart is that this is planet Earth, and we do not have any way of producing a bigger planet. We could, though, feed more people by sacrificing more nature.

Meanwhile too, any such decisions take place inside this 1/5-gets-4/5ths, 4/5ths-gets-1/5 picture. So it is not just the Brazilians and the South Africans, but all of us in the United States, Europe, and Japan as well that have to face an if-then, go-to decision point, reaffirming and or letting stand the wealthy-over-poor division of the Earth's pie that we enjoy. This is what stings when we see the

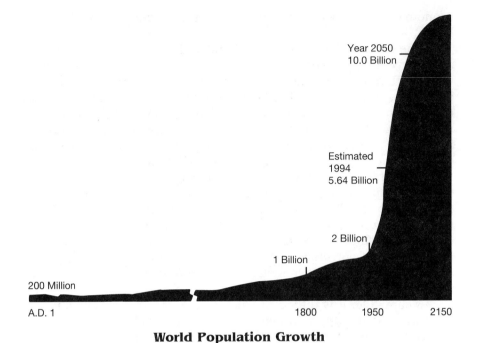

World Population Growth

Figure 2   Adapted from data in U.S. Bureau of the Census, *Statistical Abstract of the United States: 1994* (114th edition). Washington, DC, 1994. Page 850.

bumper sticker ethical injunction: "Live simply that others may simply live."

Escalating Human Populations

Consider human population growth. (See Figure 2.) Not only have the numbers of persons grown, their expectations have grown, so that we must superimpose one exploding curve on top of another. A superficial reading of such a graph is that humans really start winning big in the twentieth century. There are lots of them, and they want, and many get, lots of things. If one is a moral humanist, this can seem a good thing. Wouldn't it be marvelous if all could get what they want, and none hunger and thirst any more?

But when we come to our senses, we realize that this kind of winning, if it keeps on escalating, is really losing. Humans will lose, and nature will be destroyed as well. Cultures have become consumptive, with ever-escalating insatiable desires, overlaid on ever-escalating population growth. Culture does not know how to say "Enough!" and that is not satisfactory. Starkly put, the growth of culture has become cancerous. That is hardly a metaphor, for a cancer is essentially an explosion of unregulated growth. Feeding people always seems humane, but, when we face up to what is really going on, by just feeding people, without attention to the larger social results, we could be feeding a kind of cancer.

One can say that where there is a hungry mouth, one should do what it takes to get food into it. But when there are two mouths there the next day, and four the day after that, and sixteen the day after that, one needs a more complex answer. The population of Egypt was less than 3 million for over five millennia, fluctuating between 1.5 to 2.5 million, even when Napoleon went there in the early 1800s. Today the population of Egypt is about 55 million. Egypt has to import more than half its food. The effects on nature, both on land health and on wildlife, have been adversely proportional.

If, in this picture, we look at individual persons, caught up in this uncontrolled growth, and if we try to save nature, some persons will go hungry. Surely, that is a bad thing. Would anyone want to say that such persons ought not to sacrifice nature, if needs be, to alleviate such harm as best they can? From their perspective, they are only doing what humans have always done, making a resourceful use of nature to meet their own needs. Isn't that a good thing anymore? Such persons are doomed, unless they can capture natural values.

But here we face a time-bound truth, in which too much of a good thing becomes a bad thing. We have to figure in where such persons are located on the population curve, and realize that a good thing when human numbers are manageable is no longer a good thing when such a person is really another cell of cancerous growth. That sounds cruel, and it is tragic, but it does not cease to be true for these reasons. For a couple to have two children may be a blessing; but the tenth child is a tragedy. When the child comes, one has to be as humane as possible, but one will only be making the best of a tragic situation, and if the tenth child is reared, and has ten children in turn, that will only multiply the tragedy. The quality of human lives deteriorates; the poor get poorer. Natural resources are further stressed; ecosystem health and integrity degenerate; and this compounds the losses again—a lose-lose situation. In a social system misfitted to its landscape, one's wins can only be temporary in a losing human ecology.

Even if there were an equitable distribution of wealth, the human population cannot go on escalating without people becoming all equally poor. Of the 90 million new people who will come on board planet Earth this year, 85 million will appear in the Third World, the countries least able to support such population growth. At the same time, each North American will consume 200 times as much energy, and many other resources. The 5 million new people in the industrial countries will put as much strain on the environment as the 85 million new poor. There are three problems: overpopulation, overconsumption, and underdistribution. Sacrificing nature for development does not solve any of these problems, none at all. It only brings further loss. The poor, after a meal for a day or two, perhaps a decade or two, are soon hungry all over again, only now poorer still because their natural wealth is also gone.

To say that we ought always to feed the poor first commits a good-better-best fallacy. If a little is good, more must be better, most is best. If feeding some humans is good, feeding more is better. And more. And more! Feeding all of them is best? That sounds right. We can hardly bring ourselves to say that anyone ought to starve. But we reach a point of diminishing returns, when the goods put at threat lead us to wonder.

Endangered Natural Values

Natural values are endangered at every scale: global, regional, and local, at levels of ecosystems, species, organisms, populations, fauna and flora, terrestrial and marine, charismatic megafauna down to mollusks and beetles. This is true in both developed and developing nations, though we have under discussion here places where poverty threatens biodiversity.

Humans now control 40 percent of the planet's land-based primary net productivity, that is, the basic plant growth that captures the energy on which everything else depends.[11] If the human population doubles again, the capture will rise to 60 to 80 percent, and little habitat will remain for natural forms of life that cannot be accommodated after we have put people first. Humans do not use the lands they have domesticated effectively. A World Bank study found that 35 percent of the Earth's land has now become degraded.[12] Daniel Hillel, in a soils study, concludes, "Present yields are extremely low in many of the developing countries, and as they can be boosted substantially and rapidly, there should be no need to reclaim new land and to encroach further upon natural habitats."[13]

Africa is a case in point, and Madagascar epitomizes Africa's future. Its fauna and flora evolved independently from the mainland continent; there are 30 primates, all lemurs; the reptiles and amphibians are 90 percent endemic, including two thirds of all the chameleons of the world, and 10,000 plant species, of which 80 percent are endemic, including a thousand kinds of orchids. Humans came there about 1,500 years ago and lived with the fauna and flora more or less intact until this century. Now an escalating population of impoverished Malagasy people rely heavily on slash-and-burn agriculture, and the forest cover is one third of the original (27.6 million acres to 9.4 million acres), most of the loss occurring since 1950.[14] Madagascar is the most eroded nation on Earth, and little or none of the fauna and flora is safely conserved. Population is expanding at 3.2 percent a year; remaining forest is shrinking at 3 percent, almost all to provide for the expanding population. Are we to say that none ought to be conserved until after no person is hungry?

Tigers are sliding toward extinction. Populations have declined 95 percent in this century; the two main factors are loss of habitat and a ferocious black market in bones and other body parts used in traditional medicine and folklore in China, Taiwan, and Korea, uses that are given no medical credence. Ranthambhore National Park in Rajasthan, India, is a tiger sanctuary; there were 40 tigers during the late 1980s, reduced in a few years by human pressures—illicit cattle grazing and poaching—to 20 to 25 tigers today. There are 200,000 Indians within three miles of the core of the park—more than double the population when the park was launched, 21 years ago. Most depend on wood from the 150 square miles of park to cook their food. They graze in and around the park some 150,000 head of scrawny cattle, buffalo, goats, and camels. The cattle impoverish habitat and carry diseases to the ungulates that are the tiger's prey base. In May 1993, a young tigress gave birth to four cubs; that month 316 babies were born in the villages surrounding the park.[15]

The tigers may be doomed, but ought they to be? Consider, for instance, that there are minimal reforestation efforts, or that cattle dung can be used for fuel with much greater efficiency than is being done, or that, in an experimental herd of jersey and holstein cattle there, the yield of milk increased ten times that of the gaunt, free-ranging local cattle, and that a small group of dairy producers has increased milk production 1,000 percent in just 3 years. In some moods we may insist that people are more important than tigers. But in other moods these majestic animals seem the casualties of human inabilities to manage themselves and their resources intelligently, a tragic story that leaves us wondering whether the tigers should always lose and the people win.

When Nature Comes First

Ought we to save nature if this results in people going hungry? In people dying? Regrettably, sometimes, the answer is yes. In 20 years Africa's black rhinoceros population declined from 65,000 to 2,500, a loss of 97 percent; the species faces imminent extinction. Again, as with the tigers, there has been loss of habitat caused by human population growth, an important and indirect cause; but the primary direct cause is poaching, this time for horns. People cannot eat horns; but they can buy food with the money from selling them. Zimbabwe has a hard-line shoot-to-kill policy for poachers, and over 150 poachers have been killed.[16]

So Zimbabweans do not always put people first; they are willing to kill some, and to let others to go hungry rather than sacrifice the rhino. If we always put people first, there will be no rhinos at all. Always too, we must guard against inhumanity, and take care, so far as we can, that poachers have other alternatives for overcoming their poverty. Still, if it comes to this, the Zimbabwean policy is right. Given the fact that rhinos have been so precipitously reduced, given that the Zimbabwean population is escalating (the average married woman there desires to have six children),[17] one ought to put the black rhino as a species first, even if this costs human lives.

But the poachers are doing something illegal. What about ordinary people, who are not breaking any laws? The sensitive moralist may object that, even when the multiple causal factors are known, and lamented, when it comes to dealing with individual persons caught up in these social forces, we should factor out overpopulation, overconsumption, and maldistribution, none of which are the fault of the particular persons who may wish to develop their lands. "I did not ask to be born; I am poor, not overconsuming; I am not the cause but rather the victim of the inequitable distribution of wealth." Surely there still remains for such an innocent person a right to use whatever natural resources one has available, as best one can, under the exigencies of one's particular life, set though this is in these unfortunate circumstances. "I only want enough to eat, is that not my right?"

Human rights must include, if anything at all, the right to subsistence. So even if particular persons are located at the wrong point on the global growth graph, even if they are willy-nilly part of a cancerous and consumptive society, even if there is some better social solution than the wrong one that is in fact happening, have they not a right that will override the conservation of natural value? Will it not just be a further wrong to them to deprive them of their right to what little they have? Can basic human rights ever be overridden by a society that wants to do better by conserving natural value?

This requires some weighing of the endangered natural values. Consider the tropical forests. There is more richness there than in other regions of the planet—half of all known species. In South America, for example, there are one fifth of the planet's species of terrestrial mammals (800 species); there are one third of the planet's flowering plants.[18] The peak of global plant diversity is in the three Andean countries of Columbia, Ecuador, and Peru, where over 40,000 species occur on just 2 percent of the world's land surface.[19] But population growth in South America has been as high as anywhere in the world,[20] and people are flowing into the forests, often crowded off other lands.

What about these hungry people? Consider first people who are not now there but might move there. This is not good agricultural soil, and such would-be settlers are likely to find only a short-term bargain, a long-term loss. Consider the people who already live there. If they are indigenous peoples, and wish to continue to live as they have already for hundreds and even thousands of years, there will be no threat to the forest. If they are cabaclos (of mixed European and native races), they can also continue the lifestyles known for hundreds of years, without serious destruction of the forests. Such peoples may continue the opportunities that they have long had. Nothing is taken away from them. They have been reasonably well fed, though often poor.

Can these peoples modernize? Can they multiply? Ought there to be a policy of feeding first all the children they bear, sacrificing nature as we must to accomplish this goal? Modern medicine and technology have enabled them to multiply, curing childhood diseases and providing better nutrition, even if these peoples often remain at thresholds of poverty. Do not such people have the right to develop? A first answer is that they do, but with the qualification that all rights are not absolute, some are weaker, some stronger, and the exercise of any right has to be balanced against values destroyed in the exercise of that right.

The qualification brings a second answer. If one concludes that the natural values at stake are quite high, and that the opportunities for development are low, because the envisioned development is inadvisable, then a possible answer is: No, there will be no development of these reserved areas, even if people there remain in the relative poverty of many centuries, or even if, with escalating populations, they become more poor. We are not always obligated to cover human mistakes with the sacrifice of natural values.

Again, one ought to be as humane as possible. Perhaps there can be development elsewhere, to which persons in the escalating population can be facilitated to move, if they wish. Indeed, this often happens, as such persons flee to the cities, though they often only encounter further poverty there, owing to the inequitable distribution of resources which we have lamented. If they remain in these areas of high biological diversity, they must stay under the traditional lifestyles of their present and past circumstances.

Does this violate human rights? Anywhere that there is legal zoning, persons are told what they may and may not do, in order to protect various social and natural values. Land ownership is limited ("imperfect," as lawyers term it) when the rights of use conflict with the rights of other persons. One's rights are constrained by the harm one does to others, and we legislate to enforce this (under what lawyers call "police power"). Environmental policy may and ought to regulate the harms that people do on the lands on which they live ("policing"), and it is perfectly appropriate to set aside conservation reserves to protect the cultural, ecological, scientific, economic, historical, aesthetic, religious, and other values people have at stake here, as well as for values that the fauna and flora have intrinsically in themselves. Indeed, unless there is such reserving of natural areas, counterbalancing the high pressures for development, there will be almost no conservation at all. Every person on Earth is told that he or she cannot develop some areas.

Persons are not told that they must starve, but they are told that they cannot save themselves from starving by sacrificing the nature set aside in reserves—not at least beyond the traditional kinds of uses that did leave the biodiversity on the landscape. If one is already residing in a location where development is constrained, this may seem unfair, and the invitation to move elsewhere a forced relocation. Relocation may be difficult proportionately to how vigorously the prevailing inequitable distribution of wealth is enforced elsewhere.

Human rights to development, even by those who are poor, though they are to be taken quite seriously, are not everywhere absolute, but have to be weighed against the other values at stake. An individual sees at a local scale; the farmer wants only to plant crops on the now forested land. But environmental ethics sees that the actions of individuals cumulate and produce larger scale changes that go on over the heads of these individuals. This ethic will regularly be constraining individuals in the interest of some larger ecological and social goods. That will regularly seem cruel, unfair to the individual caught in such constraints. This is the tragedy of the commons; individuals cannot see far enough ahead, under the pressures of the moment, to operate at intelligent ecological scales. Social policy must be set synoptically. This invokes both ecology and ethics, and blends them, if we are to respect life at all relevant scales.

These poor may not have so much a right to develop in any way they please, as a right to a more equitable distribution of the goods of the Earth that we, the wealthy, think we absolutely own.

Our traditional focus on individuals, and their rights, can blind us to how the mistakes (as well as the wisdom) of the parents can curse (and bless) the children, as the Ten Commandments put it, how "the iniquity of the fathers is visited upon the children to the third and fourth generation" (cf. Exodus 20.5). All this has a deeply tragic dimension, made worse by the coupling of human foibles with ecological realities. We have little reason to think that misguided compassion that puts food into every hungry mouth, be the consequences whatever they may, will relieve the tragedy. We also have no reason to think that the problem will be solved without wise compassion, balancing a love for persons and a love for nature.

Ought we to feed people first, and save nature last? We never face so simple a question. The practical question is more complex.

> If persons widely demonstrate that they value many other worthwhile things over feeding the hungry (Christmas gifts, college educations, symphony concerts),
>
> and if developed countries, to protect what they value, post national boundaries across which the poor may not pass (immigration laws),
>
> and if there is unequal and unjust distribution of wealth, and if just redistribution to alleviate poverty is refused,
>
> and if charitable redistribution of justified unequal distribution of wealth is refused,
>
> and if one fifth of the world continues to consume four fifths of the production of goods and four fifths consumes one fifth,
>
> and if escalating birthrates continue so that there are no real gains in alleviating poverty, only larger numbers of poor in the next generation,
>
> and if low productivity on domesticated lands continues, and if the natural lands to be sacrificed are likely to be low in productivity,
>
> and if significant natural values are at stake, including extinctions of species,

then one ought not always to feed people first, but rather one ought sometimes to save nature.

Many of the "ands" in this conjunction can be replaced with "ors" and the statement will remain true, though we cannot say outside of particular contexts how many. The logic is not so much that of implication as of the weighing up of values and disvalues, natural and human, and of human rights and wrongs, past, present, and future.

Some will protest that this risks becoming misanthropic and morally callous. The Ten Commandments order us not to kill, and saving nature can never justify what amounts to killing people. Yes, but there is another kind of killing here, one not envisioned at Sinai, where humans are superkilling species. Extinction kills forms (*species*)—not just individuals; it kills collectively, not just distributively. Killing a natural kind is the death of birth, not just of an individual life. The historical lineage is stopped forever. Preceding the

Ten Commandments is the Noah myth, when nature was primordially put at peril as great as the actual threat today. There, God seems more concerned about species than about the humans who had then gone so far astray. In the covenant re-established with humans on the promised Earth, the beasts are specifically included. "Keep them alive with you...according to their kinds" (Genesis 6.19–20). There is something ungodly about an ethic by which the late-coming *Homo sapiens* arrogantly regards the welfare of one's own species as absolute, with the welfare of all the other five million species sacrificed to that. The commandment not to kill is as old as Cain and Abel, but the most archaic commandment of all is the divine, "Let the earth bring forth" (Genesis 1). Stopping that genesis is the most destructive event possible, and we humans have no right to do that. Saving nature is not always morally naive; it can deepen our understanding of the human place in the scheme of things entire, and of our duties on this majestic home planet.

NOTES

1. *Rio Declaration on Environment and Development*, Principle 1, UNCED document A/CONF.151/26, vol. I, ps. 15–25.
2. *Rio Declaration*, Principle 4.
3. *Rio Declaration*, Principle 5.
4. Insurance Institute for Highway Safety (Arlington, Virginia), *Status Report*, vol. 29 (no. 10, September 10, 1994):3.
5. Ruth Leger Sivard, *World Military and Social Expenditures*, 15th ed., Washington, DC: World Priorities, Inc., 1993.
6. Jonathan Power, 1992. "Despite Its Gifts, Brazil Is a Basket Case," *The Miami Herald*, June 22, p. 10A.
7. The empirical data below are in: Brian Huntley, Roy Siegfried, and Clem Sunter, *South African Environments into the 21st Century*, Cape Town: Human and Rousseau, Ltd, and Tafelberg Publishers Ltd., 1989; Rob Preston-Whyte and Graham House, eds., *Rotating the Cube: Environmental Strategies for the 1990s*, Durban: Department of Geographical and Environmental Sciences and Indicator Project South Africa, University of Natal, 1990; and Alan B. Durning, *Apartheid's Environmental Toll*, Washington, DC: Worldwatch Institute, 1990.
8. Huntley, Siegfried, and Sunter, p. 85.
9. Mamphela Ramphele, ed., *Restoring the Land: Environment and Change in Post-Apartheid South Africa*, London: Panos Publications, 1991.
10. The pie chart summarizes data in the *World Development Report 1991*, New York: Oxford University Press, 1991.

11. Peter M. Vitousek, Paul R. Ehrlich, Anne H. Ehrlich, and Pamela A. Matson, "Human Appropriation of the Products of Biosynthesis," *BioScience* 36(1986): 368–373.

12. Robert Goodland, "The Case That the World Has Reached Limits," ps. 3–22 in Robert Goodland, Herman E. Daly, and Salah El Serafy, eds., *Population, Technology, and Lifestyle*, Washington, DC: Island Press, 1992.

13. Daniel Hillel, *Out of the Earth*, New York: Free Press, Macmillan, 1991, p. 279.

14. E. O. Wilson, *The Diversity of Life*, Cambridge, MA: Harvard University Press, 1992, p. 267; Alison Jolly, *A World Like Our Own: Man and Nature in Madagascar*, New Haven: Yale University Press, 1980.

15. Geoffrey C. Ward, "The People and the Tiger," *Audubon* 96 (no. 4, July–August 1994):62–69.

16. Joel Berger and Carol Cunningham, "Active Intervention and Conservation: Africa's Pachyderm Problem," *Science* 263(1994): 1241–1242.

17. John Bongaarts, "Population Policy Options in the Developing World," *Science* 263(1994):771–776.

18. Michael A. Mares, "Conservation in South America: Problems, Consequences, and Solutions," *Science* 233(1986):734–739.

19. Wilson, *The Diversity of Life*, p. 197.

20. Ansley J. Coale, "Recent Trends in Fertility in the Less Developed Countries," *Science* 221(1983):828–832.